Studies in
The Book of Acts
VOLUME TWO

—⚜—

COURAGEOUS
CHRISTIANITY

MARTYN LLOYD-JONES

CROSSWAY BOOKS • WHEATON, ILLINOIS
A DIVISION OF GOOD NEWS PUBLISHERS

Courageous Christianity

Copyright © 2001 by Elizabeth Catherwood and Ann Beatt

Published by Crossway Books
        A division of Good News Publishers
        1300 Crescent Street
        Wheaton, Illinois 60187

Cover design: David LaPlaca

Cover photo: © Photo Disc

First U.S. edition published 2001

First British edition published by Banner of Truth, Edinburgh, 2001

Printed in the United States of America

All Bible quotations are taken from the *King James Version.*

Library of Congress Cataloging-in-Publication Data
Lloyd-Jones, David Martyn.
   Courageous Christianity / Martyn Lloyd-Jones.—1st U.S. ed.
     p. cm. — (Studies in the book of Acts ; v. 2)
   Includes bibliographical references.
   ISBN 1-58134-309-4
   1. Bible. N.T. Acts IV, 8-V, 18—Sermons. 2. Sermons, English—20th century.
3. Congregational churches—Sermons. I. Title. II. Series: Lloyd-Jones, David
Martyn. Studies in the book of Acts ; v. 2.
BS2625.54 .L57   2001
252'.058—dc21   2001004760
                                      CIP

15	14	13	12	11	10	09	08	07	06	05	04	03	02	01
15	14	13	12	11	10	9	8	7	6	5	4	3	2	1

CONTENTS

1

THE TRAGEDY OF UNBELIEF

Then Peter, filled with the Holy Ghost, said unto them, Ye rulers of the people, and elders of Israel, if we this day be examined of the good deed done to the impotent man, by what means he is made whole; be it known unto you all, and to all the people of Israel, that by the name of Jesus Christ of Nazareth, whom ye crucified, whom God raised from the dead, even by him doth this man stand here before you whole.

—Acts 4:8-10

Before we begin to consider this amazing statement of Peter's, it is important, obviously, that we should bear in mind its context. We are told in the previous chapter[1] of a remarkable incident that took place at Jerusalem. One afternoon at the hour of prayer, the apostles Peter and John were going up to the temple to pray. As they were entering the Beautiful Gate of the temple, they passed a man sitting on the ground, a man who had been born lame. His friends and relatives used to carry him there every day and seat him on the pavement, where he would beg alms from the people who were going into the temple. He was just a poor beggar. The world could do nothing for him; so his friends left him there, and he sat all day, hoping that people would offer a few coins.

When the lame man saw Peter and John, he asked for alms, but then something unusual happened. Luke writes: "Peter, fastening his eyes upon him with John, said, Look on us. And he gave heed unto them, expecting to receive something of them" (Acts 3:5).

Then Peter said those immortal words: "Silver and gold have I none; but such as I have give I thee: In the name of Jesus Christ of Nazareth rise up and walk" (v. 6). Peter reached out and grasped the lame man's right hand. We are told, "Immediately his feet and ankle bones received strength" (v. 7). Leaping up, he went with them into the temple, "walking, and leaping, and praising God" (v. 8).

The result was that a great crowd gathered. Whenever a thing like that happens, you always get a crowd! People came rushing to see what had taken place and saw the man they knew so well walking, leaping, and praising God—a man who had never walked in his life. Then they looked at the men who had done this, and as Peter saw them staring in amazement (v. 10), he began to preach to them (Acts 3:12-26).

Now we come to the sequel of these events. Peter had preached—he had explained what had happened, but the effect of that miracle and the preaching upon the priests and Sadducees and the captain of the temple was that they arrested Peter and John and put them on trial. In the first twelve verses of chapter 4 we have an account of what they did to the two apostles, what they said, and what Peter said to them in reply. Here we have a description of the first persecution that was ever endured by the Christian church, a persecution that arose because the authorities rejected the message of the Gospel.

Now this is most important, even when considered merely as history. It is the first persecution, and that gives it tremendous significance because, as I want to try to show you, it has all the characteristics of every subsequent persecution. That is why it still speaks to us today. Persecution always arises as the result of unbelief, and here in Acts 4 we see a rejection of the Gospel—unbelief. In this story we are given the characteristics, the elements, of unbelief. I call attention to these elements because what is recorded here accounts precisely for the unbelief that so marks the present time.

Only 10 percent of the people of this country even claim to be Christian, and we are told that only half of those attend a place of worship with any regularity. So when we go to church, we are doing something that is done by only about 5 percent of the people of this country. Why are the others, the 95 percent, outside?

In this story we are given the answer to that question. There is something surely quite astonishing about this attack on Peter and John, especially when you take it in its context. The arrest comes soon after the events of the great day of Pentecost when the Holy Spirit fell upon the church. Is it not amazing that anybody could have reacted to these events in the way that these people did? But that is still the case with all who are not Christian, who still do not believe. This reaction is almost incredible, but it is a fact of history.

But, of course, we must realize that in another sense this unbelief is not astonishing at all. For what happened here to these apostles was simply a repetition of what had happened to our blessed Lord Himself. If you read the four Gospels, you will find the same astonishing reaction. You look at the Son of God, you see what He did, you hear what He said, and yet you see the antipathy that He aroused—the opposition, the bitterness, and the rejection. The end of it all was that the leaders and the crowd joined in crying out, "Away with Him! Crucify Him!" And they killed Him.

He had prophesied in John 15 that persecution would be the lot of all His followers, too—and it did happen to them. It happened here at the very beginning. There is nothing new about unbelief. It is as old as the preaching of the Gospel. Men and women today are being fatuous when they say that it is modern to reject the Gospel. Unbelief is old, really ancient!

The idea that we ought to feel disappointed when people do not believe the Gospel, that we ought to think that something has gone wrong, is altogether mistaken. The idea that the Gospel is a message that must appeal to men and women is all wrong. By nature people have always hated and rejected it. But in doing so, they do not realize that they are proving the truth of the Gospel and of our Lord's prediction. The tragedy is that the world does not realize that in rejecting this message, it is rejecting the only thing that can save it.

Why do I preach the Gospel when people do not want to hear and I face many hardships and discomforts in doing so? I will tell you why. Take this world of ours. We have already had two world wars, and look at the present international situation. What is the matter with the world? What is the matter with men and women? Is there nothing that can put things right? I say that only one thing can even touch the problems of the human race—it is this Gospel. Yet people are militantly opposed to it; they ridicule the Gospel.

The world is refusing the only thing that can put it right. This statement applies as much to individuals as to international politics. If there is trouble in your life; if you feel you have gone to pieces, and all your prospects have been shattered; if you think that you have made a mess of life and that you are a failure—then I urge you, consider the Gospel with all your being. Ask God the Holy Spirit to give you the ability to listen with a far greater intensity than ever before. Here is something that can put you right.

The world today thinks it is clever in rejecting Christianity. The greatest tragedy in the world is not the nuclear bomb but humanity's rejection of the Gospel. If people only believed the Gospel, there would be no bombs. But why has the Gospel been rejected? Are you somebody who has blasphemed the name of Christ and dismissed Christianity? Why did you do it? Our Lord's answer is, "They hated me without a cause" (John 15:25). Or, as He said when He was dying upon the cross, "Father, forgive them; for they know not what they do" (Luke 23:34).

So it is in order to try to enlighten you that I am asking you to consider with me the case of these people of Jerusalem who persecuted the apostles, this first persecution in the long history of the Christian church. There is an advantage in looking on objectively; it helps us to see more clearly. In other words, I am simply trying to adopt the method used by Nathan the prophet in the case of David. David had done a terrible thing, but he was not aware of it. So Nathan concocted a story that portrayed the very sin committed by David, though using a different situation. Then Nathan said, "Now I would like you to give a judgment on this," and David, burning with righteous indignation, condemned the man who had done such a terrible thing.

Then Nathan looked at David and said, "Thou art the man" (2 Sam. 12:7). David had condemned himself. He had been able to see the sin in somebody else but not the same sin in himself. We are all like that, and that is why we should thank God for the historical details that we have in the Bible.

So I trust that as you look with me at these rulers in Jerusalem, you will be amazed and, if you are not a Christian, will recognize that you have been just like them. God grant that as we look objectively at the people in this story, we may see something of ourselves and the terrible nature of unbelief in all generations. In this most important passage, we are given the key to the problem of modern men and women and their rejection of Christianity. Here the whole situation is analyzed for us.

So, first of all, let us look together at what unbelief rejects. Later we shall consider the reasons for the rejection, but here is a good starting point. This whole world of ours, which is so proud of itself in its rejection of Christianity, is in terrible trouble. Let us see what it is rejecting; let us see how ridiculous, how tragic, it is that anybody should reject for a moment this amazing Gospel set here before us.

Now it seems to me that this subject subdivides itself very naturally into three main headings. First, the rejection of the messengers by these rulers. "They laid hands on them [Peter and John], and put them in hold unto the next day: for it was now eventide" (Acts 4:3). And we are told that the next day they "set them in the midst" and began to cross-examine them. It was a persecution of the church and, in particular, of the two leading apostles, Peter and John, through whom this incident had taken place. It was Peter's preaching that led to the trouble. The crowd had gathered and had listened with amazement as Peter expounded the Gospel to them. So the authorities were annoyed with them. I want to show you that anyone who is not a Christian, anyone who rejects the Christian message, the Christian faith, is also, incidentally, rejecting its messengers throughout the ages and the centuries.

Now why do I emphasize this? It is because we are told in verse 13: "Now when they saw the boldness of Peter and John, and perceived that they were unlearned and ignorant men, they marvelled; and they took knowledge of them, that they had been with Jesus." But that is where the contradiction, the blindness of unbelief, comes in. Why did they arrest Peter and John and put them into prison? Why did they not allow their own sense of wonder and amazement to lead them on in clear, inevitable, logical thinking? Why did they not ask, "What makes these men what they are?"

That is always the trouble with unbelief. It does not know how to think, and this is the result of prejudice, as I shall show you. Here was an extraordinary phenomenon—the lame man, who had never walked in his life, walking and leaping and praising God. These two men had apparently done it, and the previous day one of them had preached a most astonishing sermon there in Solomon's porch in the temple courtyard. Yet the authorities missed the whole point.

Who were Peter and John? They were just fishermen—ordinary, ignorant men—nobodies (v.13). Some people might have heard of them during the past three years because they had been followers of Jesus of Nazareth, but who was He, in any case? He was only a carpenter, and these were men who had no learning. Their speech was probably rough, lacking the refinement and sophistication that counts so much with rulers and authorities. Yet here they were, the cause of the excitement.

Now the record tells us that the rulers were aware of a kind of power when they saw the boldness of Peter and John (v. 13). So why did they not ask themselves, "What is this extraordinary phenomenon?" First, why did they not ask: "How do we account for their *preaching*?" We are told in the record, "Then Peter, filled with the Holy Ghost . . ." (v. 8), and when a man is filled with the Holy Spirit, people know it. Even people who do not believe what the preacher says know that power is there; they see a reality, a strength, a force; they feel something dealing with them, and these rulers undoubtedly felt it and marveled. But they did not think it through. They did not say to themselves, "What is it that enables these unlearned and ignorant men to preach in this way? From where do they get this understanding of the Scriptures? From where do they get this power and ability to expound and explain? From where do they get this conviction?"

It was a well-known fact that on the day of Pentecost, as the result of that first sermon preached by the apostle Peter, three thousand people had been converted and added to the church. Now in those days people were not invited to come forward at the end of a sermon—that was unheard of. It just happened that three thousand people were really changed, and everybody became aware of it. Now becoming a Christian was not the thing to do. You might have been persecuted; you might have been turned out of your home and your name taken out of the family records. The Jews hated the Christian message. Yet three thousand were converted and joined the church. We are told, "They continued stedfastly in the apostles' doctrine and fellowship, and in breaking of bread, and in prayers" (Acts 2:42). They were daily with one another.

Moreover, the number of converts increased. Two thousand more were added as the result of Peter's sermon there on the temple porch by the side of the man who had been healed, so that now there were five thousand people! Why did the authorities not look at this and say to themselves, "What is it that enables these unlearned and ignorant men to speak in such a way that thousands of people are completely changed, with new life and a new understanding so that they are filled with joy and are praising God and finding favor with all the people?" But, you see, they did not do that. "Throw them into prison," had been their response.

And why did these rulers not raise the same questions with regard to the *miracle*? The miracle was a fact, and they could not get away from it. We are told in the fourteenth verse of chapter 4: "Beholding the man which was healed standing with them, they could say nothing against it." If they could have explained it away, they would have. But the man was standing. There was the evidence, the fact, and throwing the disciples into prison could not change what had happened.

But unbelief does not face the facts; unbelief dismisses them. It says, "There's nothing in Christianity. Throw it out. Throw it into prison. Throw it out through the back door—there's the end of it." But it is not. You have not explained it, you have not answered it, you have not given a reason for it. You may get rid of the messengers, but you do not get rid of the facts. You do not get rid of the truth.

And men and women today are as guilty of evading the facts as were those rulers in Jerusalem so long ago. To dismiss Christianity is the clever thing to do, is it not? People say, "What? People still believe that? Incredible! In the light of all our modern knowledge and science? It's ridiculous. Nobody of any intelligence or learning believes that kind of thing any longer." So the

Christian faith is dismissed. "Throw them into prison. Get rid of the witnesses. Get rid of the messengers."

But do you not realize what you are doing in dismissing Christianity with a wave of the hand? You are really trying to dismiss the greatest people, the noblest souls, that this world has ever known. You are not only dismissing the apostles, but the martyrs and the confessors. You are dismissing many of those early witnesses in the first three centuries who laid down their lives for this Gospel. You are dismissing the people who were able to turn that ancient world upside down, who were so able to shake even the Roman Empire that it became politic for an emperor to become a Christian and to bring his empire in with him. That is what you are dismissing.

Have you ever tried to analyze it? There they were, ignorant and unlearned men—just a handful of people in the great Roman Empire with Greece and her philosophy against them, Rome against them, the Jews against them. What was it that changed this handful of people into a mighty power that turned the Roman Empire upside down and became the leading force in the life of the world? Can you dismiss it as easily as that? But that is what people do in their ignorance.

Think of some of the individuals you are dismissing. Think of that mighty man, Saint Augustine of Hippo. I mention him because a great problem confronting the thinkers of today is the problem of history, the problem of time, the problem of what is happening to the universe. Well, I suppose the single greatest treatise ever written on that subject is Augustine's *The City of God*. All those long centuries ago this man saw it all, and the book he wrote has remained throughout the running centuries and is still studied today. Augustine was one of the profoundest philosophers the world has ever known. He had a deeper insight perhaps into the problem of history and its meaning than anyone else. Here was a man, a pagan philosopher, who, by the power of the Holy Spirit, came to believe in this same Jesus. As a result, his thinking was revolutionized, and he was given the understanding to produce that masterpiece. It is interesting to notice how modern thinkers are turning back to him and are increasingly ready to listen to him. They are republishing his works, though he lived as far back as the fourth century.

I could go on giving a list of these men and women whom you are rejecting if you reject the Christian faith. You are dismissing a mighty man like Martin Luther, who could stand against fifteen centuries of history and bring about a change, a turning point. You are dismissing the gigantic intellect of John Calvin, one of these great architectonic minds that seems to span truth under the illumination of the Spirit and opens out vistas of thought that go on stretching endlessly into the future. That is the sort of person you are dismissing.

Another great man is Oliver Cromwell. Recently I have been reading about him again. He was the man—let us never forget—who laid the foundations of the greatness of Great Britain, and he was who he was because he was a Christian. So in saying there is nothing in Christianity, you are rejecting this mighty succession of men and women who figured in the Christian church, saints and martyrs, apologists and confessors. These messengers are all dismissed as people of no significance.

Let me sum this up by repeating an anecdote that one of my predecessors in this pulpit[2] was fond of telling. I am referring to the Reverend Dr. John A. Hutton, who often said that when he was a student, one of his professors, when confronted by a class of people who did not believe the Gospel because of their great intellects, would preface his remarks with some such words as these: "Gentlemen, I suggest to you that a Gospel and a teaching that produced a Paul, an Augustine, a Luther, a Calvin, and a Knox, the great Puritans, Oliver Cromwell, Whitefield and Wesley, Gladstone and Newman, and the rest—I suggest to you, gentlemen, that such a Gospel is at any rate worthy of your respectful consideration."

But then, having rejected the messengers, these rulers in Jerusalem rejected the message. And what a message they rejected! What is this Christian message? In this introduction I can only put it before you in broad terms, but Peter sums it all up for us. He says, "Be it known unto you all, and to all the people of Israel, that by the name of Jesus Christ of Nazareth, whom ye crucified, whom God raised from the dead, even by him doth this man stand here before you whole" (4:10). Indeed, in Acts 4:2 Luke tells us that the leaders were grieved because the apostles "taught the people, and preached through Jesus the resurrection from the dead." So here is the great theme. What are modern men and women rejecting? What are they dismissing with scorn and contumely? What is it that they suggest is almost an insult to "modern educated people"? It is this extraordinary message concerning the person here described as Jesus Christ of Nazareth.

"But I thought," says somebody, "that Christianity was a matter of who Cain's wife was or what the strange fish was that swallowed Jonah."

But it is not. Those are not the questions; that is not the essence of Christianity. You do not start there. Those are peripheral questions. But asking those questions is the clever thing people do, is it not? "Christianity?" they say. "Oh, science has disproved it—nothing in it at all. It's absolutely ridiculous. Who was Cain's wife?" So on we go, on with the dance, on with the war, on with the bombs, on with hell.

Is it not about time that the world began to consider this message? It is a message about Jesus Christ of Nazareth. It tells us that into this old, sinful, unhappy world of ours a baby was once born to whom they gave the name Jesus. He was born in a stable, in a little city called Bethlehem. Why was He born in a stable? It was, we are told, "because there was no room for them in the inn." His mother had to go to Bethlehem with the others because there was a census. She was pregnant, on the verge of giving birth to her first child, but there was no room in the inn, and nobody was going to make room for her. Why should they? They had booked months ago, every man for himself. "I'm all right, Jack. What does it matter if the woman is pregnant? This is my room. I've booked it." The world has always been like that; it is like that today. So this child was born in a stable amidst the straw and the lowing of the cattle, and they had to put His little body in a manger.

"What's all this?" you say. "The world is in trouble, and I'm concerned about the possibility of a war." But I am, too, and I tell you that there is no more relevant fact for you to know at this moment than just this—that that baby was born in Bethlehem. Who was He? He was the Son of God. The only hope for this world today lies in the fact that God is concerned about this world and sent His Son into it. That is what the apostles were preaching; that is what the authorities were rejecting. They were rejecting this baby born in poverty and in lowliness—this young man who worked with His hands as a carpenter for some eighteen years and then suddenly set out on His public ministry. They were rejecting this preacher and healer.

What did Jesus of Nazareth preach? To me, this is the extraordinary thing about unbelief. His teaching can be found in the Sermon on the Mount. Is this not the very teaching the world needs to know? "Love your enemies, bless them that curse you, do good to them that hate you, and pray for them which despitefully use you, and persecute you" (Matt. 5:44). Pray for those who treat you in a malign manner.

Did you know this? If only every man and woman in the world today lived the Sermon on the Mount, all our problems would be solved—every one of them. This is His message; this is His way of life. He preached it; He commended it; He practiced it; He gave an illustration of it and pleaded with people to live it. They rejected that, and if you turn away from Christianity, that is what you are rejecting. You are rejecting a teaching that condemns adultery and murder and malice and spite and hatred. You are rejecting a teaching that commands love and mercy and compassion and kindness and mutual regard and help. The people of our Lord's time rejected it. They rejected Him. They said, "Away with Him! Crucify Him!" They threw the apostles into prison. This is the message they rejected. But what is the matter with it, I ask you? This message is the very thing the world stands most in need of.

These Jewish leaders rejected one who was "a friend of publicans and sinners." He was not like the Pharisees. If He had been, I could understand people rejecting Him. The Pharisee was a very proud, self-righteous man. The Pharisee said that he had never sinned; he claimed to be a good man. He gave a tenth of his goods to the poor, he fasted twice in the week, he had never committed adultery, he had never committed murder. He was a paragon of all the virtues, and when he saw a tax collector, he drew his skirts in and kept as far away as he could. He felt that such men—thieves and cheats—were lepers. That was the Pharisee.

But our Lord was the exact opposite. He condemned the Pharisees. He sat down with tax collectors and sinners; He spoke with them; He ate and drank with them; He sympathized with them; He defended them against those wretched Pharisees who were always condemning them.

Furthermore, the authorities rejected our Lord's miracles and His kindly deeds, His sympathy for suffering, and His eye of compassion and mercy. He never missed a sad case. When even the disciples were annoyed at Him, He insisted on stopping; there was somebody in need, and He could not pass by. That is the one they rejected—Jesus Christ. Have you ever really looked at Him? You have used His name as an oath perhaps, but I am asking, have you ever looked at the portraits of Him in the four Gospels? Have you ever really stood and contemplated Him? Do it, my friends. This is the one you are rejecting.

But wait a minute—there He is, nailed to a cross. He has been arrested. What for? Nobody can bring a charge against Him. No, they try to trump up some evidence. They try to concoct a charge, but it will not hold water for a second. There is no witness (Mark 14:55-56). He has done nothing wrong. But they condemn Him and lead Him up a little hill called Golgotha. They try to make Him carry His cross for a while, but it is too heavy for Him. He is staggering under it, and somebody has to take His place and carry it for Him. At last they reach the hill, and there they nail Him to a tree. In agony and suffering He dies.

That is the message. The one who had never done any harm, the one who had always done good, who had taught and preached in the manner that I have indicated to you—He died upon a tree in the most shameful manner conceivable, in indescribable agony and suffering. And after He died, they took down the body and put it in a tomb. They rolled a stone in front of it and put a seal on it and set some soldiers on guard.

But that is not the end of the story! The lame man would still be sitting helplessly on the pavement outside the Beautiful Gate if the story had ended there, and Peter would never have been able to preach as he did. No, no, this Jesus—what happened? Oh, He burst asunder the bands of death; He rose from the grave. Jesus and the Resurrection! This is a fact. There would never have been an apostle but for the Resurrection. There would never have been a Christian church at all but for this. We are even told by these honest records that His own followers completely lost hope when they saw Him dying. They were utterly disconsolate; they thought the end had come. If He had not risen from the dead, there would never have been a Christian Gospel.

But He arose! He showed Himself to the disciples. He gave them a commission. He ascended into heaven in their presence and sent down the Holy Spirit upon them on the day of Pentecost as He had promised. And so miracles happened, and they were able to preach with the Spirit and with power. That is the message. "That is what you are rejecting," said Peter, in effect, to these people. "That is what you seem to be unaware of. We are nobodies. We are unlearned and ignorant men. We have nothing to say for ourselves or in and of ourselves. We are just witnesses of these things. We are simply reporting facts."

And what is the meaning of all this? Here is the vital part of the message. It means that "God was in Christ, reconciling the world unto himself, not imputing their trespasses unto them. . . . He hath made him to be sin for us, who knew no sin; that we might be made the righteousness of God in him" (2 Cor. 5:19, 21). Listen to this—this is what it all means. God is the great eternal God who made the whole universe and who made men and women in His own image—the God who owns everything, the God who is over everything, the God who is going to judge everything, the God against whom men and women have rebelled and sinned and, as a result, have brought down misery and shame upon themselves.

Nothing in the world today is as it originally was in God's creation. God made man upright and perfect. He made a woman, a helpmeet for man, equally upright and perfect. There was no sin in Adam and Eve, no lust, no evil desire, no hatred, malice, spite; there was nothing ugly or unclean. They were perfect and righteous before God.

So where has the evil come from? Oh, it is the result of that rebellion against God. Think of all the unhappiness in the world, all the misery and the heartache, the broken marriages, the broken homes—little children breaking their hearts as they see their parents separating—the agony of life as the result of sin and evil. And men and women are totally incapable of doing anything about it. All your education cannot deal with it; the politicians cannot put it right. No, the message that the world is rejecting is that the everlasting God, against whom we have all rebelled and sinned, still loves the world in spite of its sin. "God so loved the world, that he gave his only begotten Son, that whosoever believeth in him should not perish, but have everlasting life" (John 3:16).

It was "when the fulness of the time was come" that "God sent forth his Son, made of a woman, made under the law, to redeem them that were under the law" (Gal. 4:4-5). It is God who sent His Son into the world; it is God who sent Him to the cross; it is God who "laid on him the iniquity of us all" (Isa. 53:6). It is God who has taken your sins and put them on Him and punished them in Him and is offering you a free pardon. That is what Peter and John were preaching. That is the message that was being rejected: Jesus Christ of Nazareth.

Is this not the tragedy of the world? We see men and women interested in romance, ready to believe any novel, ready to believe any film, getting excited about mere fantasy that is not true to life. Yet they reject the fact of Christ—the Incarnation, God visiting and redeeming His people, the glory of the cross, the way of salvation and reconciliation to God—Jesus Christ, "who hath abolished death, and hath brought life and immortality to light through the gospel" (2 Tim. 1:10). Jesus Christ is the vanquisher of all the enemies of humanity, the devil and sin and evil. He has even conquered death, the last enemy—"Jesus and the resurrection"! Is there anything more tragic than unbelief that not only rejects the messengers but also rejects such a message?

But, thirdly, unbelief not only rejects the messenger and the message; it rejects the results of the message. Notice how Peter puts it: "Ye rulers of the people, and elders of Israel, if we this day be examined of"—what?—"*the good deed* done to the impotent man" (4:8-9, emphasis mine). Now this rejection is the most astonishing and amazing of all.

"You have thrown us into prison," said Peter, in effect. "You have us here on trial now, but why are we here? Why did we spend last night in prison? Why are we now standing in the court? What have we done? Were we drunk? Have we committed murder? Have we been blasphemous? Have we wrought havoc in Jerusalem? No, we have not; we are on trial because of a good deed that we have done."

Can you not see unbelief? What it rejects is a good deed! Later on in the house of Cornelius, Peter said that Jesus "went about doing good" (Acts 10:38). The crowd said, "Away with Him! Crucify Him!" But what had He done? The answer is that He had done nothing but good. The world had never seen and will never again see such a benefactor. He lived to do good. He relieved suffering and trouble. He was compassionate, He was sympathetic. There was nothing that He would not do for people who were in need and who looked to Him, and yet He was crucified. Good deeds! And that is the astonishing thing about unbelief. Peter and John had been put in prison and were on trial because they had enabled a man who had been born lame to rise, to stand, to walk, to leap, and to praise God.

This is but a faint picture of all the blessings that our blessed Lord and Savior has brought into this world of time, and this is where the world shows its madness. When Jesus was preaching and teaching, John the Baptist, who had been thrown into prison, began to doubt. He sent two emissaries to Christ saying, "Art thou he that should come, or do we look for another?" The answer our Lord sent back was this: "Go and show John again those things which ye do hear and see: The blind receive their sight, and the lame walk, the lepers are cleansed, and the deaf hear, the dead are raised up, and the poor have the gospel preached to them" (Matt. 11:3-5)—good deeds. It was for these that they rejected Him.

But all that is just a picture of the blessings that come to all who believe this blessed Gospel of the glorious God—the blessings in the Christian life. What are you rejecting if you do not believe the Gospel? You are rejecting rest of mind. He stands saying, "Come unto me, all ye that labour and are heavy laden, and I will give you rest" (Matt. 11:28). Rest from your useless quest for truth apart from Christ. Rest from all your intellectual perplexity. Rest in your endeavor by your own strength to be righteous and holy and clean and pure. Rest in the search for God. Rest in all your difficulties.

Or let me put it in terms of light. Our Lord said, "I am the light of the world: he that followeth me shall not walk in darkness, but shall have the light of life" (John 8:12). These are the good deeds. These are the things that He has come to do and to bring. He gives light—light on God, light on ourselves, light on the world, light on the way to be reconciled to God.

But above rest and light, He gives me life. This is what we stand in need of above everything else. Had you realized that if you reject this Gospel, as these rulers did of old in Jerusalem, what you are really rejecting is forgiveness of sins? Do you know that in Jesus Christ, the Son of God, you are offered free pardon and forgiveness? You may have sinned to the very gates of hell—it does not matter. If you repent and believe this great message now, you will be forgiven immediately.

> *Only believe and thou shalt see*
> *That Christ is all in all to thee.*
>   —J. S. B. Monsell

Forgiveness is what the world is rejecting. Men and women have uneasy consciences. They are afraid of life, afraid of death, afraid of eternity, and very rightly so, because we must all die and stand before God in judgment. That is why these people in Acts did not like the message of the Resurrection. Peter preached that through Christ there is a resurrection for all people. They saw it and did not like it, but it is true.

Yes, but the moment you see that and are terrified, the blessed message comes to tell you that your sins can be blotted out, freely forgiven. "Though your sins be as scarlet, they shall be as white as snow" (Isa. 1:18). Though you have sinned yourself into the depths and the dregs and gutters of existence, if you believe on the Son of God, your sins will be blotted out like a thick cloud, and you will be reconciled to God. Not only that, but you will be given a new life immediately; you will have a new start. Here is a Gospel that can say this. Here is a Gospel of the prodigal son; it is a Gospel of rebirth, of regeneration and renewal.

When men and women reject this message, this Gospel, they are rejecting all that—not only the forgiveness and reconciliation, but the new life, the new power, the new start. Paul puts it like this to the Corinthians—here is a word for the modern world in which we live: "Know ye not that the unrighteous shall not inherit the kingdom of God? Be not deceived: neither fornicators, nor idolaters, nor adulterers, nor effeminate, nor abusers of themselves with mankind, nor thieves, nor covetous, nor drunkards, nor revilers, nor extortioners, shall inherit the kingdom of God. And such were some of you"—they *were* that—"but ye are washed, but ye are sanctified, but ye are justified in the name of the Lord Jesus, and by the Spirit of our God" (1 Cor. 6:9-11). Here is a Gospel that is the power of God for salvation, that can cleanse men and women and make them saints in the kingdom of God and give them an everlasting hope.

"If you want to know," says Peter, in effect, "about the good deed that was done to the impotent man, here is the explanation." And, my beloved friend, if you have rejected this Gospel, you have rejected all that. The Gospel is your only hope of heaven and eternity, your only hope of forgiveness, peace of conscience, peace of mind and heart, tranquility, new life, new power, new vigor, new strength. Go back to the same old world, and where you always went down, you will stand. You will walk; you will leap; you will praise God. That is what the world is rejecting.

All the greatest benefits that humanity has ever known have come through this Gospel. Good deeds! Where did hospitals come from? The Christian church. Where did education come from? The Christian church. Where did relief for the poor and suffering come from? The Christian church. Look at the great missionary enterprise. Look at the light that has been taken to the dark places of the earth. What is the basis of liberty in England? The Magna Carta. Yes, but that did not gain for us very much, according to the best historians of today. Do you know where our modern liberty has really come from? I can tell you. It came through the Puritans of the seventeenth century—Oliver Cromwell and the rest. Where did liberty in the United States come from? From the same place—the Puritan fathers. And did you know that the trade unions are a direct outcome of the evangelical revival of two hundred years ago?

Where has morality come from? Where have the noblest periods in the history of this country come from? The answer is that they have always come in the wake of religious revivals. So as the world in its cleverness turns away from this message and its messengers, the world is hurtling itself back into what two modern writers have rightly called "the cult of softness," with ever-increasing immorality, vice, and dishonesty. When men and women reject the Gospel, they are rejecting the best, the noblest, the greatest things.

I do trust that as you have looked at these rulers in Jerusalem, God the Holy Spirit has been revealing you to yourself through them. See the folly of unbelief; see its blindness; see its tragedy; see its utter hopelessness. Did you know that you can be forgiven now? Oh, repent and believe the Gospel. Then you will begin to praise the God who has done this "good deed," this wonderful work for and in you, through His blessed Son, Jesus of Nazareth.

2

THE CHARACTERISTICS OF
UNBELIEF

*And as they spake unto the people, the priests, and the captain of
the temple, and the Sadducees, came upon them, being grieved
that they taught the people, and preached through Jesus the
resurrection from the dead. And they laid hands on them, and put
them in hold unto the next day: for it was now eventide. . . . And
it came to pass on the morrow, that their rulers, and elders, and
scribes, and Annas the high priest, and Caiaphas, and John, and
Alexander, and as many as were of the kindred of the high priest,
were gathered together at Jerusalem. And when they had set them
in the midst, they asked, By what power, or by what name, have
ye done this?*

—Acts 4:1-3, 5-7

I hope to consider this entire incident with you, but we shall concentrate
first on the particular aspect brought out in the above verses. We have here
the account of the first persecution endured by the early Christian church.
I showed you that there is something almost incredible about the way these
Jewish leaders reacted to the healing of the lame man. But their reaction is
a fact of history, and there is a sense in which what happened then has been
happening ever since, to a greater or lesser degree.

Now in these verses we have a picture not only of persecution, but of
unbelief, and that is why I am calling your attention to this passage. We are

not interested merely in the history. The times in which you and I are living are too desperate for any of us to indulge in some historical or antiquarian interest. We are looking at all this because unfortunately the attitude we see here is still true of so many men and women today. As I am trying to show, this attitude is the supreme tragedy of the world. Our world is a world in trouble, a world in confusion, a world toying with forces and powers that could put an end to civilization as we know it. But to such a world there still comes the message of the Christian Gospel. It is the only hope for that world, and yet the world is rejecting it.

Now we have looked at this incident and have considered together what it is that the world rejects. This rejection is surely something that should make us pause and ask: Why does this happen? Why did those Jewish leaders react like this? Why do men and women still react like this? That is the subject to which I am now calling your attention.

There is something very remarkable about this book of Acts. It is a book of history, but it is more than that. In this book we are given, in embryo, as it were, practically the whole history of the Christian church. So in these verses we see an extraordinary portrayal of the nature and causes of unbelief. We see the reasons why men and women turn against the Gospel. As we have already said, the advantage of having the Scriptures is that they enable us to look at things objectively. The danger always is that we tend to protect ourselves. Things we recognize as being wrong in others, we tend to excuse in ourselves, and so the moment a subject becomes personal, we are on the defensive and no longer listen. But here we find ourselves, seated, as it were, and looking at something that is happening before us. Here are the apostles, and here are the rulers throwing them into prison, putting them on trial, and dealing with them in a most abominable manner. Whatever made them do that? That is the picture, and as we analyze the reasons for their actions, we shall find that we are arriving at the explanation of why men and women still do precisely the same thing today.

So what does this passage teach us? Now this is an important matter. The welfare of every individual, both in this life and in the world to come, depends upon his or her reaction to the truth of the Gospel. That is what makes the preaching of the Gospel such a solemn responsibility, something that is almost too great a burden. The great apostle Paul, looking at himself and his ministry, says, "Who is sufficient for these things?" (2 Cor. 2:16). Why does he ask this? Well, he says that we are either "the savour of death unto death" or "the savour of life unto life." No man or woman is ever the same again after hearing the Gospel. Here is a Gospel that offers you salvation; it offers you life; it offers you everything that is noblest and best in this world and in the world to come. Is there anything more important, therefore, than that we should consider together what it is that makes anybody reject it? And here in Acts 4 we are given some of the answers.

The first thing I find is that there is nothing new about rejecting the Gospel, about unbelief. I start with that because most people today who are not Christians—and that, unfortunately, means the majority of people—think that they are not Christians because they are "modern," because they live in the twenty-first century. Is that not how they put it? "What," they say, "you still believe that? You mean to say that in these enlightened times you are a Christian and go to church?"

They are aghast. And in reply our first point is that the century has nothing to do with it at all! These people in Jerusalem were guilty of the same unbelief. They not only refused to believe the words of the apostles, but they refused to believe the Lord Himself. It is quite fatuous and ridiculous to think that the hallmark of modernity is to reject this Gospel. Unbelief is as old as the Gospel itself. From the very beginning there were people who would have nothing at all to do with it. History itself establishes that fact beyond any doubt. So if you are not a Christian, do not claim that you are being modern. You are ancient, very ancient indeed. You belong to the company that we read of in these first twelve verses of the fourth chapter of Acts.

But let us move on to something much more interesting. My second point is that we are shown here the extraordinary manner in which unbelief brings together people who are essentially different from each other and even antagonistic. One of the greatest unifying forces the world has ever known has been unbelief. This is to me a most fascinating aspect of the story that we are looking at together, and I want to show you how entirely up to date this is. I was reading recently an article by a well-known writer in this country, a very brilliant person, Miss Marghanita Laski. She is not a Christian. She says she is an atheist, but she was writing an article on these subjects, and in it she says something like this: "I cannot speak for people like me—most unbelievers have little in common." Now that is the very point I had already decided to make before I read her article.

I want to show you this from two standpoints—first, what unbelievers do *not* have in common, and then what they *do* have in common. Again my point is nothing new: Unbelievers were very different from each other in the first century also. Consider what we are told here; it is really quite remarkable: "As they spake unto the people, the priests, and the captain of the temple, and the Sadducees, came upon them." And in Acts 4:5-7: "And it came to pass on the morrow, that their rulers, and elders, and scribes, and Annas the high priest, and Caiaphas, and John, and Alexander, and as many as were of the kindred of the high priest, were gathered together at Jerusalem. And when they had set them in the midst, they asked . . ." That was the Sanhedrin, the great council, and that was the composition of the council.

Now this was an extraordinarily interesting collection of people. Here were men who, as Miss Laski says, had practically nothing in common. Indeed, they were very bitterly divided against one another, especially the Sadducees and the elders and the scribes. This gathering is a perfect illustration of what I am trying to show you. Who were these people? Take the priests first. They were just the ordinary priests who had to do their duty daily in the temple. They were divided into companies, and each company was responsible for a week's duty in the temple once every six months.

The "captain of the temple" was the head of the special group of Levites (temple assistants) who were chosen to act as policemen to keep order within the temple. He belonged to one of the chief priestly families, and his authority was second only to that of the high priest.

Then we come to these most interesting people called the Sadducees. Fortunately, we know all about them. The Sadducees may be described as the priestly aristocracy. They were primarily and essentially politicians, the people who were concerned about positions and government and order and the relationships between their country and other countries. They were schemers and plotters. Even politicians do not change from century to century! The authorities tell us that when it paid the Sadducees to be religious—and it did, of course, in those days—they were interested in religion. But they were not interested in it personally. Indeed, they were indifferent to it in and of itself.

The Bible is a wonderful book, is it not? When we read secular history books, we see people becoming Christians because it paid them. Constantine became a Christian purely for political reasons. I do not think the man was ever converted, but it suited him to become a Christian, and he brought the Roman Empire in with him. Watch such people down through the centuries—men and women who were not at all interested in God or the condition of their souls and yet who conformed to religious ceremonies. Why? Oh, expediency! It moves me with a righteous indignation to see men and women attending religious services on certain official occasions who never darken the doors of a place of worship at any other time. Church attendance is part of the game, political opportunism; they are making use of religion. That was the great characteristic of the Sadducees.

The Sadducees did not believe in the oral tradition that had been developed by the great teachers, by the fathers, but held only to what was written in the Torah, the first five books of our Old Testament that had been given to Moses. They rejected all teaching concerning a resurrection of the body, and neither did they believe in any future rewards and punishments. They said that when a person dies, that is the end. Indeed, we can go further—they did not believe in angels; they did not believe in spirits; they did not believe in a supra-mundane world; they did not really believe in the spiritual realm at all. They were materialists, political materialists, and they believed that our future in this life is determined solely by our own free will.

But the list does not stop there. Caiaphas, the high priest, was just a Sadducee writ large. It was his job to preside over the Sanhedrin. Annas, the father-in-law of Caiaphas, had been high priest but had been deposed by the Romans. The Jews, however, still regarded him as high priest. Both Annas and Caiaphas were well in with one another. Also present were John and Alexander, but we know nothing about them. Then, "and as many as were of the kindred of the high priest." These were all part of the great council, the Sanhedrin, and they were gathered together at Jerusalem.

In other words, you gave yourself to this game, and you worked it so well that you were not only in a high position yourself, but you brought your relatives in. Nepotism, we call it, do we not? I am talking about the first century, remember, not the twenty-first! Is it not astonishing how people can say, "I'm not interested in the Bible, that old book of yours"? But can you not see that this is the book of life? This is God revealing Himself. This is the exposure of men and women fallen and in sin. People do not change, and here they were.

Then there were the scribes. Who were they? They were the teachers of the law, the experts in the oral tradition, the teaching of the fathers. The scribes belonged mainly to the party of the Pharisees. They believed in the resurrection, in angels, in judgment, and in rewards and punishments. They were an absolute contrast to the Sadducees—and yet they were all together in their opposition to Peter and John. Is this not interesting? Of course, exactly the same thing had happened to our blessed Lord Himself. A most interesting statement toward the end of Luke's Gospel puts it like this: "The same day Pilate and Herod were made friends together: for before they were at enmity" (Luke 23:12). They hated one another, but when Jesus became the topic of discussion, Herod and Pilate became friends and joined in opposing Him.

St. Paul, writing to the Corinthians, points out that it was exactly the same in his time: "The Jews require a sign, and the Greeks seek after wisdom" (1 Cor. 1:22). Jews and Greeks—again a great contrast. The Jew, the Hebrew, with his practical, historical, and factual way of thinking, and the Greek with his ideas and philosophy. The Greek despised the ignorant Hebrew, while the Hebrew regarded the Greek as a dog—someone outside the pale, someone cut off from God, who did not have His oracles. You cannot imagine a greater contrast than that between the Greek and the Jew, the children of Israel and everybody else. But, as Paul points out, the Gospel brings them together. The Jews require a sign, and the Greeks seek after wisdom, but they both agree in rejecting the Gospel.

The Gospel is still having exactly the same effect as it had there at the very beginning. But this is what people today do not realize. Unbelievers reject the Gospel because they are intellectuals. "The great intellectuals," they say, "don't believe the Gospel, and I am an intellectual. I am a thinker, a reader. I have a brain, and that's why I'm not a Christian." But you are not the only people who do not believe the Gospel. It is equally rejected by people who do not even know what the word *intellectual* means.

"But," you say, "look at those people on the television. Look at the people whose articles I read—they reject the Gospel."

Yes, but for every one of them I suppose I could produce ten thousand whom you have never heard of, who have never written an article and probably have never read many, who also reject the Christian faith. Intellectuals and ignoramuses join together in unbelief just as the Sadducees and the Pharisees did of old. We tend to take these things for granted, but is it not important that we should examine them?

Let me give you another strange combination of people who reject the Gospel. Take these modern moralists of ours. There are many of them, and let me grant that they are very able. Let me further grant that many are very good men and women. But they are interested in morality only. They do not believe the Gospel; they do not believe this supernatural teaching; they do not believe these facts about Jesus and about His death. No, they say that in the interests of morality, they have to reject the supernatural element in the Christian faith.

But side by side with them, I see the libertines. It is not only the moralists who reject this Gospel. The people who frequent the nightclubs also reject it. The people who live to indulge their lusts and their passions and their baser desires are unanimous with the moralists in rejecting it.

Might I go even a step further and say that this simple Gospel is rejected by traditional Roman Catholics and liberal Protestants ultimately for exactly the same reason. All these apparently disparate units, all these people who Miss Laski says have little in common, are brought to a common denominator. They are one; they all combine together to persecute the apostles of Christ, to reject the Gospel of salvation.

So there is nothing new in unbelief itself; there is nothing new in the way that unbelief unites diverse people; and, thirdly, and perhaps most strikingly, there is nothing new in what unbelief objects to about the Gospel. The argument is that because we are in the twenty-first century, we have come of age. We have wonderful knowledge and information, and so we cannot believe certain things. But these certain things are exactly what the people in Acts objected to: "As they spake unto the people, the priests, and the captain of the temple, and the Sadducees, came upon them, being grieved that they taught the people, and preached through Jesus the resurrection from the dead." What was the teaching that these people objected to? Well, here it is: *Jesus!* It was the apostles' essential testimony that this carpenter who had been born in Bethlehem, who had been brought up in Nazareth, was none other than the eternal Son of God. It was a stupendous claim. "This is not only a man," they said. Peter had argued this at length in his sermon on the day of Pentecost. He had said, in effect, "David prophesied of this one whose soul would not be left in hell and whose flesh would not experience corruption. David could not have been speaking about himself because we know that he died; he was buried; his sepulcher is still with us; he never rose from the dead. But this one has. Therefore," Peter argued, "I tell you that this person is none other than the Son of God."

And you remember that Peter had made the same point in his sermon at the Beautiful Gate of the temple:

> *The God of Abraham, and of Isaac, and of Jacob, the God of our fathers, hath glorified his Son Jesus; whom ye delivered up, and denied him in the presence of Pilate, when he was determined to let him go. But ye denied the Holy One and the Just, and desired a murderer to be granted unto you; and killed the Prince of life, whom God hath raised from the dead; whereof we are witnesses.*
> *—Acts 3:13-15*

But the authorities objected to that. Jesus the Son of God? Monstrous! Impossible! There is God; there is man; there is no such thing as God-man. They objected to the teaching about the person of Jesus, and that is the very objection being made today. People are prepared to believe in Jesus as a teacher, a moralist, a pacifist—they will believe in a man. But they will not believe that He is the Son of God, that a great miracle took place, that a virgin's womb was visited by the Holy Spirit, that "that which is conceived in her is of the Holy Ghost" (Matt. 1:20). God-man: two natures, one person. That was the first bone of contention—Jesus, Son of God.

The second objection centered on Peter's preaching about the death of Jesus of Nazareth. "We preach Christ crucified," said Paul to the Corinthians, "unto the Jews a stumblingblock, and unto the Greeks foolishness; but unto them which are called, both Jews and Greeks, Christ the power of God, and the wisdom of God" (1 Cor. 1:23-24).

The Jews said, "What? Preaching a dead Savior? Saying a man saves by being put to death? Impossible! Ridiculous! The Messiah, the Deliverer—when He appears—will come as a mighty military chieftain. He will be strong and powerful. He will be born in a palace, surrounded by pomp, and He will set Himself up as king in Jerusalem. He will conquer the world, and Israel shall head the nations—that is, the Messiah. And are you telling us that someone who was crucified in utter weakness and died in shame and ignominy is the Son of God and the Savior? What nonsense!"

The cross, the death, was a fatal stumbling block. Peter had dealt with Christ's death in his sermon at the Beautiful Gate of the temple. He had said, "[Ye] killed the Prince of life. . . . But those things, which God before had showed by the mouth of all his prophets, that Christ should suffer, he hath so fulfilled" (Acts 3:15, 18). And on the day of Pentecost he described the death of Christ in this way:

> *Ye men of Israel, hear these words; Jesus of Nazareth, a man approved of God among you by miracles and wonders and signs, which God did by him in the midst of you, as ye yourselves also know [notice] him, being delivered by the determinate counsel and foreknowledge of God, ye have taken, and by wicked hands have crucified and slain.*
>
> —Acts 2:22-23

But remember it was "by the determinate counsel and foreknowledge of God." It was God's plan—salvation through a crucified Savior. The Jews were aghast.

And to the Greeks, of course, this was the height of folly. The world, they said, will be saved by a thinker, by a philosopher, by one who propounds a great theory—not by an ignorant carpenter, an unknown in a little land like Palestine. The world's savior will belong to the great succession of Greek sages and will have a great delivering word. Dying on a cross? This is a fantasy, childishness.

But is that not what men and women are still saying? Is there anything that a modern unbeliever objects to more than our Lord's death upon the cross? They say, "Yes, we are interested in the person, and we are interested in his teaching, but when you come to that cross and tell us that that's the climax and the most glorious thing that's ever happened, you're talking rubbish! It's immoral. One man dying for another, our sins being put on him? A God who does that is unjust. Such teaching is sentimental rubbish."

And then, thirdly, and in particular, the authorities objected to hearing that this crucified man had come alive again: ". . . being grieved that they taught the people, and preached through Jesus the resurrection from the dead." The apostles kept on saying that they were witnesses of the fact that He had indeed literally risen in the body from the tomb on the morning of the third day. That is not what the modern church preaches, I know, and that is why it is driving people away. But the apostles preached the fact of the Resurrection. They said that the tomb was empty, the body gone. Our Lord had appeared to them; He had come into a room and had spoken to them; He had eaten broiled fish and honey in their presence; He had spoken to them; He had breathed the Holy Spirit upon them. Later they had seen Him ascending into heaven. They preached all these things as facts, and the Jewish leaders were furious. That is why they arrested the apostles; that is why they threw them into prison; that is why they put them on trial. "Resurrection?" they said. "It cannot happen. The Sadducees have always said so."

People are still saying the same things. They are prepared to believe in the continuing influence of the teaching of Jesus. Some are even prepared to believe that He still exists in the spiritual realm and may have a certain amount of influence upon us, but the great thing, they say, is the memory of Him and His teaching—that is what matters. But as for saying that He has literally risen—well, science makes the whole thing impossible.

But modern-day scoffers not only reject the resurrection of Christ. They reject all miracles, and they reject the teaching that we must all stand before the judgment throne of Christ and before God in a final judgment. They hate the notion of judgment and of punishment and of rewards, just as the Sadducees did. They say that religion is all right on a state occasion or if some great person dies. Have a state funeral. Include a religious element— that's fine. But they add, "When you ask us to believe that God is going to judge the whole world and that men and women go to heaven or hell, then we cannot believe it; it's unintelligent." But the same thing was said in the first century. That was exactly the viewpoint of the Sadducees. So we have established this point, have we not? There is nothing new about unbelief. Therefore, give up the statement that you are not a Christian because you belong to the twenty-first century.

Let me come, then, to a second great principle. It should be obvious to all of us, therefore, that belief or unbelief are not matters of the intellect. The argument that rejection of the Gospel is purely the result of modern knowledge is invalid because the same objections were raised in the first century. You say, "I cannot believe in the Resurrection because of modern science." But the Jewish leaders could not believe in the Resurrection because of their supposed knowledge. Modern knowledge makes no difference at all.

Similarly, intellectual ability makes no difference. I need not belabor this because I have a simple proof—the apostle Paul. Paul (at first called Saul) was brought up as a Pharisee. He excelled in his studies. But he was an unbeliever. He hated the Gospel of Christ with all the intensity of his brilliant, erudite nature, and he did his utmost to put an end to the faith and to all preaching about Christ. There he was, Saul of Tarsus, a man of flaming genius.

But you remember what happened to Saul on the road to Damascus. He turned around and became an apostle of the Jesus he had reviled. He became a preacher of this salvation that he had ridiculed and rejected. But—and here is the point—he was still the same man. He still had the same intellect, the same genius, the same knowledge, the same ability as a writer, as a logician.

If you could prove to me that after what happened to him on the road to Damascus, Saul of Tarsus just became a fool, a kind of psychopath—that he suddenly went mad and lost his faculties, that he became an idiot who sat in a corner staring into the fire and never did anything again—well, you would have a plausible argument. But that is not the case. We fortunately know a great deal about this man after the incident on the road to

Damascus, and what do we find? When we read his letters, we find the same brilliant intellect, the same man with the same powers.

Is that not enough to show that unbelief obviously has nothing to do with intellect? I could prove this to you in the case of every other conversion that has taken place. I could prove to you that from the standpoint of ability, some of the greatest geniuses that the world has ever known have been Christians.

"But," you say, "look at people today. Surely there is no man or woman of ability who is a Christian."

That is not true. There are scientists who are Christians. In most walks of life are men and women gifted in an exceptional manner who are Christians. Unbelief has nothing to do with intellect or with how much you know.

So what is it that makes people unbelievers? Here is the vital question. Miss Laski, I remind you again, says that most unbelievers have little in common. She says that they are all different, and looked at from the surface, that is quite right—Sadducees, Pharisees, politicians, teachers of the law, dreamers—all different types. "There is," you say, "nothing in common." Ah, but this is where Miss Laski's statement breaks down. This is where all unbelievers stop thinking and fail to understand. She says that they have little in common. But can you not see that there must be *something* in common? What brings them all together? What makes them unbelievers? What made these people in the first century join together—and people do the same ever since then?

Now here we come to the essential cause of unbelief, and the first seven verses in Acts 4 seem to me to expose it perfectly. What is it that makes a man or woman reject the Gospel? The condition of the heart and the spirit. The cause is not in the mind; it is deeper; it is in the very center of the personality; it is in the realm of feeling, in the realm of emotion—not knowledge, not understanding, but something more elemental. Here is the common denominator. So you get your musicians and your scientists, your poets and your practical people—all these types who are different on the surface and in the realm of intellect have a common base that unites them in opposing the Gospel.

How do I prove that? Well, notice this: "As they spake unto the people, the priests, and the captain of the temple, and the Sadducees, came upon them, being grieved . . ." There it is—*grieved*. Somebody has translated it as "so troubled, very upset, very annoyed, moved." Can you not see at once that you are in the realm of feeling? Oh, I know how one likes to think of oneself as an unbeliever. You can scarcely ever look at the television without finding it in some shape or form; you find it in your morning newspapers, and this is the joke, is it not? Christians? What are they? Just emotionalists, just sentimentalists—people who live entirely in the realm of feeling, moved by emotions. They are not people who sit down calmly and examine the facts dispassionately.

And the unbeliever? A rational being, a calm, unmoved, dispassionate person with a scientific bent. Unbelievers are never moved, never disturbed; they just look on objectively from their Olympian heights and calmly evaluate the facts. They say, "I cannot believe it; I have to reject it." But that is not true! "Being grieved," we are told. If you read these modern unbelievers, you will find that they always reveal their feelings; they cannot think about these things without sneering, without laughing, without making fun. But the moment they behave like that, they are out of the realm of intellect, and they are governed by their feelings. There was nothing dispassionate about those Jewish leaders—quite the reverse. We see vehemence.

There is vehemence on both sides. A man or woman does not believe the Gospel without passion. There is no such thing as a calm, cool, collected, quiet Christian; it is not possible. If men and women believe that God has indeed sent His only Son into the world and even to the cross, why, they are bound to shout. They are bound to be filled with passion; they must be moved. To believe is to be passionate; to disbelieve is to be passionate. Yes, they were "grieved."

Notice, too, the contempt with which the Jewish leaders spoke. Unfortunately, the Authorized Version does not bring this out as powerfully as it should. In verse 7 we read, "When they had set them in the midst, they asked, By what power, or by what name, have ye done this?" Let me give you an alternative, more literal translation: "When they had set them in the midst, they asked, By what power or by what name this did you?" They ended on the word *you*. Do you see the sarcasm and the contempt and the bitterness? "You?" they said. "Are *you* the center of the excitement and the interest? Are people crowding to listen to *you*? Who are *you*?" But again, you notice, they were not speaking with calm, dispassionate intellectualism. No, no, the contempt creeps in and the innuendo, the suggestiveness, and the ridicule. These things always characterize unbelief. It is not just a matter of annoyance. It is deeper, something elemental; it is passionate.

But let us go on with our analysis—why were those Jewish leaders like this? The answer is here on the very surface of the passage: Their pride was wounded. Why did they arrest these two simple men, throw them into prison, and put them on trial? They were concerned about their own authority. Here were the leaders of the nation—the Sadducees and the Pharisees, the scribes, the Herodians, and the temple guards—these were the people on top, and the ordinary populace had always looked up to them. Now the leaders were concerned about their whole position as teachers, about their own reputation. Fancy a Sadducee listening to preaching that said that Jesus had risen from the dead when they had always said that there was no such thing as resurrection!

This is where the passion comes in. Modern men and women believe that science has a complete explanation of the universe and that everything has to be within the limits and terms set by science. Suddenly this Gospel comes and breaks into it all—miracles, Virgin Birth, two natures in one person, a demonstration of power, rising from the dead, ascension. "Nonsense," they say. "Impossible!" Why? Because it makes them look silly; it is a denial of their very teaching.

And that is how these authorities felt at the very beginning. They were jealous because the apostles taught the people and preached through Jesus the resurrection from the dead. The whole of Jerusalem was crowding to listen to these men—these men, of all people! Everyone was turning away from those in authority and listening to these tub-thumpers, these nonentities who had set themselves up as authorities. The situation was impossible!

That is how it has always been. It is not a bit surprising that the Greek philosophers were annoyed with the Gospel and with Jesus Christ. The world had always sat at their feet and looked to them for wisdom. Then came this upstart, this carpenter, this fellow who had never had any training at all, who said, "I am the light of the world." "I am the way, the truth and the life." Where was the Greeks' authority now—their dignity and their status?

Let me be perfectly fair. When Christianity became a religion, it behaved in exactly the same way. By the time of the Middle Ages, the Roman Catholic Church had turned Christianity into a religion, so that when a man like Martin Luther appeared, the authorities turned on him and tried to silence him. "Who is this fellow who stands up against fifteen centuries of teaching?"

And you will find that nearly all religious leaders have done the same thing in turn. Roman Catholicism tried to put an end to Protestantism in Europe and to the early Church of England. But then, in turn, the Church of England tried to suppress the Puritans, and today the official bodies are trying to silence all those who have not got their stamp upon them and their authority. It is all a matter of pride, jealousy, and envy. How can anyone possibly be a teacher unless *they* have taught him? What authority has a person got unless *they* have given it to him? That is the essential cause of unbelief. It is not in the mind; it is deeper down. "No intelligent person believes that old Gospel today," you say—but that is speaking from pride; that is speaking with passion and with contempt. It is not the understanding speaking; it is not knowledge. You feel that you are in a position of authority, but here is a Gospel that seems to smash that authority. That is why men and women hate the Gospel and reject it.

Look at the smallness of unbelief. I am trying to show you what a contemptible thing unbelief is when you truly understand it. Look at these men in Acts. A most notable miracle had just taken place. A man who had never walked in his life was not only walking but leaping and praising God—an amazing thing, a wonderful deliverance. But listen to these men: "When they had set them in the midst, they asked, By what power, or by what name, have ye done this? Then Peter, filled with the Holy Ghost, said unto them, Ye rulers of the people, and elders of Israel, if we this day be examined of the good deed done to the impotent man, by what means he is made whole . . ."

You see the mentality of the authorities? I suggest to you that this smallness is always true of unbelief. It is so petty. It misses the glorious miracle, but it is very interested in the authority by which the miracle was done. "By what power, or by what name, have ye done this? What is your authority? Where are the regulations giving you a right to do this?" Unbelief is not interested in the great fact but in the qualifications! Unbelievers come along as inspectors and say, "What are your degrees? What school have you been to? Where were you trained? Who gave you this authority?" The miracle is staring them in the face, but they cannot see it.

Unfortunately, this attitude is being manifested in the Christian church today. We are told that the world is desperately in need, that the greatest tragedy is a disunited church, and that we must all come together to fight the common enemy. Then we hear: "Yes, but you must accept episcopacy. Have you been ordained?" It does not matter that a man can preach with fire and the Holy Spirit. It does not matter that hundreds may be converted under his ministry. What is asked is: "Have the hands of a bishop been on his head? What is his authority? What is his right? Has he conformed to the regulations? Has he passed through our colleges?" Oh, the tragedy of unbelief that misses the glorious fact and in its pettifogging legalism cares only for the trappings.

Finally look at the unreasonableness of it all. If the apostles had hit the lame man on the head, I could understand why the authorities threw them into prison. But fancy throwing them into prison because they had healed a man! What is it that makes people do such things? There is only one answer: It is the blindness and the deadness that is ever produced by prejudice. Something in human nature is malignant. The Bible tells us that this is the effect of sin upon the human race so that men and women have become perverts, rejoicing in evil and hating the good. And this is still the tragedy of the unbeliever at this moment.

3

FOOLISH AND FUTILE BUILDERS

This is the stone which was set at nought of you builders, which is become the head of the corner.

—Acts 4:11

In a world such as this, the one vital thing is for all of us to know the Gospel and to feel its power. I do not say this because I have some kind of antiquarian interest in the history of the Christian church. Life is too desperate for that. I say this because I, like you, am in the midst of life. We are all here today and gone tomorrow, and we are faced with such momentous decisions that we cannot afford merely to take an academic, theoretical, passing interest in these matters. We are all of us living souls, facing God and eternal judgment, and this is the only message that can help us.

To me, there is nothing more tragic than unbelief. You get the impression from many people that the most tragic thing in the world is the nuclear bomb. But there is something even more tragic. There is something within people that makes them make the bomb. This is where people are so superficial. I am not only referring to the politicians, but I am also referring to those in the church who always speak like the politicians; their guilt is infinitely greater. The question that should confront us is not what people do, but why they do it. The business of the Gospel is to ask this question.

The world is as it is, unhappy and in trouble, simply because it rejects this Gospel. And the same holds true with the individual. Are you in some grievous trouble? Are you ashamed? Are you cast down? Are you disappointed? Are you defeated? It is all because you do not believe the Gospel of salvation and deliverance. That is why we are paying attention to this terri-

ble condition of unbelief. I am saying all this for one reason only. God forbid
that anyone should think that I am just putting up these targets in order to
shoot them down. I have neither the energy nor the time to do that. No, I am
sorry for people who are unbelievers. I see what they are doing, and I see what
they are. But they do not see it, and it is my commission to open their eyes.

So I am trying to do what Peter did. "If you really want to know," he
said, in effect, to the authorities, "I will tell you. You want to know by what
authority and power this lame man has been healed. The answer is the power
and authority of the one you rejected. Can you not see what you are doing?"
Peter was concerned for their souls. He was not just getting back at them; he
was not trying to be clever. He, with John, was on trial, and they knew that
their lives were in the hands of these authorities, who could do whatever they
liked with them. Peter was not acting. He was speaking the truth, and he
wanted these people to understand. And it is in the hope that, by the blessing of the Spirit, those who hitherto have rejected this Gospel may be given
to see exactly what they are doing. For this reason I am calling your attention to these words in Acts.

This is the remarkable thing about the Bible. It is timeless; it belongs to
every age. You cannot say that about any other book. Of course, people in
their folly say the exact opposite. Modern men and women do not read the
Bible. "Old-fashioned! Out of date!" they say. But it is modern books that
become out of date; books on science constantly need to be revised. In almost
every subject textbooks of forty years ago are useless today. But the Bible
never dates. This book, which is a book of history, is also a book that shows
us the state of the human heart in sin. It tells us the truth about men and
women since the Fall. As we have seen, what was true of these people in Acts
is equally true of everyone who does not believe this Gospel. So we are looking at this passage together because, as we have also seen, it is always easier
to see something in someone else than it is to see it in yourself.

So then, having looked at the nature of unbelief, let us now go a step further. As we consider this eleventh verse, I want to try to show you two more
aspects of unbelief—its folly and its futility.

Now Peter brought out these elements by quoting from Psalm 118—a
quotation he slightly modified. The key word in the quotation is *builders*.
"This is the stone which was set at nought of you *builders*." Remember that
he was addressing the most important people in Israel—the scribes, the
priests, the high priests, the Sadducees, the politicians. They were all there;
they constituted the Sanhedrin. They were the "builders," the leaders. So the
apostle could have produced no more apposite quotation.

The problem confronting the human race is the task, if you like, of building a city, a city in which we can dwell. That is what is meant by civilization. And men and women are convinced that they can do it. But here is God's plan. He is building a city, and it is the conflict between these two cities that we are called upon to consider by this quotation from Psalm 118. Peter quotes this verse in order to show that God has always ridiculed these builders and always will. If ever this word was appropriate, it is so today. I find here in one sentence the whole of the modern problem.

First of all, let us look at the folly of unbelief as it is put before us here. Now the Bible has many things to say about unbelievers. It says that they miss the mark, that they are blasphemers. But most frequently it says that ultimately they are fools. "The *fool* hath said in his heart, There is no God" (Psa. 14:1, emphasis mine; 53:1). Our Lord said the same thing in His parable about a rich man, a man who congratulates himself on his wonderful ordering of his own life, a man whose barns are overflowing with produce, so much so that larger barns have to be built. He is typical of successful people today. But God says, "Thou fool, this night thy soul shall be required of thee" (Luke 12:20). The sinner, the unbeliever, is, above everything else, a fool.

But the Bible does not merely state that unbelievers are fools; it demonstrates this fact. The Bible shows that the particular form this folly takes is self-deception. If people are deceived by someone else, then you can say that they lack understanding perhaps or have not been careful enough. But the real fools are those who deceive themselves, and that, as this word *builders* shows, is the essential trouble with unbelievers. Peter was saying: "You people proudly describe yourselves as builders. Yet this is what you have done: 'This is the stone which was set at nought of you builders.'"

Now the people to whom Peter was speaking were, remember, the people who had rejected the Lord Jesus Christ. The Son of God had appeared among them. They had looked into His blessed face, heard His gracious words, seen the miracles He had performed, seen Him dying on the cross, and yet they had reviled Him, rejected Him, and turned their backs upon Him. They had been so blinded by prejudice that they had missed the glory and the miracle. And now they were persecuting these followers of His because they thought that the Gospel was wrong and what they had was right. They were the builders!

But the apostle exposed their folly. He showed them how guilty they were of self-deception. And he did this first by showing that they were hopeless judges of themselves. They had put a label on themselves. They had said, "We

are builders. We are men of understanding." But Peter showed that their esti-
mate of themselves was entirely false.

How did Peter show this? He did it by showing that they were guilty of
the sin of intellectual pride. Why did they call themselves builders? It was
because they were confident that they could solve their problems. They said
to the common people: "Here is the position. We have to build a city.
Everything has been chaotic hitherto. There has been struggle and confusion.
Now we must build a perfect society. We can do it. We have the plans and the
specifications. We are the people to do it—we are the builders. Listen to us."

It was there that their false self-confidence emerged. There was no limit
to their pride. They not only thought that they could deal with the situation,
but they also claimed that human beings were creatures of such understanding that nothing was beyond them.

And is not this the very root cause of the modern rejection of the
Christian faith? Are we not being told that we are living in a scientific age in
which men and women only believe what they can see and demonstrate and
prove and check by experimentation? Modern people will not believe anything beyond that. They say, "The human mind is capable of encompassing
all truth." And if you tell them about the supernatural or the miraculous, they
say, "We don't believe that because we cannot understand it; it doesn't fit into
our system." They are the builders; they have confidence in their intellects.
They say, "Man is the center of the universe; there is nothing outside human
knowledge." You must not talk about mystery; you must not talk about
supernatural intervention; you must not talk about God acting apart from the
laws of nature—this is intolerable. Man! He must have everything before
him, and he must encompass it with his mind. He is a builder!

Is this a caricature? I think you will agree with me that it is not, that I am
giving you an accurate description of the attitude of modern men and women
toward the Christian faith. They claim that there is nothing that they are not
competent to deal with. They have the power to evaluate everything, God
included. Everything is down on the table for their dissection and analysis.
They sit as judges. Builders!

So, you see, in this false view of themselves, people reveal their folly. They
admit that the human race is in trouble, but they are confident that they can
put it right. They can solve the problem because they have the ability and the
brains and the knowledge and the confidence. They reject the Gospel because
they have their own remedies. What is needed? According to them, only the
application of reason. You have only to put the case to men and women. They
are such fine creatures, and they have such great intellects that you have only

to explain to them, to show them the evil effects of certain sins, and they will do them no more. If people understand that statistics can prove that too much alcohol does harm, then they will stop drinking too much alcohol. Show them what sexual indulgence leads to, and they will stop indulging. Appeal to them—reasonable animals!

So you preach morality and inculcate ethics; you teach social ideas; you introduce philosophy and the thinking of the great minds of the century. To sum it up in a word—education! That is all people need. Once they are educated, they will no longer be guilty of excesses. Once they are educated, they will see that it is ridiculous for people to attempt to solve problems by killing one another, and they will banish war. So you bring in your leagues to put an end to war—the League of Nations, the United Nations (call them what you will)—and people are quite certain it can be done. They say, "Don't talk to us about the supernatural; we don't need things like that. Human beings are rational creatures, and this is the way to put their world in order." But it never is!

Have I not just described the position of all the humanists at the present time? They are confident that they have the power of diagnosis and the ability to produce the appropriate remedies. But I would sum it all up by saying that this is sheer overestimation of the self. The builders! Humanity writ large! And it has taken the place of God. This is how self-deception shows itself.

But wait a minute, men and women show the same folly in another way, and it is another part of the self-deception. They are not only hopeless judges of themselves, but they are hopeless judges of stones! What a builder wants, does he not, is the appropriate stones? Especially when you come to the great "cornerstone" that will hold together the greatest walls and be a basis on which everything can be built. The cornerstone! Ah, builders need to have an eye for stones. Of course, amateurs do not know or understand, but builders have knowledge. They know about stresses and strains; they know about weight and suspension. They are experts on stones. Show the builder the right stone, and he will jump at it. "Just the thing," he says.

But according to the teaching of the Bible, that is exactly what these religious leaders did not and could not do. "This is the stone that was set at nought of you builders." They rejected it. Here was a great stone, as it were, offering itself to them, and they looked at it and turned away in disdain. "Useless," they said. "We cannot be bothered with it. Cast it away."

Now this is the tragedy depicted in the four Gospels and also frequently here in the Acts of the Apostles, especially at the very beginning. Peter speaks of "the stone" here and again in his letter (1 Pet. 2:4, 6). What is he talking about? Oh, he is talking about Jesus of Nazareth. Suddenly He stands in their own land of Palestine, this blessed person, Jesus of Nazareth—the one born in a stable, the boy who at the age of twelve could confound the doctors of the law in the temple, the man who at the age of thirty became the miracle worker, the amazing preacher and teacher.

Yet here are the experts, the religious teachers, Pharisees, politicians, Sadducees, doctors of the law, high priests, the leading men, and they all look at him and say, "Who is this fellow who stands up and claims that he is a teacher?" "How knoweth this man letters, having never learned?" (John 7:15). "By what authority doest thou these things?" (Mark 11:28). The apostle Paul has summed it all up for us in 1 Corinthians 2:8: ". . . none of the princes of this world knew: for had they known it, they would not have crucified the Lord of glory."

Here is the test of a good builder: Can he choose something solid, durable, that can stand strain and stress? These Jewish leaders, who called themselves "builders," wanted something big enough and great enough to make their world and civilization, but they rejected the Son of God. It is the supreme tragedy of all history that when men and women are confronted by the only one who can solve the problems and answer the questions, they reject Him with scorn and derision.

Not only did the Jewish leaders reject Jesus of Nazareth and His teaching, but they regarded the apostolic teaching about His death as the height of folly: "unto the Jews a stumblingblock, and unto the Greeks foolishness" (1 Cor. 1:23). They jeered at the idea that someone dying on a cross could be the Savior of the world. They thought it monstrous, ridiculous! "The blood of Christ," they said, "don't talk such rubbish!"

Men and women still say this, but they are rejecting God's way of salvation. It is interesting to see the things that people object to about the Gospel. This is always where the builders have given themselves away. Many today believe that Jesus was a perfect man, but tell them that He is God, and they hate it. They will accept His moral teaching but not His miracles. They will believe that He died the death of a pacifist, that the world did not understand Him and tragically and wrongly put Him to death. That is all right. There is even something beautiful and wonderful about it. But if you tell them that God "laid on him the iniquity of us all" (Isa. 53:6), they will rise in fury and say that it is insulting and immoral. If you say that "with his stripes we are healed" (Isa. 53:5), they will revile you. When you tell them that He taught the doctrine of the rebirth and that He did not come into the world merely to teach and improve men and women, but to give them new life by enabling them to be "born again," born from above of the Spirit, then they will bare their teeth at you and say that you are insulting them. "Are we so bad," they ask, "that we need this?"

These are the doctrines that people object to, and they revile all who preach such things. Rebirth, regeneration, the power of the Holy Spirit in us—these are the truths that cause the builders to betray themselves as hopeless judges of the stones offered to them.

And, lastly, these builders are exposed as frauds by the common people. Verse 3 says, "They [the authorities] laid hands on them, and put them in hold unto the next day: for it was now eventide." Now notice the fourth verse in this chapter: "Howbeit many of them which heard the word believed; and the number of the men was about five thousand." This response is wonderful. The apostle Paul saw the same thing happen in Corinth. "The wisdom of this world" is always shown to be the folly that it really is (1 Cor. 3:19).

Our Lord Himself had taught that the world would reject Him. In His parable of the man who had two sons, the father told both sons to go and work in the vineyard. One son said, "I will not!" But afterwards he changed his mind and went. The second son said, "I'll go." But he did not go. Then our Lord put the question: "Which son did what his father wanted?" Our Lord's listeners replied, "The first." Then we read:

> *Jesus saith unto them, Verily I say unto you, That the publicans and the harlots go into the kingdom of God before you. For John came unto you in the way of righteousness, and ye believed him not: but the publicans and the harlots believed him: and ye, when ye had seen it, repented not afterward, that ye might believe him.*
> *—Matt. 21:31-32*

There were the authorities refusing, staying outside, and the common people, the tax-collectors and prostitutes, crowding into the kingdom. And this pattern was being repeated here in Acts.

So the apostle Paul reminds the Corinthian Christians that it was "the wise and prudent" who rejected the Gospel:

> *For ye see your calling, brethren, how that not many wise men after the flesh, not many mighty, not many noble, are called: But God hath chosen the foolish things of the world to confound the wise; and God hath chosen the weak things of the world to confound the things*

*which are mighty; and base things of the world, and things which are
despised, hath God chosen, yea, and things which are not, to bring
to nought things that are.*

—*1 Cor. 1:26-28*

This has been the wonderful story of the Christian church and the
Christian faith throughout the running centuries. What the wisdom of this
world has not been able to do, the Gospel of Christ has done. While the wise
and the prudent have remained on the outside, criticizing and despising, living a life of sin and shame and dying in hopelessness, simple, ignorant, ordinary people, sometimes from the gutters of life, have been entering into the
kingdom and have become saints and have died triumphantly. Oh, the unutterable folly of the builders, these clever people who think they understand
and know! Oh, the fatal self-confidence that believes it can put things right
and that everything must submit to the criticism of its intellect! Oh, the folly
of it all!

But let me now go on to say a word about the futility of unbelief, and
this, of course, is still more serious. There is nothing in the world so futile as
unbelief. It is all talk, nothing but talk; that is what Peter was exposing in his
quotation from Psalm 118. Here were these clever authorities, these people
who talked so much and who taught others. What did they do? The answer
is—nothing!

Am I exaggerating? Well, let us put it to a simple test. The business of a
builder is to build. There is such a thing as a "jerry-builder," is there not? And
he is always a good talker! But you do not test him by his talk but by the
building he erects. So look at the people today who reject the Gospel with the
kind of scorn and derision these authorities expressed in Jerusalem at the
beginning of the Christian church. People today are builders. They are concerned, they say, about society, about people, about the state of the world.
These are the humanists who reject the Gospel in the belief that they can put
things right.

So let us ask a simple question: What has civilization done? It has
existed for a long time now—what has it actually succeeded in producing?
Is it not time that we began to examine the building? We do not want talk;
we want results. About sixty or seventy years ago the Christian church
began to preach a new gospel. It was called the "social gospel," and the
church has been preaching it ever since. It says: "That old Gospel, that old
evangelical message, was always personal. But that is wrong; it is even
unscriptural and immoral. We need a social gospel, a gospel that will put

things right in Vietnam, not this talk of a personal relationship with God. No, no, we need the big view, a concern about the state of society and the affairs of the nation."

So the old Gospel is put aside. Preachers of the social gospel say that you do not need the miraculous and the supernatural, that primitive people invoked the supernatural out of ignorance, but science has shown that the miraculous is impossible. So they preach morality, good conduct, the importance of education, and the inculcation of right principles. They say, "Do that, and the world will become perfect."

Well, all I would ask here is: "Where is the building?" The builders have said: "We have the plans, the specifications. We can tell you exactly what to do. You have only to do it, and you will have this durable building. You will have a perfect world. With the parliament of man and the federation of the world, war will be abolished." They have taught the people to stop attending places of worship. They have said that the world can be improved through politics. You need not believe in a supernatural God. All you need to do is put your back into political action and pass Acts of Parliament. You can legislate a paradise—and they have been trying to do it.

But our world today is the answer to those builders. What wonderful talkers they are, but what have they done? What has all this education led to? I see figures showing increasing juvenile delinquency. What has been the result of all the ethical teaching? Look at the statistics in the divorce courts. What has civilization produced? Where is this city? And the answer is that there is nothing to be seen. The builders are fools; they are talkers; they are boasters; they are always bringing up plans, but nothing happens. Let me sum it all up in a verse from a hymn:

> *Pride of man and earthly glory,*
> *Sword and crown betray his trust;*
> *What with care and toil he buildeth—*
> *Tower and temple fall to dust.*
> Joachim Neander

Is not that what is happening to our civilization? The whole world is rotting and shaking. There is no place of safety. There is no residence where you can sit down and be quiet and enjoy yourself. The world is crumbling. There is nothing but talk and talk and talk. Oh, the futility of the talk of unbelievers that leads to no building! And the only answer is this:

But God's power,
Hour by hour,
Is my temple and my tower.
                    Joachim Neander

Still worse, these builders do not realize that they are fighting against God's plan and purpose, and that, of course, is what Peter was driving home. With regard to the question about the apostles' power and authority, Peter stated, "Be it known unto you all, and to all the people of Israel, that by the name of Jesus Christ of Nazareth, whom ye crucified, whom God raised from the dead, even by him doth this man stand here before you whole" (Acts 4:10). That is the answer.

"Can't you see what you are doing?" said Peter, in effect. "You are defying the living God; you are standing up to the Almighty. You are trying to build, and you are ignoring God's building. You have nothing, but His building is continuing. You are such fools that you do not realize that the one whom you rejected is the very cornerstone of the edifice. Jesus of Nazareth is the Savior; He is the Messiah. Don't you know?" asked Peter. "Why don't you read your own history. God has announced His plan—the seed of the woman shall bruise the serpent's head (see Gen. 3:15). There it is—there is the basis. Why don't you realize this? Read your prophets; see them pointing to the one who was to come. And He has come, He is the cornerstone, and you don't realize it. You say that you want a building. Don't you see that your need is a 'city which hath foundations, whose builder and maker is God' (Heb. 11:10)?

"When are you going to give up this fatal self-confidence that produces nothing, and when will you begin to consult and listen to the heavenly Architect? Forget your little plans that always come to nought and crumble to the dust, and humble yourselves under the mighty hand of God. God revealed His plan in the Garden of Eden. He renewed it and made it plainer in Abraham, Isaac, and Jacob. With Moses, He produced the specifications. Read your own prophets.

"You blind fools!" said Peter. "This is God's plan, God's edifice, God's city. Can you not see that God has revealed to you the cornerstone, the head of the corner, the only stone that can bear the weight and stand the stresses and bind the walls together? Oh, you builders, there you are, interested in your nothings, and you are ignoring this amazing plan of God. He has put it before you, and you have not seen it."

Oh, the blindness of unbelief, the futility. It always comes to nothing. But let me remind you of this before we leave it. Here is a message that also tells us about the certain and inevitable menaces that await unbelief—the destruction. Peter was also saying in effect: 'Can you not see that God is ridiculing you? You have set at nought this head stone of the corner, and God has shown you your folly. Can you not see it? He is exposing you to yourselves ere it be too late. Can you not see that you are fighting not only against the wisdom of God, but against the power of God?"

This is the truth that the Bible teaches everywhere about unbelievers. They are like King Canute's servants, so confident of his great power that they thought he could defy the ocean. He took his seat and said, "Stop—don't come any nearer." But the waves did not listen; they came in. To think otherwise was madness; it was to be drunk with self-confidence and power. But that is the picture of unbelievers. They are fighting what is certain; they are pitting themselves against something irresistible.

That is what makes Peter's words so desperately serious and urgent for all of us. "Listen," said Peter. "Who has done this miracle? Let me tell you. It is the Jesus whom you crucified, whose body you laid in a tomb. He has done it! You could not kill Him. He is alive, and alive forevermore. The stone you builders have set at nought has been made the head stone of the corner." And this is the message of the whole Bible.

Before the Flood the people laughed at Noah. They thought it funny that a man should be building an ark and should go on saying that there would be a great deluge. This was a wonderful joke. All the people had enjoyed themselves. "They were eating and drinking, marrying and giving in marriage" (Matt. 24:38). But it made no difference to the coming of the flood. God carried out His threat.

Was it not exactly the same with Pharaoh, the dictator of Egypt, who defied the living God? Here he comes, chasing after these little people, and he says, "I've got them. Who is this God? I'll show them who God is. I'll show them who has the power!" And there he is, counting his chariots and horses and galloping after this band of people. "There's the Red Sea! I've got them." No, no, the Red Sea opens, the children of Israel walk across the sea bed, and Pharaoh and his hosts are drowned. The builders are shown to themselves in their utter futility.

Look at a man like Nebuchadnezzar. He sets himself up as a god and wants people to worship him. But God strikes, and there he is, like a beast in the field, living with animals, eating grass—a monster.

But the most striking illustration of all is the very one that Peter put before the people. In His love and mercy and compassion, God sent His own Son into the world. Oh, He gave signs of his Son's godhead. Even the temple guards said, "Never man spake like this man" (John 7:46). Here was God incarnate, sent to save the world, but the builders of the world rejected Him and said cleverly to one another, "The only thing to do with Him is to put Him to death." So they conspired together. They said, "If we put Him to death, that's the end, and then we can go on as before." And they killed Him. But He rose! "The stone which the builders refused is become the head stone of the corner" (Psa. 118:22).

> *Vain the stone, the watch, the seal,*
> *Christ hath burst the gates of hell:*
> *Death in vain forbids His rise,*
> *Christ hath opened Paradise.*
>   Charles Wesley

He burst asunder the bands of death and rose triumphantly even from the tomb, and here He was, still at work. They had rejected Him, but He was there. They could not get rid of Him. God had made Him the head stone of the corner. The very healing of the lame man was an absolute proof of this fact, and a few years later the destruction of Jerusalem was a further proof.

But the persecutions continued. Humanity does not change. The Roman emperors thought they could exterminate the Christian church. But what happened? Well, the more they killed the Christians, the more the church grew. "The blood of the martyrs is the seed of the church." The stone the builders rejected always becomes the head of the corner. And is this not the great story of all the revivals in the history of the church? Just when people are confident that Christianity is coming to an end, God sends revival. The moribund church is awakened, filled with life anew, made strong with power, and goes on to greater conquests. "The stone which the builders refused is become the head stone of the corner."

You cannot win against God; you are fighting against the eternal and omnipotent God. The very world of today is proof positive of all these things. The work of the builders is a shambles throughout this universe. Oh, the cleverness and ingenuity of men and women! How they boast of their science and knowledge! And see the results! But God goes on, and He will go on. The Christ is being preached, and men and women are being saved. He comes "conquering and to conquer."

So we look to the future, and what we see is just this same principle: "The stone which was set at nought of you builders is become the head of the corner."

He sits at God's right hand
Till all His foes submit,
And bow to His command,
And fall beneath His feet.
Charles Wesley

Unbeliever, you are going to see Him. "Every eye shall see him" (Rev. 1:7). He is coming again. Let the clever men and women deride Him; let the builders laugh at Him and reject Him; let philosophy scoff at Him. A day is coming when "at the name of Jesus every knee should bow, of things in heaven, and things on earth, and things under the earth; and that every tongue should confess that Jesus Christ is Lord, to the glory [and the honor] of God the Father" (Phil. 2:10-11).

My dear friend, cannot you see the futility of it all, the madness? You are defying the living God. He has given you final proof of it in the resurrection of His dear Son. "You fools," says Peter, "can you not see that the Christ whom you rejected is alive? He has healed this man. It is this Jesus of Nazareth and the power of His name that has given this man perfect soundness in the presence of you all."

You cannot get rid of him. Kill Him—He comes back! Bury Him—He rises! He is seated at the right hand of God, and all power is given to Him. He is carrying out his program; the specifications are being worked out in detail. He knows His people, and He is saving them generation by generation until "the fulness of the Gentiles be come in. And so all Israel shall be saved" (Rom. 11:25-26). Then He will come and judge the world in righteousness, and all who have rejected Him will go to eternal perdition. But all who have believed and trusted in Him will shine with Him like the sun and share His eternal glory and reign with Him.

4

THE ONLY SAVIOR

Neither is there salvation in any other: for there is none other name under heaven given among men, whereby we must be saved.

—Acts 4:12

In his address to the people, Peter has shown the folly and the futility of unbelief, and then he comes to this great climax. Verse 12 is a great, positive affirmation. Indeed, it is a summary of the Christian message. It is, of course, the very thing our Lord Himself had said many times during His earthly ministry. He had said, for example, "The Son of man is come to seek and to save that which was lost" (Luke 19:10). "I am come a light into the world" (John 12:46). And, in particular, after His resurrection when He had called His apostles together and explained the Old Testament Scriptures to them, He had said, "Thus it is written, and thus it behooved Christ to suffer, and to rise from the dead the third day: and that repentance and remission of sins should be preached in his name among all nations, beginning at Jerusalem. And ye are witnesses of these things" (Luke 24:46-48). He had told them He would give them power to go and preach the Gospel to the uttermost parts of the earth, and now here they are, beginning to do that.

So now we find ourselves face to face with the great central affirmation of the Christian church. This verse is obviously, therefore, the statement by which anything that claims to be Christian teaching must always be judged. There is much confusion in the world today as to what Christianity is, but here, in this one verse, we have the ultimate test. If anything that claims the name of Christian does not conform to this verse, it is false. This is essential

Christianity. The church is "built upon the foundation of the apostles and prophets" (Eph. 2:20), and here is that foundation in this most succinct and convenient form for us all to remember always.

Now at the present time it is obvious that that which calls itself "modern Christianity" or "radical Christianity" not only differs from Peter's words here in verse 12, but it seems to go out of its way to deny them at every single point. That is almost incredible, but it is the truth.

What is it that people object to about this old Gospel? Above everything else, they dislike its exclusive claim. They say, "You people are arrogant. You say that you alone are right, that you alone have the truth of God. But what about Hinduism or Confucianism or Islam? Why do you say that this message, and this alone, is true? You must not claim that." Then they add, "We must not send missionaries to India and Africa and Asia and say to the people, 'Listen, this alone is the truth.' No, no! We must go and say, 'What you have is all right, but we think you ought to know something about this as well.' And you must not say that anybody is a 'non-Christian.'" Modern theologians never tire of telling us that we need the insights of other religions and the help of philosophy and modern learning, and that taken all together, somehow or another, sometime or another, these will bring us some glimpse of the truth.

That is the modern position, and you are familiar with it. This view offers itself to the world as something that will appeal to today's intellectuals. Its advocates say, "People no longer believe in God who is a person, a personal God. They do not believe in the supernatural; they do not believe in the miraculous. We are scientific now. So if you really want to appeal to the intellectual, cultivated, scientific mind, you have to present this new, radical Christianity." But this one verse is sufficient to answer all that. This verse shows that "radical Christianity" is not Christianity at all, but denies it, as I shall show you, at every single vital point.

Furthermore, what is so interesting to me is that far from appealing to the intellectuals, the humanists, the atheists, and others who are outside the Christian church, this "radical Christianity" does not interest them at all. Now I am not just giving my opinion. I read recently, strangely enough, in *Punch*, another important article by that brilliant atheistic humanist, Marghanita Laski. She writes that the modern Christianity that is being offered to people like herself is, to start with, not Christianity at all. She adds that she does not understand why contemporary theologians still go on talking about Jesus and having their sacraments, because these practices bear no relationship to their teaching. She does not hesitate to say that though she does not believe the old presentation, it is at least consistent with itself, whereas the new interpretation is not.

Theologians are trying to produce a Gospel that will appeal to the modern intellectual, but modern intellectuals see through it and respond, "You are now saying what we've always said." So "radical Christianity" is not Christianity at all; that is the simple truth. Now I want to explain why I say this in terms of this great statement made by the apostle Peter in Acts 4:12. *This* is Christianity; this is what has saved men and women throughout the centuries, and it is the only thing that can save them now.

What do Peter's words tell us? Let me give you two propositions. Here is the first: The Lord Jesus Christ is the Savior. Look at the way Peter puts that: "Neither," he says, "is there salvation in any other: for there is none other name under heaven given among men, whereby we must be saved." Here is the first great affirmation of the Christian faith. Its emphasis is upon what the Lord Jesus Christ does. Oh, how blind we all are to this by nature!

Peter had an obvious illustration that he could use. He was on trial because of the lame man who had been healed. Peter turned to the authorities and said, in effect, "You are examining us because of the good deed done to the impotent man. You want to know by what means he was made whole. I will tell you. We have not done it by our own power; indeed, we have not done it at all." So who has done it? And Peter said, "Be it known unto you all, and to all the people of Israel, that by the name of Jesus Christ of Nazareth, whom ye crucified, whom God raised from the dead, even by him doth this man stand here before you whole" (v. 10).

What had healed the man? It was the name of Christ. In the Bible the words "in the name of" mean "by the power of." That is why the authorities had asked, "By what power, or by what name, have ye done this?" (v. 7). Peter had said to the lame man, "In the *name* of Jesus Christ of Nazareth rise up and walk" (Acts 3:6, emphasis mine). So he was saying here that it was the power of Christ that had done this miracle. Christ had healed the man. Christ had given him the power to stand and walk. "And listen," said Peter, "salvation also is entirely the result of the work of Christ. He does it all."

Now I emphasize that it is Christ who brings salvation because there is such grievous misunderstanding with respect to this truth. Some people think of our Lord as someone who teaches us how to save ourselves. "Ah, yes," they say, "Jesus was a great teacher. I like reading the Sermon on the Mount. That is what I want, and I'm trying to put His ethical teachings into practice." Their idea is that if you take His teaching and apply it, then you will make yourself a Christian, and you will get to know God.

Others emphasize the importance of His example. They say that He not only taught, but He practiced what He taught. He gave a visible demonstration of the truth of the principles of His own teaching. There you see a life that is right and perfect, and what you have to do is imitate it. So they set out upon the task of "the imitation of Christ." They express this idea in various other ways, but it comes down to the fact that they regard Him as someone who has come to teach us how we can save ourselves. He tells us what we must and must not do, and then, as we put His words into practice, we shall gradually feel better and will increasingly deliver ourselves.

But that is an utter contradiction of what the apostle says. The illustration proves it, does it not? Peter and John did not tell the lame man to start on a course of exercises. They did not say, "Well, now, my good man, you have never been able to walk in your life, but we can put you right. We have a course of treatment here. You see, you've made a mistake, you've lost hope, you've not tried to use your muscles. You must try. At first it will seem useless, but you must concentrate and use your willpower. You must move the muscles of your right leg first. Slowly start with your feet and gradually work up. Then go to the left and do the same, and you will slowly find yourself getting better and stronger. And ultimately, we assure you, you will be able to stand." No, no. Peter said the exact opposite of that.

Christianity is not a course of treatment. It does not give us instructions on how we can put ourselves right. To a man who was completely paralyzed, who was born lame, the apostle said, "In the name of Jesus Christ of Nazareth rise up and walk." And the lame man did. Immediately! Christ healed the man there and then. The very first principle of this Gospel is that Christ is the Savior. He came into the world not to tell us what to do, but to do it for us. He came not to teach us how to save ourselves, but to save us. Salvation is His work; He is the Savior. "The Son of man is come to seek and to save that which was lost" (Luke 19:10). Primarily and essentially, He is not an instructor, not a teacher, not an example, but, as this illustration demonstrates and as Peter used it, he is a Savior. It is by *his name* that we are saved: "For there is none other name under heaven given among men, whereby [by which] we must be saved."

There is the first proposition. Are you clear about that, or are you still trying to make yourself a Christian? Do you think you can ever do that? Do you think that by going through a course of training, you can make yourself good and reconcile yourself to God? Well, in that case, you need not go any further. You are altogether wrong. The beginning of this message is that Jesus saves by the power of His name. He is the healer, the one who delivers us.

Salvation is entirely His action. You do not give instructions and rules to a man born lame who has no power and can never generate it. No, a miracle is needed, and our Lord came to work that miracle.

Secondly, our Lord, says Peter, is the *only* Savior. "Neither is there salvation in any other: for there is none other name under heaven given among men, whereby we must be saved." Peter says it twice for emphasis. Again this second point is absolutely vital. This, as I said, is the point the modern clever people object to most of all. "All right," they say, "we are interested in your Christianity, but when you say it is the only way, you are just arrogant and narrow-minded." But the whole of the Gospel depends upon this claim, as I shall show you.

Our Lord Himself constantly claimed to be the only Savior. He did not hesitate to say, "I am the light of the world" (John 8:12; 9:5). Now that is as exclusive a claim as you could ever make. Then he said, "I am the bread of life," (John 6:35, 48) and, "I am the way, the truth, and the life: no man cometh unto the Father, but by me" (John 14:6). Now either these statements are true, or they are the most arrant nonsense ever uttered. That is what Jesus said, and Peter and John were saying the same thing. The apostle Paul puts it even more strongly in writing to the Galatians when he says, "Though we, or an angel from heaven, preach any other gospel unto you than that which we have preached unto you, let him be accursed" (Gal. 1:8).

When Peter said, "there is none other name," he was insisting that no other individual who has ever lived in this world, or who ever will live here, can make this claim for himself. We maintain that Jesus of Nazareth is unique. He does not belong to any category; you cannot put anybody else in the same class. He is on His own. He is not one of many. He is not simply the best of many. There are people who talk about him like that. They have a list. They talk about Plato, Socrates, Aristotle, Moses, Jeremiah, Jesus, and then various other great thinkers since then. But that is utterly to deny Him. There is no other; there is no second. It is not a question of whether He is better than everybody; He is different. He and he alone saves.

We can put that in another way also: The apostle is not only asserting that nobody else can ever save or deliver us, but also that our Lord needs no help. Jesus alone saves, and He saves perfectly. Let me say it with reverence: He does not need the help of the Virgin Mary. She is not a "co-redemptress," because He is the full, sufficient, complete Redeemer in Himself. He is all and in all, and to add anybody to Him, even His mother, is to deny Him, and it is blasphemy.

To talk, therefore, about syncretism or eclecticism is to deny the Gospel.

To talk about a "World Congress of Faiths" and to say, "Yes, we're very interested to hear about the contribution of Hinduism, and we're anxious to hear what Islam has to say, and we're interested in the insight that comes from Confucianism," is to deny Him. If you add anything to Him, you take away from Him altogether. No, there's "none other name." He, in and of Himself and alone, is the Savior of the world. As this is a point that is most hotly contested and seems to the so-called impartial, balanced intellectual of today to be an amazingly arrogant assertion, let us examine it. Let us see why the apostle said it and why our blessed Lord Himself ever said such a thing. The reason is given fully here and elsewhere in the New Testament. And, as we look at this teaching, we shall see where modern men and women go astray. We shall see also why they reject the Gospel. It is all put before us here so simply and plainly.

Why, then, is it that objections are raised when we say that Christ alone is the Savior? The answer is quite simple: It is entirely due to a failure to realize the nature and depth of the problem. Let me show you what I mean. Why are any of us ever unhappy? Why do we do things that we bitterly regret afterwards? Why do we fail as we do in life? Why is there so much misery and pain? Why is the world as troubled as it is? Those are the great questions, and I repeat that the reason why people do not believe this message concerning Christ as the exclusive Savior is that they have never, never understood the nature and the reality of the problem. So what is it? Now that is the great message of the whole Bible, and it is summarized here for us by Peter. It is also summarized in his sermons immediately after healing the lame man and on the day of Pentecost.

When we try to understand the problem, we have to start with God, with the nature of God. Unbelievers do not start here. They always start with a human situation, with men and women, and they end with them. They propose this and that, and nothing comes of it. The builders, as we have seen, never succeed in producing anything. They are great talkers, but they do not help us. All their talk is useless because they do not start at the right place—with God.

If people believe in God at all, they think of Him as someone like themselves, and they say, "If there is a God, then he must be a God of love; and because he is a God of love, he will always smile upon us. And if we misbehave? Oh, like a modern parent, he will never punish us. He will just say, 'Don't do it again.'" There is no discipline, no sense of justice, no righteousness—just indulgence. "We do not need to live moral, clean, decent, pure lives," they say. "Love never punishes but always forgives; love is always kind, tender, long-suffering, and patient. Everybody will go to heaven. You must not talk about justice when you are talking about love." These people get their idea of love from films and romantic novels. But others conclude that there cannot be a God at all, because, if there were, He would not allow terrible things to happen in this world.

And so the world goes from bad to worse simply because men and women do not know God. Our Lord Himself said in His high priestly prayer at the end of His life: "O righteous Father, the world hath not known thee" (John 17:25). My friends, if you want to understand the problem of humanity, you start with God, the everlasting and eternal God—holy, pure, righteous, just.

Oh, yes, God is a God of love and mercy and compassion, but not at the expense of His justice, holiness, and righteousness. He is a God of law; He revealed the law to Moses. Moses did not concoct the Ten Commandments. God gave them to him. God said, "I am the LORD thy God. . . . Thou shalt have no other gods before me. Thou shalt not make unto thee any graven image. . . . Thou shalt not take the name of the LORD thy God in vain. . . . Remember the sabbath day, to keep it holy. . . . Honour thy father and thy mother. . . . Thou shalt not kill. Thou shalt not commit adultery. Thou shalt not steal . . ." (Ex. 20:2-15). This is *God* speaking.

And God went further. He said that if we did not keep His commandments, He would punish us. The Old Testament is nothing, in a sense, but the record of God punishing His own chosen people for breaking His law. When He first made the man and woman, He put them in a place called Paradise and told them quite plainly that if they kept His laws they would grow in their knowledge of Him, and He would give them immortality. But if they sinned against Him, He would drive them out of the Garden. And God did drive them out when they sinned by rebelling against Him.

Now there is no need to argue about these things. You cannot mix light and darkness; you cannot mix holiness and sin; you cannot mix everlasting purity and filth—it is impossible. God cannot tolerate evil because He is what He is. The modern idea of God is a travesty—a projection of the evil hearts of men and women. Forgiveness of sins is not an easy thing for the almighty God. He cannot deny Himself. He is "the Father of lights, with whom is no variableness, neither shadow of turning" (James 1:17). We human beings often contradict ourselves. We lay down a rule: "If you do that, this will be the consequence." But when we are disobeyed, we say, "All right, I'll forget about what I said." I say it with reverence here and now that God cannot do that. He would not be God if He could. He would not be worthy of our worship and respect and adoration. No, He is unchangeable and always consistent with Himself. But the modern world does not know that, so it has already gone wrong.

The world is equally wrong in its understanding of the condition of men and women and the problem resulting from that condition. Modern people have such a high opinion of themselves; they think they are so good, so much better than their forefathers. They think nothing is beyond their competence. They are confident, proud, and assured, and because of this pride, they do not realize the truth about the Lord Jesus Christ. What do I mean? Well, the condition of humanity is only truly discovered as we read the Bible, and here it is: Men and women are guilty before God. They have forgotten him and denied Him. They utter blasphemous statements concerning Him. They break His laws; they ignore His holy commandments. They are guilty sinners. They know it in their hearts because their consciences tell them, but they will not listen. They have a feeling that they are guilty, and they are afraid of God, but they stifle these feelings.

Modern men and women are not only guilty, but they are also fallen. Each of us has a polluted nature. That is where the notion that all that is needed is instruction and education and guidance and example so completely fails. It is not simply that people do wrong, but that they love it; they revel in doing wrong. As our blessed Lord Himself put it: "This is the condemnation, that light is come into the world, and men loved darkness rather than light, because their deeds were evil" (John 3:19). Men and women are not good; they are not pure; they are fallen and polluted. They love the darkness; they delight in it; it ravishes their hearts; they are twisted, perverted creatures.

The result of all this is that we are under the power of sin, under the power of the devil, under the power of the world and the flesh. Now there is no question about our condition if we are only honest with ourselves. Why is it that we go on repeating the same sin, though we always experience remorse? We know the behavior is wrong; yet we do it. We promise we will never do it again, and yet we repeat it. What is the matter? It is that we are not only polluted, but we are tyrannized by the devil, the world, and the flesh. We are under the dominion of sin, and we are weak and helpless. "To will is present with me," wrote Paul, "but how to perform that which is good I find not. . . . For I delight in the law of God after the inward man: but I see another law in my members, warring against the law of my mind, and bringing me into captivity to the law of sin" (Rom. 7:18, 22-23). Beyond this, there is the fear of death and of life slipping away. We are unready. We are unprepared, and we feel left to ourselves, lost and forlorn. Is that not our condition?

So if that is a true description, then it follows that our need is, as the apostle Peter says, for "salvation." What is needed? It is not help, not advice, not a good example, not to be improved. We need to be delivered; we need salvation.

But there is something else that we need: We need someone to speak to God for us. How can I speak to God? At last I come to see that I am wrong. I am disappointed, unhappy, a failure, and, oh, then I begin to think about God. But how can I address Him? God is in His heaven; I am on earth. God is holy; I am unworthy and vile. God is light, and I am darkness.

> *Oh! how shall I whose native sphere*
> *Is dark, whose mind is dim,*
> *Before the Ineffable appear,*
> *And on my naked spirit bear*
> *That uncreated beam?*
>
> Thomas Binney

How can I? Job lamented that there was no daysman between him and God (Job 9:33). Is there nobody who can arbitrate between me and God? I need someone to introduce me. I am afraid to enter Buckingham Palace and approach the queen without an introduction, so how can I approach God? Is there no one who can act as an intermediary and introduce me? I am unworthy. Is that not it?

Then I need to get rid of the guilt of my sin. I cannot undo the past. I cannot erase the blots in the journal of my life. I am guilty; I am condemned by the law, and I know it. The philosophers do not help me; they are guilty themselves. Nobody helps me; they have all failed. Who can help me? "How should a man be just with God?" (Job 9:2). How can I be reconciled to God? That is also what I need to know.

What else do I need? Well, I obviously need a new nature. In my better moments I feel unhappy and say I must live a better life. I must be a better person. Somebody dear to me dies. I stand over an open coffin or grave and say I am going to be different. But there is something wrong inside me; all my resolutions come to nothing. Every year on the first day of January, I make New Year's resolutions, but I only keep them for a few days, if even a day. I want to be better, but I cannot be better; I need a new nature.

The fault is not really in what I do, but in what I am. Oh, that I could make myself anew! But I cannot. "Can the Ethiopian change his skin, or the leopard his spots?" (Jer. 13:23). It cannot be done. "That which is crooked cannot be made straight" (Eccl. 1:15). "It's no use," says the world. "You are what you are, and you have to live with yourself." So here I am, left with my own fallen, perverted nature. I cannot produce a new nature; no human being can give it to me. I need power to stand against the world and the flesh and the devil, and I do not have it.

We are all defeated. As we read of the saints and the patriarchs conquered by the devil, overcome by the subtlety of his temptations, we know that the same is true of us. We need help and strength in this terrible fight, the fight to be moral and clean and good, the fight to live a worthy life, the fight so to live that we may die without fear and apprehension. Advice, teaching, instruction, and example do not help but throw us back on ourselves. The philosophers are great men, but they cannot give us their understanding. We see examples of great people living good lives, and we say, "How wonderful to live like that!" Can they give us their morality? Can the best people in the world help us when we fall into sin? They may give sympathy, though they are more likely to offer criticism, but they cannot impart anything of themselves to us. As we look at all this, we simply have to confess:

> *Not the labors of my hands*
> *Can fulfill Thy law's demands.*
> *Could my zeal no respite know,*
> *Could my tears forever flow,*
> *All for sin could not atone.*

Is that not your problem? Is that not the problem of the whole world in spite of our education, our good books, our universities, and all the cultural agencies? Why are we all in trouble? There is only one answer: These things cannot save us.

> *All for sin could not atone,*
> *Thou must save, and Thou alone.*
>   Augustus Toplady

It comes to this: Once you realize the true nature of the problem of men and women, you will soon agree with Peter that there is only one who can deal with it. Peter says, "Neither is there salvation in any other: for there is none other name under heaven given among men, whereby we must be saved." He says, "Listen, there is only one, the one you rejected. He has been made the cornerstone. He is the only Savior. Believe in Him; for as He did this for the lame man when nobody else could do it, so He alone can save your soul."

But why can He alone save me? Well, He is the only one who in His person is adequate to meet my needs. We have seen that we each need someone who can represent us before God. But no one can represent me because no one is better than I am. I am a sinner, but so is everyone else. No one can be an intermediary between me and the God whom I long to know. Every man and woman is fallen. Even a perfect man, like Adam at the beginning, fell. So no one is adequate to represent me, and yet my representative must be a human being because I am a human being.

Have you ever thought of that problem? Here is humanity—fallen, sinful, alienated from God. Who can speak for humanity to God? No polluted and unworthy human being can have that right, so there must be someone beyond, but that someone must be human because we are flesh and blood, and a representative must belong to those represented.

Can there be such a representative? You see the answer? There is only one. Here is one who is fully God and fully human. He is the eternal Son of God. Yes, but as the eternal Son of God, He could not save us. In order to save us, He had to become "a son of man." That is why we have the birth in Bethlehem. That is the meaning of the Incarnation. He is God, but He had to become man. Hebrews 2:14 says, "Forasmuch then as the children are partakers of flesh and blood, he also himself likewise took part of the same" in order that He might represent us. Do you see it? We must have one who can stand in a position of equality before God and speak for us in the presence of God. Yet He must also be man and share with us in our problems and difficulties. And there is only one solution: the Son of God became the Son of man. "The Word was made flesh, and dwelt among us" (John 1:14). Two natures in one Person—the Lord Jesus Christ, the Son of God.

> *Who, being in the form of God, thought it not robbery to be equal with God: but made himself of no reputation, and took upon him the form of a servant, and was made in the likeness of men: and being found in fashion as a man, he humbled himself, and became obedient unto death, even the death of the cross.*
>
> —*Phil. 2:6-8*

This person alone satisfies my need. He must be God; He must be man. There is none other; He is alone. Confucius was a man, Mohammed was a man, Buddha was a man—but none of these could save me. I need God as well as man, and here is the God-man in all the perfection of His glory.

So He satisfies my need in His person, but, oh, thank God, He also satisfies my need in His ability. I have told you what we need—someone who can not only represent us before God, but also someone who can do something about the guilt of our sin. That guilt is there, and, I say it with reverence that even God's love cannot deal with it directly by a word. No, God is just, and sin must be punished. God cannot pretend He has not seen sin; that would be a lie, and God cannot lie. Oh, the guilt of my sin—what can be done about it? No human being can bear it because everybody is already guilty, but here is one who can. Here is "the Lamb of God, which taketh away the sin of the world" (John 1:29). Here is one who has never sinned; here is one who is spotless; here is one who has never broken a commandment. He has pleased His Father in all things and in all ways. And, "the LORD hath laid on him the iniquity of us all" (Isa. 53:6). None other could bear it; none other could take the punishment and yet live. But He has; He is great enough. He is God and man, and He bore our sins in His body on the tree.

And because He bore our sins, He is able to give us the new nature that we need. He took upon Himself human nature in order that He might give us a new nature. Here is one who talks about a rebirth. Here is one who says, "Ye must be born again" (John 3:7). Here is one who can make us partakers of the divine nature. He has linked humanity to the Godhead, and He gives us this new life. We are born of the Spirit, born from above, born of God. He gives us a new life, a new beginning, a new nature, and a new start.

What else do we need? We need someone who can help us in the terrible fight against sin. We cannot win this conflict ourselves; there is only one who can enable us. He met the devil in single mortal combat; the devil produced his last reserves, but our Lord defeated him. Jesus Christ is Master of the world, the flesh, and the devil.

But still more wonderful, Jesus sympathizes with us. You may think of Him as the Son of God—holy, spotless, undefiled, separate from sinners—and say, "What does someone like that know about me and the tragedy of my failure and weakness?" But listen! He knows all about you: "In that he himself hath suffered being tempted, he is able to succour them that are tempted" (Heb. 2:18). "We have not an high priest which cannot be touched with the feeling of our infirmities; but was in all points tempted like as we are, yet without sin" (Heb. 4:15). He has been in this world. He has shared the strain, the tension, and the agony of your life and mine. The enemy has attacked Him in a way that you and I can never know. He has been through it all, and He sympathizes even though He is holy God. He has promised to aid us, and He says, "I am with you alway, even unto the end of the world" (Matt. 28:20).

Most wonderful of all, perhaps, is this: He has conquered our last enemy—the fear of death. As Hebrews 2:15 puts it: "[He might] deliver them who through fear of death were all their lifetime subject to bondage." Oh, what a thought! He has taken the sting out of death—the end, the dissolution of the body, the departure into an unknown eternity. He has taken the terror out of the grave. He has conquered every enemy, and He has risen triumphantly and taken His seat at the right hand of God in the glory everlasting.

Do you not see? He is the only one who could do all these things. It takes a God to represent us before God. It takes a man. He is both. It takes one strong enough to bear my guilt. He has done it. It takes one who can impart His own nature to me. He does it by the Spirit. He is the only one who has ever conquered the world, the flesh, and the devil. He has even conquered the last enemy—death. There has only been one in this world who could say, "It is finished" (John 19:30). Finished! Everything necessary for our salvation He has done, and He alone has been able to do it. That is why Peter said, "Neither is there salvation in any other: for there is none other name under heaven given among men, whereby we must be saved."

Have you realized that what you need is to be saved? Did you think you could save yourself? Did you fondly imagine that all you needed was to be improved a little bit? Have you seen your real condition? You do not need instruction. It is of no use to you. You do not need an example. It cannot help you. You do not need improvement. You need to be forgiven. You need to be born again. You need to be renovated. You need to be made a child of God and an heir of eternity.

Have you realized that Christ is the only Savior? It comes to this: Either like the clever builders you reject Him, or else you believe in Him. It is one or the other. Standing before you is the one and only Savior. Reject Him, and you will go on being as you are. Only you will get worse and worse, and at the end of your life, you will be completely without hope, filled with horror. You will go on to an eternity of misery and shame and useless remorse. You will find that your cleverness was of no value. The fact that you belong to the twenty-first century makes not the slightest difference. Reject Him—the builder, the cornerstone—and you are left to yourself, to your wretched failure and the eternal misery that follows it.

Believe in Him. Listen to His voice. Listen to the message of His apostles. Confess your sin. Acknowledge your utter helplessness and hopelessness and cast yourself solely upon His name. Say, "Yes, He is the only one; He is the Savior of the world, and He is *my* Savior." Turn to Him now and say this:

> *O Christ, in Thee my soul has found*
> *And found in Thee alone*
> *The peace, the joy I sought so long,*
> *The bliss till now unknown.*
> *Now none but Christ can satisfy.*
> *None other name for me.*
> *There's love and life and lasting joy,*
> *Lord Jesus, found in Thee.*
>
> Anonymous

In the name of Jesus Christ of Nazareth, rise up and walk now. He has done it all. In His name I command you—believe now, rise up out of your sin, and go through the remainder of your life walking and leaping and praising God.

5

THE AUTHENTIC MARKS OF CHRISTIANITY

Now when they saw the boldness of Peter and John, and perceived that they were unlearned and ignorant men, they marvelled; and they took knowledge of them, that they had been with Jesus.

—Acts 4:13

My whole object in this book, let me remind you, is to show what Christianity really is. It may seem strange to some of you that we still have to do that. The Christian faith began nearly two thousand years ago, and there has been a Christian church ever since. Someone may say, "Surely it is no longer necessary to should spend any time telling us what Christianity is." But unfortunately it is necessary. Our whole world is in a state of confusion—political confusion, moral confusion, international confusion—but there is no greater confusion than with respect to this one great question: What is the Christian message?

Something happened during this last week, that, it seems to me, increases the confusion and makes it very urgent that we should know exactly what this passage in Acts 4 tells us. I am referring, of course, to the visit of the pope to the United Nations and his address and his reception there—all that was shown us at great length, with much repetition, on the television and wireless. Here is the pope, who claims to be the direct successor of Peter—the modern Peter, as it were—addressing the United Nations and being received as the head of a state.

Here in the book of Acts, we have the apostle Peter, with John, confronting the worldly states and authorities and powers. Here is Peter himself. Then consider what the one who claims to be his successor is like when he appears before similar principalities. I will not spend time pointing out the contrast but leave that to your intelligence. I have not arranged these circumstances; it is extraordinary how these things happen, is it not? I believe in the guidance of God and in the presence and the power of the Holy Spirit. God forbid that anybody should think this sermon is about Roman Catholicism. It is not, but it *is* about true Christianity. The world, as I say, is confused and unhappy. Individuals are in trouble. We are so perplexed that we are ready to believe almost anything that offers itself to us. Because I have a concern for bewildered men and women, because of my sympathy with them and for them, I am calling your attention to this whole question.

How can we tell what real Christianity is? There are two main ways. The first is to go to the New Testament. We do not know anything about the church, nor about the Christian message, nor about our Lord, apart from what we have here. It is no use telling me that a modern thinker says this and that; a modern thinker does not know any more than I know. He was not there! If you want to know what Christianity is, if you want to know what the church is meant to be, I suggest that you are in honor bound to go back to the New Testament. Here is the account, the only account we have.

You want to know what Christian preaching is? Go back and listen to the first preachers. You do not start with modern opinions because they are only human, and one is as good as another. If you want an authority, you must go back to this New Testament. As you do so, you will find how the Christian church came into being and what happened to her. You have the whole history here. You have the descent of the Holy Spirit and the first things the apostles began to say and do. Here is Christianity in its origin, in its purity. This is what turned the ancient world upside down. This is what conquered even the Roman Empire within some three centuries. Here it is—authentic Christianity.

But reading the New Testament is not the only way. That is a positive way. There is another, sometimes very helpful, way of finding out exactly what Christianity is—a way that is negative. You can tell whether a message that claims to be Christian is true or not by observing the reaction of the world to it. The world reacts in different ways to the true and to the false message. Here in Acts 4 we see the apostles, the church, facing the worldly powers, and we see the reaction of those powers. That reaction is still the same today.

As we look at this passage, we shall, incidentally, be noting the true marks of the Christian faith and of the Christian church. Here is authentic Christianity put before us in a graphic and dramatic manner. What are we taught? I have tried to reduce it to a number of principles that are easy to remember. Here is my first proposition: Christianity is a phenomenon. It is not merely a teaching, nor an outlook, nor a point of view. It is a phenomenon, and a phenomenon is a fact; it belongs to the realm of history. And that is Christianity. That is the whole point about the New Testament; indeed, it is the point of the whole Bible.

Now there are other so-called religions in the world, and there are philosophies and points of view. How have they come into being? Well, one person, or perhaps a number of people, have thought about life and have put up ideas and theories. They have taught them and argued with others about them, and then perhaps these ideas have been reduced to a book that other people read. So this teaching gains currency and becomes known. But that is not the situation with regard to the Christian message. Christianity is not merely some theory or idea; it is based entirely upon things that have happened and upon the activity of God. First and foremost, the Bible is a history book. It is an account of things taking place, of God intervening, of God entering into time.

But not only that, the Bible is an account of something remarkable, unusual, startling—something that attracts attention. That is the whole point, is it not, of the incident we are studying? Jerusalem was in a turmoil; everybody was excited; everybody was filled with curiosity; all the people were gathering together. What was going to happen next? The rulers were amazed and alarmed because they had a situation to deal with—that is, the effect of Christianity. This faith is living, dynamic, challenging. It confronts you with a problem. You have to face it and make a decision. Christianity compels that decision and insists upon it. Everybody facing these events honestly must take a stand on one side or the other.

Now it is essential that we should emphasize the historicity of Christianity, because the opinion of the average person is that it is nothing but some sort of lifeless tradition. Of course, there are some people who do not have enough intelligence even to think about it. As children, they were brought up to go to chapel or to church or to Sunday school, and they have continued, but there is no life in their religion. It is a dead, weary tradition—just a handful of people trying to sing together in a pathetic manner. Everything is dull and drab. Dead faith is an insult to the intelligence. Those people who still claim to be Christians and members of the Christian church are merely pathetic continuers of a lifeless custom. Is that not the impression?

But can you not see that that situation is all wrong? That is not Christianity, and if there are people who give the impression that it is, then I take leave to question whether they are Christians at all. Christianity is a startling phenomenon. It fills people with amazement and wonder. "What's this?" they say.

We are living in a dangerous world. We never know what is going to happen next, and, therefore, I make no apology for putting a simple question to you at this point: Has Christianity ever come to you as a challenge? Has it come to you as something dynamic, something that has compelled you to pay attention and that has driven you to make a decision? If it has not, you really do not know anything about it. You may have thought of it in terms of drab and dead ritual, but that idea is entirely wrong.

There is nothing that has so affected this world as the Christian message. Indeed, further on in the book of Acts, the apostles are described as, "These that have turned the world upside down" (Acts 17:6). Has anything in the modern world turned anybody or anything upside down, let alone the world itself? No, a lifeless religion is not Christianity. New Testament Christianity is life-giving, dynamic, and challenging—a phenomenon.

Then the second point is that Christianity is a phenomenon that the world does not understand. This is most important, and this is where the negative test comes in. It is the whole point, of course, of the healing of the lame man. These authorities were confronted by the fact of this healing. Everybody in the community knew that poor, lame beggar, and suddenly they actually saw him standing before them: "And beholding the man which was healed standing with them" (Acts 4:14). They could say nothing to deny it, and yet they did say everything against it—not against the healing but against the way in which it had happened. That response characterizes the Christian message. The world is perplexed by it.

Now this is how the world lets us know whether our message is truly Christian or not. There are false representations of the Christian message that not only do not perplex the world but that the world understands very well and likes and commends. If the Christian church were to stand before the governors and the authorities and the powers with a political message, it would receive a standing ovation. The world is not perplexed by political pronouncements. It understands them. They are its own currency, its own thought, its own language and idiom. So if the church talks to the world about peace and about war and about stopping bombs and so on, the world will listen, accept it, and commend it. But that is not the reception Peter and John got.

Or again, when the church gives the impression that the Christian Gospel consists solely of ethical teaching and says that her message is an appeal to people to live a better life, and adds that it can help the authorities deal with the problems of juvenile delinquency, sexual immorality, and social injustice, then the world, the authorities, understand it perfectly well. They are always having to deal with things like that. They have to pass acts of Parliament and set up institutions and clubs and societies, and they spend the whole of their time in trying to deal with these multiplying moral problems. So if the church comes and says, "That is exactly what we are concerned about—we are here to teach people how to live decent, good, and upright lives," the world will give it a standing ovation. It understands that; it is the coin of its thinking and expression.

Or when the church gives the impression that the Christian message is just a matter of a little moral uplift, giving people beautiful thoughts to start the day with, positive thinking, a bit of idealism in a materialistic world, then the world likes it. The world likes to think it is idealistic, and not altogether bad, that it likes the good. So when the church talks about idealism, and appeals to people in the name of idealism and friendship, and when she says that this is the Christian message, the world acclaims it and accepts it and is grateful for it. But that was not the reception that was given to Peter and John.

Or if the church stands before the world and gives the impression that the Christian message is nothing but psychology—expressed, of course, in Christian terminology—the world will be very ready to listen because it is in trouble. People are suffering from insomnia; the drug bill is going up. There is the tension of daily life and the problem of how to live with one's neighbors—how, indeed, to live with one's own wife or husband. The world is breaking down, and so if the church comes along and says, "We can help you with all that; we will teach you how to think and perhaps even teach you how to deal with your own aches, pains, ailments, frustrations, and loss of confidence. We will teach you psychology so that you can understand human nature," giving the impression that her message is some kind of applied psychology, then again she will have a standing ovation. But that was not the reception Peter and John got.

Or, finally, some may give the impression that the purpose of the Christian church is to provide some sort of vague worship, some kind of refined paganism. You know the sort of thing that the pagan does when he is ill: He offers up a prayer, or if he is frightened of what is going to happen to him, he performs his rites and ceremonies. If the church seems to be a state organization that can function very well on Memorial Day, or call for a national day of prayer in time of war when battles are being lost, or arrange some wonderful ceremonies with dim religious lights and some suggestion of unseen powers at a coronation or on the death of a member of the royal family or a great prime minister—if the church gives the impression that that is Christianity—well, the world will accept it. It will like it. It will praise and thank the church and offer—I say again—a standing ovation.

But observe the contrast. The world is always perplexed by the true message, as here in Acts. That is why the reaction of the world is one of the best tests of the message. If the world accepts the message readily, you can be certain it is not Christianity. If the world is perplexed and astonished, you can be fairly certain that, at any rate, the message is approaching that which is true. This is a message that has always startled the world, for it does not understand the language.

But I must go even beyond that. The true message is not only a message that perplexes; it also angers the world. The world always hates the true message and tries to put a stop to it, as here at the beginning. Is this not the whole story of the Bible? Look at the way the world treated Noah, the preacher of righteousness, the man appointed by God to preach to that ancient world and to call it to repentance. Look at the treatment it gave him. Look at the treatment that the people of Sodom and Gomorrah gave to Lot. Poor Lot—he had lowered his standards, but even he was a righteous man in those degenerate cities of the plains. Read the account of the treatment meted out to him by the people of Sodom and their rulers when he tried to remonstrate with them and to call them to repentance before it was too late.

Read the Old Testament and look at the way the prophets were treated. In Israel there were always large numbers of false prophets, and there was an occasional true prophet. The false prophets were always praised and well received. Why? Well, because they said, "Peace, peace; when there is no peace" (Jer. 6:14; 8:11). When the church says to the world, "It's all right; you only have to appeal to people, and they will put an end to war, and we really must all join in," then it is saying, "Peace, peace; when there is no peace." That is the message of a false prophet, but the world likes it. This message makes people feel a little happier and postpones the calamity, and so it always has a wonderful reception.

But look at the way the true prophets were treated. They were thrown into dungeons, hated, persecuted, and put to death. Look what the world did to John the Baptist. They chopped his head off because he ventured to tell a king that adultery was wrong. That is how the powers have always treated the true message and the true preachers. See how they treated the apostles. Peter was put to death, and so was James. Read the story of the martyrs, the confessors, the people who were thrown by the thousands to the lions in the arena in Rome and in other places—the massacre of the saints. It has been the treatment of Christians throughout the centuries. The Protestant Reformers, the Covenanters, the Puritans, the early Methodists—these all were persecuted.

> *Truth forever on the scaffold,*
> *Wrong forever on the throne.*
> J. R. Lowell

Above all, consider the Son of God. He came into this world to save it. He came "to seek and to save that which was lost" (Luke 19:10). He is the greatest benefactor the human race has ever known, one who forsook the courts of heaven and humbled and abased Himself, endured the contradiction of sinners against Himself, and was ready even to die for them. And what treatment did they mete out to Him? Did He have a standing ovation? No, they said, "Away with Him! Crucify Him! Let's get rid of Him." They rejected Him. He was set at naught. He was "despised and rejected of men" (Isa. 53:3). That is how the world has always treated the true message.

Let me put it like this. I sometimes meet Christian people who are really troubled and frightened because they find that so many of today's eminent people—the thinkers, philosophers, and scientists—are not Christians. These Christians develop a kind of inferiority complex, and they feel rather ashamed that they believe a message that is rejected by the great and the mighty and the noble of the world. My dear friend, how stupid that is! If you believe something that they reject, you are in very good company. That is why, as I said, the reception given by the world to a message that purports to be Christianity is one of the very best tests of all as to whether or not it is true Christianity. Look at what the world did to Peter. It is very illuminating to apply that test to every man who claims to be a successor of Peter.

But we must now go on to consider why it is that the world misunderstands and hates the Christian message. The answer can be put in one word. It is because this true message is *supernatural*. Let me expound that. Christianity is not something that we do; it is not something that is in any sense dependent upon us. Here we touch upon the greatest modern fallacy. We like to think that we can do anything and everything; we have the confidence; we have the capacity and the power. But here at the very beginning, we are told at once that becoming a Christian is in no way dependent upon us and our power and capacity. It is not a matter of our ability, understanding, and knowledge. No, notice this: "Now when they saw the boldness of Peter and John, and perceived that they were unlearned and ignorant men, they marvelled." Of course they did! It was contrary to the whole of their thinking. Thousands of people outside the church reject the Christian message because they have never understood this first principle. Because they are wrong about this first point, they are wrong everywhere.

Why do you think that our blessed Lord chose the particular men He did to be His disciples? You remember the sort of men they were? Some were fishermen. One was a tax collector. They were the most ordinary men, employed in the most everyday occupations. He did not go out to select Pharisees, scribes, doctors of the law, or leaders of political thought. Nor did He choose philosophers. When He formed his cabinet, He did not select twelve of the ablest, most educated and learned men of Jerusalem. He did the exact opposite. Why do you think He did that? I suggest that it was in order to establish once and forever that men and women do not enter His kingdom according to their ability, that one does not become a Christian by one's own understanding. That is why He chose "unlearned and ignorant men," nobodies. I know that the apostle Paul was one of the greatest geniuses of all times, but in a sense that proves the rule. God was saying that whether a man is brilliant or ignorant, it does not matter. The power is always the same. So you get the majority—unlearned and ignorant—and among them this outstanding genius. It has continued like that through the running centuries.

Of course, as we have seen, the world believes that it is dependent upon its own thinking, and therefore it admires great thinkers and believes that our only hope lies in producing great people who can think in a great way, who will have deep insight into our problems and show us the way out. But if you think that that is Christianity, you are altogether wrong before you come on to any further questions about miracles or about the person of Christ.

Because the Christian faith is supernatural, we do not need to be clever to understand it or put it into practice. This is the remarkable thing. You may call it the paradox of the Christian message. Here we have the profoundest truth in the world about everything to do with men and women, life, living, death, the cosmos, and God. Yet it this truth is never arrived at as the result of intellectual effort.

Similarly, we do not depend at all upon our moral effort in order to become Christians. You find not only unlearned and ignorant men in the church, but you find men and women who have been thieves and drunkards and revilers and braggarts, who suddenly become saints in the church of God.

Christianity is supernatural. When we become Christians, it is not because we have done something, but something has been done to us; something changes us. Here is the phenomenon: Unlearned and ignorant men could speak as they spoke, could heal the lame man, were filled with power. What had happened to them?

And there is Christianity for you in a nutshell. It does not depend upon us; it is a power acting upon us and in us and in spite of us. Listen to the apostle Paul writing to the Romans: "I am not ashamed of the gospel of Christ"—why not?—"for it is the power of God unto salvation to every one that believeth" (Rom. 1:16). Therefore he says, "I am debtor both to the Greeks, and to the Barbarians; both to the wise, and to the unwise. So, as much as in me is, I am ready to preach the gospel to you that are at Rome also" (vv. 14-15).

He does not postulate great understanding; he does not postulate ignorance. He postulates nothing but need and the power of God. It is God's power, and it acts upon men and women. Paul is never tired of saying that. "Christ," he says, "[is] the power of God, and the wisdom of God. . . . For ye see your calling, brethren, how that not many wise men after the flesh, not many mighty, not many noble, are called: But God hath chosen the foolish things of the world to confound the wise; and God hath chosen the weak things of the world to confound the things which are mighty" (1 Cor. 1:24, 26-27). God acting—a phenomenon; ordinary, ignorant, unlettered men speaking with boldness and working miracles. It is God's power—but that is Christianity.

So being a Christian does not depend upon us, but entirely upon God and His power and what He has done in the person of His only begotten, dearly beloved Son. You see God at work in these disciples. Look at the way they could stand and reason before this great council and confute them. Peter and John were fishermen. But not only that, Peter had such a craven spirit that when his greatest friend and benefactor had been in difficulty and on trial, this disciple had denied Him to save his own life. But look at Peter now, standing with boldness. What had happened? He had been changed! That is Christianity. Peter had not been reading textbooks of philosophy; he had not been studying science; he had not been acquainting himself with the great lore of the centuries. No, something had happened to him. He had been filled with power; he was a new man.

The lame man himself was also a striking example of the supernatural power of God. "Beholding the man which was healed standing with them, they could say nothing against it." And this has been the story of the Christian church throughout the long ages. Christianity is not something I take up; it is not something I grasp with my great mind. It is God dealing with me; it is God acting upon me; it is the power of God possessing me, changing me, giving me a new birth, giving me a new life, and making "a new man" of me.

How does Christianity do this? It gives men and women a new understanding. Look at these men—Peter and John. What did they know? They had never been through the schools, and yet they could expound the Scriptures. They had spiritual understanding; they had an insight into the truth. Where did they get this understanding? This is the miracle of the rebirth. You see, what makes a man or woman a Christian is that the Spirit of God deals with the person and changes his or her nature: "If any man be in Christ, he is a new creature [a new creation]: old things are passed away; behold, all things are become new" (2 Cor. 5:17). Listen to the apostle putting it again to the Corinthians: "Which none of the princes of this world knew" (1 Cor. 2:8). The leaders did not recognize and know the Christ; they did not understand. "But the natural man," writes Paul, "receiveth not the things of the Spirit of God: for they are foolishness unto him: neither can he know them, because they are spiritually discerned. But he that is spiritual judgeth [understands] all things, yet he himself is judged of no man. For who hath known the mind of the Lord, that he may instruct Him? But we have the mind of Christ" (1 Cor. 2:14-16).

That we can have the mind of Christ is astonishing, a most glorious fact. That is why a feeble man like myself can stand in a pulpit and address a congregation without knowing anything about the people in it. I do not need to know them. I am not interested in whether they are able or lacking in ability, whether they are learned or ignorant, whether they are scientists or ignoramuses—it makes no difference. I know they are human beings. I know they have a need. They have souls that they have not realized, and they are lost. I know that they are not ready to live or to die, nor to face God in the bar of eternal judgment. I know that they are lacking in an understanding of the elementary facts of life, death, and eternity.

But I preach with confidence. Why? Here is the romance and the marvel of being a Christian preacher. I know that it does not matter at all what people's condition is. I know that the most ignorant person has as much chance of being a Christian as the ablest, because salvation does not depend upon the power of either. If salvation did depend upon a person's inherent natural powers, just a few VIPs would be saved, and all the rest of us would be damned forever. Thank God, He can take the foolish people of the world and fill them with understanding. We rely on the power of God. And so the apostle John, writing to very simple early Christians says, "Ye have an unction [an anointing] from the Holy One, and ye know all things. . . . ye need not that any man teach you" (1 John 2:20, 27). There are false Christs, false apostles, false teachers. John is not worried. Believers have an unction, an understanding that the wise, the learned, and the prudent lack.

Our blessed Lord said it. I have already partly quoted Him: "I thank thee, O Father, Lord of heaven and earth, because thou hast hid these things from the wise and prudent, and hast revealed them unto babes. Even so, Father: for so it seemed good in thy sight" (Matt. 11:25-26). There it is from the Lord's own mouth. There it is still. "Ignorant and unlearned men"—it did not matter. God's power gave them understanding. These apostles had realized that they were sinners. They had realized that they had lost their souls. They had realized further that they could never save themselves, but they had been given the understanding to see that this Jesus, whom they had been following and with whom they had been working, was none other than the only begotten Son of God who had come into the world to save them.

And that is all you need to know—that you are a sinner with a desperate need and that you have an almighty Savior who is able to pay the price of your sins and bear your penalty in His own body on the cross, that He rose again to justify you before God, that He gave you a new life—a new being, a new start, a new nature—that He floods love into your heart and being and enables you to live. However much we might be paupers intellectually, morally, and in every other sense, the only capacity He postulates is the capacity to accept what He gives. He gives understanding. He changes us as He changed these men, and He gives peace and joy. He gives a happiness that no one had even imagined before. He gives a rest to the soul. He gives such an understanding of life that even when things go against us, we know that all is well. When everything is working against us, we still say, "All things work together for good to them that love God, to them who are the called according to his purpose" (Rom. 8:28). We do not merely say it; we know that it is true. We say with the apostle Paul that we not only joy in God, "but we glory in tribulations also: knowing that tribulation worketh patience" (Rom. 5:3). Even tribulations teach us and prepare us for what is awaiting us.

God's power gives us power to live, and it gives us power in many other ways. It takes weaklings and failures and puts backbone and moral fiber into them. It puts a dynamic into them that makes them new men and women so that where formerly they were defeated, they conquer. It enables little human beings to stand and to resist the devil and cause him to flee—the devil who ventured even to tempt the Son of God Himself. It gives them strength to resist him, steadfast in the faith.

As we have seen, God's power gives feeble, unlearned, and ignorant men and women power to confound learned authorities. It gives believers an understanding that is hidden from the wise and prudent and sophisticated people. And it gives Christians boldness: "When they saw the boldness of Peter and John . . ." Peter, the coward, the frightened rabbit, who ran away to save his own skin, was able to stand and defy the authorities. They did not understand these miracles; they did not know that Peter was a new man; they did not know that now he was ready to die for the Christ and the truth that he had formerly been ashamed of. He was a new man, born again, having passed through Pentecost, and filled with a power divine and ready to stand for this blessed, glorious Savior. That is Christianity. And there is only one explanation for it all: "They took knowledge that they had been with Jesus."

Here is a message that the world does not understand, and it is annoyed. Here is a message that humbles people and shows that their need is as great as that of anyone else. People do not like such a message. When the church speaks in her own true and native language, the world always senses and detects the offense of the cross. For the message of the church to the nations is not a message of praise that encourages them in their efforts to make peace. It is not a message that gets acclamation and approval from atheistic Communists and others. No, it is a message that tells all men and women and all nations that they are vile sinners, so vile that they can never improve themselves but must be born again. Their sin is so great that it necessitated the coming of the Son of God into the world to assume human nature and to humble Himself even to the death of the cross, to die as a felon, smitten by His holy Father for their sins, to be laid in a tomb, before rising again and ascending into heaven to take His seat at the right hand of God's glory in power. There Christ administers His kingdom and one day will come again and rout His enemies and to set up a new kingdom of peace.

The church does not ask the world or individual nations to make peace. That is impossible. "Ye shall hear of wars and rumours of wars" (Matt. 24:6). There is only one who can make peace and guarantee it, and He is the Prince of peace, the Son of God. Anyone who has been with Him and knows Him, anyone upon whom He has placed His mighty, recreating hand through the Holy Spirit and has been made anew by Him, has already found peace with God, peace with other men and women, and has become a fellow citizen with the saints and the household of God.

May we all learn the lesson of this old incident. Let us meet with this Jesus and listen to Him, and soon we, too, will become phenomena. We will become men and women who are enigmas to everybody else. They will not understand us; they will object to us because, without our openly condemning them, we do condemn them by being what we are and by baffling their great intellects. But, thank God, by the acknowledgement of our sinfulness and our unworthiness and our helplessness, we will have opened our hearts to the radiance of the face of God in Jesus Christ. The power of the Spirit will have come upon us, will have made us anew, made us children of God, and will be preparing us for the beatific vision and the joys of an eternal bliss.

6

THE EYEWITNESSES

But Peter and John answered and said unto them, Whether it be
right in the sight of God to hearken unto you more than unto
God, judge ye. For we cannot but speak the things which we have
seen and heard.

—Acts 4:19-20

The account of the healing of the lame man is a rich story that brings us face
to face with the great fundamentals of Christianity. What is the message of
the church? This question is clearly basic, because if there is any doubt about
this, then there will be doubt all along the line. To put it another way: What
is it that makes someone a Christian? What is our authority? What is our
sanction? What are our reasons for believing this message? Why, indeed,
should anyone believe it? These are the things about which we must be clear.
These are the great questions, I think, that agitate the minds of so many people, and the answer is given here as simply as one could ever desire. It is we
who always add the complications.

Here is the simple beginning of the church. These verses illustrate what
the church is meant to be, but people have added their traditions, their points
of view, and their philosophies until it has become the most complicated thing
in the world. Indeed, there are those who say that the common people are
not meant to understand Christianity, but only the priests, or the bishops, or
the popes, and so we must listen to their interpretations. But that is not what
we find here in Acts.

No, what stands out here first and foremost is that when we want to
know what Christianity is, we must look at the message preached by the first

apostles. Now this is a quite basic proposition. The apostle Paul says in his letter to the Ephesians that the church is "built upon the foundation of the apostles and prophets" (Eph. 2:20). There is the foundation, the beginning. The only message that I have to present is the message of the apostles, which I find in this book.

These points are crucial. If you want to know what Christianity is, you do not start by buying a textbook on philosophy; you start by reading the Bible. You do not go out into libraries and search the vast wisdom of men. You come straight to this book. John Wesley, who used to read many books, said that after his conversion, he had become "a man of one Book." Why? Because the Bible is the only book that speaks with authority on these matters. What do we know about Christianity apart from what we are told by these apostles, these first preachers? These are the witnesses; our Lord appointed them as such, and He told them that that was to be their task: "Ye shall receive power, after that the Holy Ghost is come upon you: and ye shall be witnesses unto me" (Acts 1:8).

It was the apostles who knew what Christianity was. That is why the authorities were questioning them. The authorities were not in a position to decide. They were amazed and were unable to understand. All they could do was ask questions of the apostles, and that is what we must do. I say with all respect to many a modern scholar that they may be very learned, great thinkers, but are they in a position to tell us what this message is? Of course not. They were not there. The truth is based upon the foundation of the apostles and prophets, and to try to discover what Christianity is without going straight to them, is, I repeat, already to go wrong.

Let me develop that point a little because it is all-important. This idea that Christianity is something that changes from age to age and that, therefore, it will be different in the twenty-first century from what it was in the twentieth is a denial of the Christian Gospel. Christianity is something that happened once and for all. In the third verse of his epistle, Jude refers to "the faith which was once delivered unto the saints." That is the starting point, and we must therefore consider what these men have to say. You can read about them in this book of Acts. Peter was the first and John with him. Later on the great apostle Paul appeared, and he spread the message throughout the Gentile world. These were the men who planted the churches, the men who turned the world upside down.

Then, secondly, what was the message that they preached? And, of course, it is summed up perfectly for us by the decision reached by the council: "That it spread no further among the people, let us straitly threaten them [the apostles], that they speak henceforth to no man in this name" (Acts

4:17). Then we are told that the council members called Peter and John in and "commanded them not to speak at all nor teach in the name of Jesus." Now that is a very good summary; the council members saw the point quite clearly. They were annoyed because these apostles were preaching and teaching "in the name of Jesus." Peter and John were not just giving their own ideas or the result of their own thoughts and meditations. One may express opinions under certain circumstances, but when one is preaching the Gospel, it is all wrong. The apostles did not get up and say, "Now we have been examining this whole problem, and we have had many discussions together and have come to this conclusion." Nor did they quote some other great thinkers, some authorities. They preached, they taught, "in the name of Jesus."

You will find in reading the Gospels that after our Lord had been preaching, so often the people made this comment (and it was a most discriminating observation): "For he taught them as one that had authority, and not as the scribes" (Mark 1:22). In part, they meant that the scribes were very learned men who gave the whole of their time and all their energy to the study, not only of the Scriptures, but especially of what the great commentators had said about the Scriptures. These men had given their teachings, and others had disagreed, and there were disputations, so that the teaching of the scribes was similar to attorneys' arguments in a court of law. Up to a point attorneys give their own views, but they prove their cases by pulling out books and reading from them. They will quote from paragraph something and subsection something else and then cite further authorities. Attorneys from opposing sides argue against each other, quoting different authorities. So cases go on for days and weeks and perhaps months. That is how the scribes used to preach.

The philosophers, too, have always followed this practice. They ask: "What do Plato, Aristotle, and Socrates say?" And this is regarded, of course, as learning and as the most helpful thing in life today. People say, "This man has read such a lot; he knows all about it. He's read his philosophers and will tell you what you need to know." So he puts forward his views, which someone else modifies a little, while yet another disagrees altogether. Now you have rival schools. The intellectual gymnastics are all so brilliant! But that scenario is the exact opposite of Christianity.

The apostles did not spend their time in quoting authorities. No, they only had one authority. Their preaching was entirely confined to Jesus, and they preached what He had taught them. They had nothing to say apart from what Jesus had told them. Their preaching was all in the name of Jesus and nothing else at all.

This is a very important point. Peter and John were unlearned and ignorant men, but the apostle Paul was not—quite the reverse. He could quote the Greek scholars; he had read the Greek philosophers; he was an expert on the authorities quoted by the Pharisees and scribes. He knew them better than most people because he had such a brilliant mind. Yet in writing to the Corinthians, he says, "I determined"—deliberately decided—"not to know any thing among you, save Jesus Christ, and him crucified" (1 Cor. 2:2). He put himself in the same position as these unlearned men—Peter and John, the fishermen. Why? Because he knew that all the other learning was of no avail; it was useless and a hindrance. That is why some clever people in Corinth thought he was a fool, an ignorant man. "All right," he says, "call me a fool. But I am determined. I have made myself a fool for Christ's sake, and that is the essence of wisdom."

Paul made another statement. He had been preaching in Galatia where people had believed and churches had started up. Then others had gone around after him, some of the authorities, the "Judaizers," and they had said that Paul was all right as far as he went, but, of course, he did not go far enough. He did not know that circumcision and obedience to the Jewish law had to be added on to trust in Christ. So the apostle wrote a letter to the believers in which he said, "Though we, or an angel from heaven, preach any other gospel unto you than that which we have preached unto you, let him be accursed" (Gal. 1:8).

On another occasion, Paul had to write on the same subject to the church at Corinth. There were clever people in the first century, as there are now, and some were saying that there is no such thing as the resurrection. They considered the resurrection impossible, and they thought they were still being Christian! It is not only the modern preachers who say such things. But listen to Paul's answer:

> *Moreover, brethren, I declare unto you the gospel which I preached unto you, which also ye have received, and wherein ye stand; by which also ye are saved, if ye keep in memory what I preached unto you, unless ye have believed in vain. For I delivered unto you first of all that which I also received, how that Christ died for our sins according to the scriptures; and that he was buried, and that he rose again the third day according to the scriptures.*
>
> *—1 Cor. 15:1-4*

The Gospel was a message that Paul had received; it was not his idea. Indeed, when he was standing before Agrippa and Festus, he told them what he used to believe: "I verily thought with myself, that I ought to do many things contrary to the name of Jesus of Nazareth" (Acts 26:9). But now he was a preacher, and what did he preach? He preached what had been "revealed" to him. This is what made him an apostle. He used to have his own ideas, which were contrary to Christianity. But then on the road to Damascus, he had met this risen, glorious Lord, and the Lord had said to him: "I have appeared unto thee for this purpose, to make thee a minister and a witness . . . to open their eyes, and to turn them from darkness to light, and from the power of Satan unto God" (Acts 26:16, 18). The Lord had commissioned Paul and given him a message: "I delivered unto you first of all that which I also received" (1 Cor. 15:3).

Paul says the same thing in the passage on the Lord's Supper: "For I have received of the Lord that which also I delivered unto you" (1 Cor. 11:23). The Gospel was not Paul's idea, nor the idea of any of the apostles; they did not excogitate it, as it were. It was revealed, it was given. Like Peter and John, they all taught and preached in the name of Jesus. He had made the message known; He had shown it to them. This is a tremendous point—so have you gotten hold of it? The moment you grasp it, it solves most of your intellectual problems.

In many ways, these apostles and the Old Testament prophets were in similar positions. What is your understanding of the prophets? Do you think they were just great thinkers, able men, seers, who, having meditated long and having thought seriously about the problems of life, at last came to a number of conclusions and then began to teach them? That was not their position at all, and they tell us so quite specifically. (See, for example, Zech. 9:1; Mal. 1:1). "The burden of the word of the LORD," they said. "The word of God came to Nathan" (1 Chron. 17:3). Every prophet was told what to say. Each claimed that he was not merely expressing his own ideas but was the mouthpiece of God. This is what is called "inspiration."

"Inspiration" is a term that has been misunderstood. There are people who say, "Of course, I believe in inspiration. I believe that the poets are inspired." I remember hearing of a man saying in a meeting, "I believe the Bible is inspired. I believe the men who wrote it were inspired in exactly the same way that Wordsworth and Browning and all the great poets have been inspired." But that is not inspiration in the biblical sense of the word. The apostle Paul explains exactly what inspiration is in 2 Timothy 3:16: "All scripture is given by inspiration of God." By this he means that all Scripture is *God-breathed*. God breathed into these men. The apostle Peter puts that in his own words in his second letter: "We have also a more sure word of prophecy; whereunto ye do well that ye take heed, as unto a light that shineth in a dark place, until the day dawn, and the day star arise in your hearts: knowing this first, that no prophecy of the scripture is of any private interpretation" (2 Pet. 1:19-20). Scripture is not the result of a man's long meditation and cogitation. No, Peter continues: "For the prophecy came not in old time by the will of man: but holy men of God spake as they were moved [carried along] by the Holy Ghost" (v. 21).

Again we must be clear. We all know something about the experience that sometimes wrongly passes for "inspiration." Sometimes if a politician speaks more freely than usual, our common parlance says, "He was inspired that night." What is really meant by that is that the speaker happened to be feeling well. He did not have a headache, for example. Then people had clapped and cheered him, which had put him into a good mood. He had started off well and had no hesitation in warming to his subject. So they said that he was inspired. But he was not. He was simply at his best. That is not inspiration.

What inspiration means, and what the prophets claimed, is this: "We know nothing. We have not thought out this message. It has all been given to us." The form of the message was given to them, the understanding was given, and the ability to preach it was given. We read here about Peter before the Sanhedrin: "Peter, filled with the Holy Ghost, said unto them . . ." (Acts 4:8).

Peter preached a message about Christ. He made these points: Christ is that prophet that was to come. He is the light of the world. He is the only one who can teach us about God, the only one who can teach us about humanity. He alone can teach us about life, death, and the way of salvation. He understands all, and we know nothing apart from what He has told us. He is the expositor of the Old Testament, the only one who really understands it. It was He who said, "Ye have heard that it was said by them of old time . . . but I say unto you" (Matt. 5:27-28).

That is how the apostles preached—in the name of Jesus. As Paul puts it to the Corinthians, "But of him are ye in Christ Jesus, who of God is made unto us wisdom" (1 Cor. 1:30). The apostles made it clear: "We are not giving our own wisdom or the wisdom of any other human being; we are telling you the only wisdom, God's wisdom. Christ is God's wisdom. He has given it to us, and we are passing it on to you."

That is how Christianity began. That is the origin of the Christian church; that is the authority behind the message. So to talk about the twenty-first century and the latest knowledge is completely irrelevant. If this message was given to the apostles by the Son of God, it is the only authoritative statement, and this is what they preached.

But something else is amazing about the content of the apostles' message.

Peter puts it here in wonderful and dramatic language: "Whether it be right in the sight of God to hearken unto you more than unto God, judge ye. For we cannot but speak the things which we have seen and heard." "You are telling us to stop," said Peter, in effect, "not to preach or teach any more. But we cannot help it. We must go on telling people about the things we have seen and heard." That means *facts*, does it not? These men called themselves witnesses: "We are his witnesses of these things" (Acts 5:32; see also Acts 2:32; 3:15). Our Lord, as I have reminded you, said when He sent the apostles out, "Ye shall be witnesses unto me" (Acts 1:8).

A witness is someone put into the witness box in a court and asked questions.

"Were you at such and such a place at a given time?"

"I was."

"Very well, tell the court what you saw."

A witness gives evidence of what he has seen, and each of these apostles was a witness.

Or, to put it another way, the thing that differentiates this gospel message from every other teaching is that it is historical; it consists of events that happened. The teaching of Plato is not based on history; he may think of the problem of history, but it is just his thinking. The same is true of all the philosophers and all the so-called great religions of the world. But this Gospel is a matter of facts—things seen, things heard. When the apostle Peter was an old man and knew that he was about to die, he said: "I am writing to you about these things, because though you know them already, you are in trouble because you do not always remember them."

> Yea, I think it meet, as long as I am in this tabernacle, to stir you up by putting you in remembrance; knowing that shortly I must put off this my tabernacle, even as our Lord Jesus Christ hath showed me. Moreover I will endeavour that ye may be able after my decease to have these things always in remembrance.
>
> —2 Pet. 1:13-15

What were these things? Listen:

> For we have not followed cunningly devised fables, when we made known unto you the power and coming of our Lord Jesus Christ, but were eyewitnesses of his majesty. For he received from God the Father honour and glory, when there came such a voice to him from

the excellent glory, This is my beloved Son, in whom I am well pleased. And this voice which came from heaven we heard [they heard it with their natural ears], when we were with him in the holy mount.

—2 Pet. 1:16-18

There was Peter as an old man saying the same thing that he said here at the very beginning of the Christian church. "These are not fairy tales or invented stories," he says. "We are not concocting something clever. We are witnesses of facts; we are telling you the truth. I am an old man facing death. Would I lie in such a position? Of course not. We were there. This is what I have seen and heard. This is all I have to tell you, and I want you to lay hold of it—this is Christianity."

What, then, were these things of which Peter and John spoke? Of course, we must start with our Lord Himself. They had seen Jesus. The authorities "took knowledge of them, that they had been with Jesus" (Acts 4:13). They had spent three years with Him. They had seen His face, looked into those eyes, seen the depths of His eternal deity coming out at times and all that expression of the everlasting love of God. Oh, what a privilege to look into the face of the Son of God! But you and I, let us admit, have been so clever, have we not? We have expressed our opinions though we have never seen Him. These men knew Him intimately—the person, the personality of Christ.

They had observed very closely how He lived. They had watched His reactions to things that happened; they had observed that calm, that peace, that quiet, in spite of everything—the crowds, the adulation, the Pharisees and scribes with all their bitterness and envy, their malice and hatred. They had seen Him walking through it all with the equanimity of the Son of God. They had observed Him rising up early in the morning, even before sunrise, to climb a mountain to pray to God. They had seen His obedience to God's commands. He had never done or said anything wrong. They had observed His humility. He mixed with tax collectors and sinners, the outcasts of society. He could meet the doctors of the law on their own ground, and yet He sat with the lowliest, the humblest, the most ignorant of people. They had noticed His compassion, His eye for suffering and for need, no matter how busy He was. Crowded by a great throng one day, He felt a woman tugging at the hem of His garment, and He turned around and healed her. They had seen all this—this amazing life—"the things we have seen and heard."

You and I know something about this. If we have the privilege of meeting some outstanding man or woman, we spend the rest of our lives telling people about it. We constantly describe the great person's appearance, language, and behavior. Multiply that by infinity, and this is what Peter and John were talking about—this person and the way He lived.

Then there was His teaching. This was what impressed *everybody*, not just the apostles. "The common people heard him gladly" (Mark 12:37). Why? Because they could follow Him, because His words were not a mere display of cleverness or of rhetoric or of knowledge of the law and the authorities. No, they understood what He was talking about; it was plain, it was direct, it was immediate, and they said that they had never heard anything like it. "For he taught them as one having authority, and not as the scribes" (Matt. 7:29). There was a time when the authorities sent the temple guard to arrest him. But they came back without the prisoner, and their only explanation was to say, "Never man spake like this man" (John 7:46). There was something about the way He spoke—the certainty, the authority, the assurance, and the knowledge He displayed. He was apparently but a carpenter, just an ordinary person, and yet "Never man spake like this man." They did not understand what it was, but they felt something. They were conscious of something that they had never known in their lives before. And the apostles had been with Him while all this was happening.

And then there were the miracles: "We cannot but speak the things which we have seen and heard." What had they seen? They had seen Him turning water into wine. They had seen the leper healed. These were facts. There would be no church but for these things. The miracles are manifestations of His deity and of His divine saviorhood. They had seen Him commanding the raging wind, the rolling billows, the surging sea. They had seen Him asleep in a boat when the sudden, terrifying storm had arisen. They had been convinced they were going to drown, and in terror and alarm they had awakened Him. Then He had stood up and said to the raging wind, "Peace, be still." Immediately there came a great calm. They had observed Him healing the blind and the lame and the deaf. They had even seen Him raising the dead more than once. These were the things to which they testified, these astounding miracles.

Peter and John had had many great privileges, greater than the rest of the apostles. On some occasions our Lord selected Peter and John and James, three only out of the twelve, to be with Him. On one of these occasions (as Peter tells us in his second epistle), our Lord took them with Him to the top of a mountain. While they were there, suddenly He was transfigured before them. His clothing began to shine more brightly than any bleach could ever make it—shining like the sun—and His face was aglow with His eternal deity. God appeared through the person, and they saw it. "We were with him in the holy mount," wrote Peter (2 Pet. 1:18). Then a cloud overshadowed them, and they heard a voice saying, "This is my beloved Son, in whom I am well pleased; hear ye him" (Matt. 17:5). They had seen the Transfiguration; they had heard the voice from heaven. That was why they were preaching; that is why Peter said, "We cannot but speak."

And then they had seen Him dying in utter weakness and apparent helplessness upon a cross. They had observed His agony; they had heard everything He had said upon that cross: "Father, forgive them; for they know not what they do" (Luke 23:34). They had heard His conversation with the poor dying thief. Though He was in such agony, He had time for this man. He had compassion on Him and spoke His gracious, blessed word: "I say unto thee, To day shalt thou be with me in paradise" (Luke 23:43). They had seen His body being taken down and laid in a tomb with a stone rolled in front of the entrance, a seal put on the stone, and soldiers put on guard. They had seen it all; they were eyewitnesses; they could testify.

Then Peter and John could tell how they had heard a report from some of the women who had gone early to the tomb on the morning of the third day. The women had come back and said, in effect, "We got there, but there was no body. We saw angels, but we didn't see Him. He's not there. He's gone." They had thought at first that the women were mad, but then they had raced to the tomb, John outrunning Peter, and they had looked in and seen the empty tomb. Jesus was not there. And then that night, when they were all together in the Upper Room in Jerusalem, behind locked doors because they were afraid of the Jews, suddenly our Lord appeared among them and spoke to them. In front of their eyes, He ate broiled fish and a piece of honeycomb. This had happened to them; they were eyewitnesses.

Later Peter and John, feeling rather disconsolate, had gone fishing with the other disciples. They had been out all night trying to catch fish but had not caught anything, and now they were going back to the shore in the early morning. Suddenly they had seen someone standing on the shore. Who was it? They drew a little nearer and recognized Him—Jesus! He had made breakfast for them, and they had listened to His last commandments and His prophecy about Peter's death and how John was going to go on living (John 21). Above everything else, they were witnesses of the Resurrection.

And what else? He had appeared to the disciples for forty days at different times and in different ways. Then He had taken them all to the top of Mount Olivet, and while He was speaking to them, they saw Him ascending into heaven. "We are witnesses," said Peter. They said to the authorities: "You may tell us to stop, but we cannot. We've seen such things! How can a man keep silent when he's seen things like this?"

Not only that, but the apostles had passed through the day of Pentecost. After our Lord had ascended to heaven, an angel had come to them and said: "Ye men of Galilee, why stand ye gazing up into heaven? This same Jesus, which is taken up from you into heaven, shall so come in like manner as ye have seen him go into heaven" (Acts 1:11). Then they had gone back to the Upper Room, and for ten days they and others waited together in prayer. Each day they continued in prayer, but nothing was happening. Then on the morning of the day of Pentecost, when they were still together and were praying, suddenly there was a sound—this is Christianity!—the sound of a mighty, rushing wind, coming nearer and nearer. It filled the whole place with glory and with power and wonder and amazement, filling them and giving them new languages and a joy that baffled description. They had seen; they had heard; they had felt; they were living witnesses of all these things. That was their message. It was about this Jesus. This is Christianity, you see—not a philosophy, not a teaching, but this person and all these things that literally happened in this world of time.

So the apostles told the people the things they had seen and heard. It was a reporting of facts. I have no Gospel if these things are not facts. The facts are the basis, the foundation, of the Gospel. God sent His only Son into the world.

But the question is: What is the meaning of it all? And this is my final point. The apostles preached and talked and taught in the name of Jesus. Then they gave the explanation. Wherever did they get their message? It was from the Lord Himself.

After His death, Jesus' followers had been utterly disconsolate. There they were, two of them, walking along the road from Jerusalem to Emmaus, commiserating with each other. Suddenly the risen Jesus joined them. He listened to their foolish talk, and this is what He said:

> *O fools, and slow of heart to believe all that the prophets have spoken: Ought not Christ to have suffered these things, and to enter into his glory? And beginning at Moses and all the prophets, he expounded unto them in all the scriptures the things concerning himself.*
>
> *—Luke 24:25-27*

Then He had to explain it again in the Upper Room in Jerusalem:

*He said unto them, These are the words which I spake unto you,
while I was yet with you, that all things must be fulfilled, which were
written in the law of Moses, and in the prophets, and in the psalms,
concerning me. Then opened he their understanding, that they might
understand the scriptures, and said unto them, Thus it is written, and
thus it behoved Christ to suffer, and to rise from the dead the third
day: and that repentance and remission of sins should be preached
in his name among all nations, beginning at Jerusalem. And ye are
witnesses of these things.*

—Luke 24: 44-48

He told them exactly what they must say. They had seen and heard, but
they had not understood. So after His resurrection He gave them the explanation. He had given it before, but they had not been able to take it in; now
He gave it in person, having risen from the dead. He said: "Go out, witness
to these things, tell people the meaning of it all."

And what does it mean? It is my privilege to hold it before you once more.
May God the Spirit open the eyes of all who have never seen it. It means that
this is the Son of God. The Old Testament Scriptures had prophesied about
Him. He is there in the books of Moses; He is there in the Psalms; He is there
in the prophets—they all point to Him, the Messiah, this great Prophet, this
great one who was to come—Jesus! He had come, the Son of God. That is
why they preached in His name. This was no mere man; this was God and
man, the God-man, God in the flesh. Why had He ever come into the world?
He had told them why: "The Son of man is come to seek and to save that
which was lost" (Luke 19:10). He came into this world because we have all
gone astray, we are all lost, and we cannot save ourselves. Prophets cannot
save us. Psalmists cannot save us. Philosophers cannot save us. Politicians
cannot save us. Education cannot save us. There is only one who can—Jesus,
the Son of God.

But you may ask, if He was the Son of God, why did He have to die?
Jesus explained that to His disciples after His resurrection. He said: "You
should not stumble at this. Do you not see that I had to die? My death was
not an accident. From one standpoint, it was a human tragedy, but from
another it was not. I came into the world in order to die."

So the apostles could say: "We know why He died. There on the cross
God was laying on Him the iniquity of us all. He is the 'Lamb of God'—as
John the Baptist had said—'which taketh away the sin of the world'" (John
1:29). They said: "There is no salvation in anybody but in this Jesus. He is

the only one who can deliver us. He is the only one who is great enough and powerful enough to bear the punishment of our sins and still go on living. The Son of God not only could do it, but He has done it."

So the apostles explained what they had seen, and that is why they emphasized the Resurrection. This event was proof positive that He had borne all the punishment demanded by the holy law of God. The Resurrection is God's proclamation that He is satisfied, that Christ was delivered for our offenses and raised again for our justification. In the Resurrection, God is proclaiming to the universe that His Son has borne the penalty. The Resurrection—justification by faith. God is offering free pardon to all who believe in Him.

And what else? Oh, they explained that Christ is the Savior of the whole universe and that as they had seen Him ascending into the heavens, so He would come back again, visibly, in bodily form. They would not see Him next time as a babe in a manger but as the King of kings, as the Lord of lords, riding the clouds of heaven, surrounded by the holy angels. They would see Him riding in the chariot of eternity, coming back to judge the world in righteousness, to consign all evil men who hated Him and rejected Him to the perdition that they richly deserve. He is coming to set up His holy kingdom and then to hand it back in utter perfection to His holy Father—"that God may be all in all" (1 Cor. 15:28). That is Christianity.

"We cannot but speak the things which we have seen and heard." Peter and John said to the rulers, "We respect you. You are the authorities, you are the council, but when you ask us not to preach or teach in this name, we cannot listen to you because of what we have seen, because He is who He is, because of why He came, because of what He has done, because He is the only way of salvation. We must speak of these things."

7

THE TRANSFORMING MESSAGE

And they called them, and commanded them not to speak at all nor teach in the name of Jesus. But Peter and John answered and said unto them, Whether it be right in the sight of God to hearken unto you more than unto God, judge ye. For we cannot but speak the things which we have seen and heard.

—Acts 4:18-20

The Christian message, we have seen, is the message of facts, of "things . . . seen and heard" about the Lord Jesus Christ and then the interpretation of these facts, their meaning, their relevance to every one of us. That is the essence of Christian preaching. But now we look at another equally important aspect of the Gospel. The wonderful thing about the Scriptures is that they put the one great central truth to us in so many different ways. They seem to take us by the hand and say: "Come and look at it from this angle or that angle or in this further way." Throughout the running centuries different people have been brought to a knowledge of the truth by looking at it from different angles. They look at it in a new way, and suddenly it comes home to them.

Some people see Christianity almost purely in terms of doctrine. Others will observe it working itself out in someone's life, and they are so impressed and charmed and fascinated that they begin to ask questions: "What made you like this? What has done this to you?" And so they come to the same truth in that way. We must not confine God to one way of revealing His truth. God uses many methods, and we should thank Him for it. That is why in the Bible itself, though there is only one message, one great truth from beginning to end, that truth is presented to us in a variety of ways—didactic teaching, history, illustrations, and poetry.

Now the incident we are examining is one example of God's saving power at work. We have considered the effect it had upon those who did not believe it, and now we shall look at its effect upon those who truly believed it.

This incident not only provides us with a wonderful test as to whether we ourselves are Christians, but it is also an excellent test of everything that offers itself to the modern world as a representation of the Christian message. There are "Christian agnostics," for example, these clever people who think that with their little theories they can explain everything that our Lord did and said and all that happened to Him. The point about all these supposed "new representations" of Christianity is, of course, that they are not new; they are as old as the Gospel itself! But the world thinks they are new, and they get the publicity. You will always read of such theories in the newspaper; there will probably be a session on the television, and people will be asked to give their brief opinions. Such is the world we are living in.

But if you want to know the truth about these modern ideas, a very good test to apply is to ask the question: What do they lead to? Do they do anything at all apart from being a nine-days' wonder, giving people something to write articles about, something to discuss and argue over with one another? Do they do anything really vital or worthwhile? Because our whole contention is that this Gospel is "the power of God unto salvation to every one that believeth" (Rom. 1:16). If that is so, it is bound to show itself by producing certain results. When God acts, there is something to be seen. So I am asking you to test yourselves, to test what you regard as Christianity, to test your own experience in the light of what we read here in Acts.

Now let us be clear about this. I am not saying that we must be able to reproduce in every single detail all that happened to these people. My contention is that in embryo the Gospel is all here, and in some measure we must all be able to trace the same kind of effect in us and upon us. If not, we are not Christians. This, after all, is the only standard. Here is the early church out of which everything we know of Christianity has come. The early church must ever be our norm and our standard of judgment both with regard to what is suggested to us and also to what we find within ourselves.

So, then, what effect does this Gospel have upon those who truly believe it? The answer is given us in Peter and John, the apostles of our blessed Lord and Savior. From what they said and did I shall extract principles to guide us.

First of all, it is surely obvious that Christianity is something that entirely changes us. Of course, we know a good deal about these two disciples. We read about them in the four Gospels—Matthew, Mark, Luke, and John. Anybody who has ever read the Gospels and then comes to this book of Acts must be struck at once by the astounding change that has taken place in these men.

When you look at Peter and John as they appear in the Gospels before the day of Pentecost, what strikes you is their slowness, indeed, their failure, to understand. There was the Son of God among them for three years. He had drawn them out from society. He had formed them into an inner circle of students and had taught them. They were always present whenever He taught, and they saw all His miracles. They could ask Him questions, and He was always patient with them, always ready to answer, to explain. Never did men have such a marvelous opportunity of learning and grasping the truth. And yet they were so slow to learn, so dull, so lacking in apprehension. They seemed to fumble and to stumble. Though He had explained things so often, they still failed to understand, and He had to reprimand them very sharply.

On one occasion, our Lord even turned upon Peter and said, "Get thee behind me, Satan" (Matt. 16:23). This happened at Caesarea Philippi after our Lord had said to His disciples, "Whom say ye that I am?" And Peter, with that amazing insight that had been given to him, replied, "Thou art the Christ, the Son of the living God" (Matt. 16:16). Our Lord had commended him, saying, "Blessed art thou, Simon Barjona: for flesh and blood hath not revealed it unto thee, but my Father which is in heaven" (v. 17). But then our Lord went on to tell the disciples about His forthcoming death. Peter had remonstrated with Him: "Be it far from thee, Lord: this shall not be unto thee" (v. 22). Then it was that our Lord said, "Get thee behind me, Satan"—Satan!—"thou art an offense unto me: for thou savourest not the things that be of God, but those that be of men" (v. 23).

This exchange is not the only example of Peter and John's lack of understanding. Many times you will find our Lord dealing with the same question of His death and resurrection, but none of the disciples understood it and were grieved and troubled. One afternoon they were so downhearted that He had to say, "Let not your heart be troubled: ye believe in God, believe also in me. . . . It is expedient for you that I go away" (John 14:1; 16:7). But they could not see it. That was their trouble all the way through the Gospels. Then when they saw Him dying upon the cross, they were completely upset and bewildered. And after His death you see them utterly disconsolate; they did not know what to do with themselves. Then the women reported that they had been to the tomb and found it empty. The disciples thought the women had lost their senses and did not believe the report.

You remember that in the last chapter we looked at the two followers who were commiserating with one another as they walked to Emmaus. Our Lord joined them without their recognizing Him, and He asked, "What is the matter with you? What are you talking about? Why are you so sad?"

"Don't you know" they said, "about Jesus of Nazareth? Haven't you heard what has happened? Where were you? Are you a stranger in these parts that you don't know about these things?"

"What things?" our Lord asked.

"Well," they replied, "concerning Jesus of Nazareth. We had trusted that it would be He who was going to restore the kingdom to Israel, but they have taken Him and crucified Him and laid Him in a tomb."

And again our Lord had to reprimand them and say, "O fools, and slow of heart to believe all that the prophets have spoken" (see Luke 24:13-33).

Look at the disciples again in that old setting in the Gospels. You find they were ambitious, jealous of one another, wanting the preeminence, quarreling and fighting over little details. What a miserable lot they were! Above all, look at their fearfulness. When our Lord was arrested, Peter wanted to hear the trial, and so he sneaked into the courtyard. There he was, standing by the fire, hoping that nobody would recognize him. But a servant girl challenged him and said, "This man was also with Him." An hour later, someone else said, "Of a truth this fellow also was with Him: for he is a Galilaean." Peter's speech had betrayed him. And each time Peter denied it with oaths and curses. He said, "I don't know the man. I've nothing to do with Him" (See Luke 22:54-60). Oh, the miserable cad! He was afraid of losing his life, and so he denied knowing his best friend and benefactor, his great teacher. The craven spirit, the fear, the cowardice! Indeed, the apostles' behavior is all summed up in a phrase. When our Lord was arrested, "They all forsook him, and fled" (Mark 14:50). They were terrified of being arrested and tried and perhaps condemned to death themselves.

But now look at them here in the book of Acts; you can scarcely recognize them. Now the apostles have a clear grasp of the truth and the ability to state it; they can argue, they can reason, they are in command. Not only that, but look at their boldness! Indeed, we are told that when they saw the boldness of Peter and John, even the members of the Sanhedrin were amazed. But here these two are, fearless. What caused the change?

Let me sum it up like this: Christianity is not something that you add on to your life; it changes the whole of your life beginning at the center. It is not an addendum or an appendix; it is not an afterthought or something you do on Sundays. It is not something you take up and put down. No, Christianity is a power that changes men and women through and through, as it changed

Peter and John. And, of course, as you read the whole of the subsequent history of the Christian church, you will find that when men and women truly become Christians, this is what inevitably happens to them.

Let the apostle Paul express this in his incomparable words: "If any man be in Christ, he is a new creature [a new creation]: old things are passed away; behold, all things are become new" (2 Cor. 5:17). Christians have not just adopted certain ideas from the teaching of Christ and other ideas from the teaching of Gandhi and others from the teaching of certain ancient philosophers. They are men and women who are entirely changed—a new creation, a new being. They are "born again." This principle stares us in the face on the very surface of this incident.

The second principle I find here is that Christianity is, therefore, something that masters us. This is a very important point. It is not something you take up but something that takes you up. It is not something that you control and manipulate but something that controls you and governs the whole of your life. There are many who seem to think that people are Christians because they have examined Christianity and, having listened to sermons and discussions, have decided on the whole to take it up. Then for most of their lives, in their daily work, probably they forget all about it. But Sunday comes, and this is the day when they give themselves up—to a certain point, at any rate—to their religious interests. So they decide to go to a place of worship either on Sunday morning only or on Sunday evening only. Of course, they are very interested. They want to keep "in touch" (that is the phrase), but should there be a fine summer's day and should a friend say, "What about a round of golf?" of course, the golf wins. They can take up their Christianity again when they cannot play golf, provided they do not have any pressing business. "Not today perhaps but another time certainly."

Is not that the popular idea? Indeed, there are many who do not even remind themselves of Christianity but have to be reminded by something else. There are many people who never think about it at all until they have to face illness. They have not prayed for years, but they or a dear one falls ill, or there is a death, and then they remember.

But all that is remote from what we find in Acts. Christianity is not something to which you are loosely connected, something to which you are vaguely attached. The Gospel was central to these people; it was at the very heart of their lives. Here was something that mastered them. They had to say, "We cannot but speak . . ." It was the biggest thing in their lives.

Is not that also obvious in the history of true Christianity in all the running centuries? When we read the lives of the martyrs and the confessors, we see that they were all men and women who had been mastered by Christ and this Gospel. They were slaves, they had been bought, they were no longer the ones who thought and decided, they were no longer in command. No, they were commanded by the Gospel. They were controlled by it, and their whole outlook was determined by it. So if your religious faith is on the circumference of your life, it is not the Christian faith. You can leave your philosophies, your different teachings there, but you cannot do that with Christianity.

Do you not see how important all this is? Do you not see how ridiculous it makes all this so-called dialogue and discussion? Discussion! As if you can sit down in judgment upon Christianity. Christianity is that which judges you. It is something that possesses you. You are a man or woman of one idea, one Book. It is all in Christ; Christ has mastered you. That is Christianity!

I have often quoted from my pulpit the memorable phrase spoken two hundred years ago by that great German Christian Count Zinzendorf, the man who had such an influence upon early Methodism. He said: "I have one passion; it is He, and He alone." That is Christianity.

The third principle is that when men and women are truly Christian, when they are possessed in this way by this message, by this truth, they feel that they must tell everybody about it. "We cannot but speak the things which we have seen and heard." The whole bone of contention, the point at issue between the apostles and the Sanhedrin at this stage was this one question: Should they go on preaching and teaching in the name of Jesus? The authorities had conferred together and had decided to forbid all preaching about Christ. We read: "That it spread no further among the people, let us straitly threaten them [Peter and John], that they speak henceforth to no man in this name. And they called them, and commanded them not to speak at all nor teach in the name of Jesus." But Peter and John replied that they could not but speak.

So let us analyze this. First of all, when men and women become genuine Christians, they are no longer uncertain as to what they believe. If someone says, "I cannot but speak about it," then they must know what they are talking about. People who merely speculate about truth cannot say, "I cannot but speak." Their attitude is, "Well, at the moment, we think that it is probably this, but we know that truth is always changing, and the world is developing and advancing. We know that probably in twenty years time, this will prove to be wrong, just as we can prove that those who have gone before us were wrong." So it goes on ad infinitum. Do people like that feel that they cannot help but speak? Of course not! Philosophers never know anything about this constraint because they are only speculating, only examining; they are only trying to discover truth.

But it was of the essence of these apostles that they had a very definite message—we have looked at that. It was a discrete, a concrete message. They did not get up and say, "On the whole we have come to this conclusion," and then put up rival views and give a wonderful, intellectual answer. They were men with a message, and when they repeated it, it was always the same. They knew exactly what it was; they had not understood it before, but now they did, and they were preaching it with absolute authority.

On the basis of the New Testament teaching, I do not hesitate to assert that men and women who do not know what they believe are not Christians. They may be very good people and fine philosophers, but if they cannot say, "This is the truth," they are not Christians. The position of the apostle Paul was: "I know whom I have believed" (2 Tim. 1:12). "I *know.*" The great affirmations, the great asseverations, the great certainties, the great absolutes.

This certainty is not confined to apostles and preachers. The apostle Peter, in writing his first letter, says to ordinary Christians, many of them slaves and servants: "Be ready always to give an answer to every man that asketh you a reason of the hope that is in you" (1 Pet. 3:15). A reason! And they were able to do this. The apostle John, the companion of Peter here in Acts, writes in his first letter, "Ye have an unction from the Holy One, and ye know all things. . . . ye need not that any man teach you" (1 John 2:20, 27). You see, there were false teachers then, as there are now. There is nothing new about false teaching. Those teachers were called "antichrists" then; now they often become dignitaries in the church. In the first century they went out from the church because they did not belong; now they stay in. That is the one difference that I can see in the situation.

But John tells the ordinary Christians to whom he is writing that he is not worried about them. "You know all things," he says. The Gospel was known; the apostles all preached the same message. It was the one message delivered to them, and there was no contradiction, no uncertainty.

But, further, notice also this aspect: The apostles were not apologetic or half-hearted; they were not ashamed of their message. Is there someone, I wonder, who is a bit ashamed of believing the Gospel in this modern scientific age? Do you try to hide your faith from your fellow students or the members of your profession? Do you try to hide it from your business associates? You are a Christian. You are afraid not to be, but are you apologetic? Do you try to keep it quiet or to accommodate it to the latest fashion or the latest supposed discovery?

Oh, what a contrast to these two men and to all the early Christians. These men exulted in the Gospel; they gloried in it. They said with the apostle Paul,

"God forbid that I should glory, save in the cross of our Lord Jesus Christ" (Gal. 6:14); and, "I am not ashamed of the gospel of Christ: for it is the power of God unto salvation to every one that believeth" (Rom. 1:16). When Paul found himself in Athens, he was not apologetic on Mars' Hill; he was not trying to defend his position, fighting a rear-guard action against the attack of philosophy. He charged, he attacked, he exposed. And here in Peter and John you find that fire, that enthusiasm, the "must," the constraint. "We cannot but speak."

Why? Ah, here is the question; here is the thing that leads us into the secret. Why did they rejoice and glory in the Gospel? Why did they feel they must tell everybody and that, whatever edict the Sanhedrin might pass, they would still go on? Here is the answer. They felt this because of the very glory of the facts. When you have been in the presence of the Son of God, as these men had, you cannot keep quiet about it. Look at these things that they had seen and heard; think of that glory; think of the wonder, the amazing character. They were bound to tell, especially when they had seen Him risen from the dead with something of the glory of eternity showing itself more plainly than ever before. That is the first answer.

But there are further reasons. Why did they feel they must tell everybody? It is because of what the gospel message had done to them, because of the difference it had made to them. This Gospel had not only changed them, as we have seen, but it had brought to them a joy that they had never known before. Peter later describes it as "joy unspeakable and full of glory" (1 Pet. 1:8). This joy was the result of all that had happened on the day of Pentecost when they had been filled with a spirit of exultation and of rejoicing, when God had told them, in a way they had never imagined possible, that they were His children and that the Christ was His only begotten Son. He had poured His love into their hearts—"shed [it] abroad" (Rom. 5:5)—by the Holy Spirit. They had been lifted up and transported into an ecstasy; they had never known anything like it. Unbelief had gone; melancholy had gone; uncertainty and doubt had gone; joy and happiness had come flooding in.

The apostles knew they were at peace with God, that God had had them in His heart and in His mind from all eternity and had sent His Son to die for them. They knew the power that they had received, the power to work miracles, the power in prayer, the power in speaking. They did not understand; they were amazed, and they were so enthralled and enraptured that they must tell everybody what it had meant to them—this new knowledge of God, this new understanding of life, and this subjective experience of the power of the Gospel giving them a clarity of knowledge and of understanding and a new power to see all things in the light of Christ.

But there is another even more powerful reason why the apostles were persisting in telling everybody about these things. It was because they felt compassion for the men and women who did not know. "We cannot but speak the things which we have seen and heard." Why? Because they had become a little bit like their Lord Himself. We are told that He looked out upon the multitude, and His heart felt for them, for He saw them as sheep without a shepherd (Matt. 9:36). He saw humanity in ignorance and in the grip of sin, and He had a heart of compassion. He had to tell them. He sat down with tax collectors and sinners and prostitutes, but what did it matter? He was sorry for them.

Peter and John had become like that. There were the authorities telling them to stop teaching in the name of Jesus, and they said, "We cannot stop!" They felt like a man who has had some wonderful experience of deliverance and looks at other men and women who are in the position he was in, knowing exactly what will put them right. But here are the authorities telling him not to speak, and he says, "I cannot keep quiet. I'd be a cad."

Imagine a man who has been suffering for years from some painful, crippling illness, let us say a disease of his joints. He has suffered terrible pains, and his joints have become enlarged and stiff. He cannot grip things; he cannot walk. There he is crippled and in terrible agony. He has tried a number of doctors and has been referred to specialists, but no one can help him. Then at long last he comes across a doctor who says, "Yes, I know exactly what is the matter. I can cure you." The doctor writes out a prescription and hands it to this poor patient with the words, "Now you take that regularly. It will put you right." The man starts taking the medicine, and the pain begins to ease. Then the joints become loose and supple, and after a while he is perfectly healed. He can move his joints; he can walk. He is free. The prescription has done it.

Now here he is, once more walking up and down the streets of life. One afternoon he sees a man coming up the other side of the road. He does not know the man, but he recognizes the disease. He can tell by the way the man is holding himself that he has joint trouble. The healed man says to himself, "It's obvious that that poor man doesn't know about this prescription, for if he did, he would not be like that." And he has the medicine in his pocket. What does he do? There is surely no doubt about it. He must cross the road. So he goes over to the man and says, "Sir, you don't know me, and I don't know you, but I do know what's the matter with you. Tell me, have you ever heard of this?" And he produces his medication.

Now the healed man did not have to force himself to cross the road. He said to himself, "If I don't tell that man about this certain cure when I have it in my pocket, I'm a cad, unworthy of the name of man. I'm bound to tell him. No one can stop me. Am I to allow that man to go on suffering because of some rules and regulations, some medical etiquette? Not at all! I owe that man this knowledge that I have and he lacks."

Now that is exactly what Peter and John felt as they faced the authorities. Because of what had happened to them, they saw humanity in its appalling need. The truth of Jesus had given them insight into the condition of men and women in sin. The apostles no longer saw them as they used to see them. Along with Paul, they said: "Henceforth know we no man after the flesh" (2 Cor. 5:16). They always used to know men "after the flesh"—Jew and Gentile, black and white, along with all the enmity between these types of people. Now they saw all people as slaves of the devil and the world and the flesh. They saw the misery, the unhappiness, all the ravages of sin, and they felt great compassion.

But not only that, Peter and John saw these men and women in Jerusalem under the condemnation of God's holy law. They did not see them merely as people walking up and down the streets of life; they did not now see mainly the fighting between nations and people struggling for their rights. No, they saw all people as souls. They said, "These people will have to stand before God whatever their race. They have all got to die and to stand before God in eternal judgment, and they are all under condemnation." "There is none righteous, no, not one" (Rom. 3:10). They did not see people merely doing things that were wrong; they saw their souls and the jeopardy of their eternal existence, and it terrified them. They saw the ignorance of men and women boasting about their lives but dupes of sin and Satan, moral failures socially and personally. Oh, they saw it all, and they had great hearts of compassion.

But that was not the final thing; that alone would not have made them take the trouble they did to defy the authorities. They knew that all the things these people were trusting could never help them or save them. They knew that even a rigid adherence to the Jewish law could not save anyone. The disciples had tried that themselves. They knew that all the things to which humanity was pinning its faith would ultimately be of no avail. But they knew of someone who could put people right, as they themselves had been put right. They knew that they had been saved not by anything in them but by the power of God, that Christ was the Savior, that the Spirit was the power of God. They knew that this transformation that had taken place in them could take place in others.

There is only one way of salvation, and that is all of grace. It does not matter how deeply people may be steeped in sin. Christ can lift them up. And it is all by faith, a simple act of faith, of belief: "By grace are ye saved through faith," says Paul, "and that not of yourselves" (Eph. 2:8). Peter and John knew that they had to tell people. It was the only thing that could save them; the position of the lost was desperate.

And then, I think, there was a final reason, and this was a very human one. They wanted everybody to praise Jesus. They had admired Him before. Even when they had misunderstood Him, they had loved Him. They had never met anybody like Him. But now they had seen Him as He is, as the divine Savior. They had seen the glory of His person, and now their greatest concern was that everybody should come to Him, that everybody should get to know Him, that the whole world should praise Him.

Again is not this something that we do on the human level? Take the illustration I gave you about the man who at last found a doctor who could heal him. For the rest of his life he will talk about that doctor. He wants the world to know what a wonderful physician he is. And that was the motive that imbued these apostles. They said, in effect, "You tell us not to speak or teach in the name of Jesus. We cannot but speak, because He is who He is. We've seen His glory, His majesty. We know what He's done to us and what He can do for you. We must tell the whole world; we're bound to. We cannot but speak . . ." That is always the mark of true Christianity.

But I must take that one step further. Once men and women see and are gripped and mastered by this message, they are not only entirely changed, and they not only feel that they must tell everybody about it, but they are ready to defy the authorities and to die for it. Peter and John were facing the authorities, and these authorities had it in their power to sentence them to death. The apostles were not merely arguing with equals. They were arguing with "the priests, and the captain of the temple, and the Sadducees"; they were arguing with "their rulers, and elders, and scribes, and Annas the high priest, and Caiaphas, and John, and Alexander, and as many as were of the kindred of the high priest." These were nearly all in league with Rome, and the apostles realized that they were facing the same power that had put their blessed Lord to death a few weeks back.

Yet they did not hesitate to defy these rulers. "They . . . commanded them not to speak at all nor teach in the name of Jesus." But here is the answer Peter and John gave: "Whether it be right in the sight of God to hearken unto you more than unto God, judge ye. For we cannot but speak the things which we have seen and heard." They were going on, whatever it might mean—even though it might mean death itself.

And eventually most of them had to lay down their lives for the Gospel.

Peter certainly did. There is a tradition that John died a natural death, but it does not matter. Hundreds, even thousands of early Christians gladly laid down their lives. They were challenged not only by these authorities but by the Roman Empire, which said to them, "If you go on saying that Jesus is Lord, and if you persist in refusing to say that Caesar is Lord, we will cast you to the lions in the arena, or we will put you on the rack and tear you limb from limb. Are you going on?" And they said, "We are!" They counted it the greatest privilege to lay down their lives for the name of this blessed Jesus.

Christians throughout the centuries have been ready to do the same thing. Go and visit Smithfield. The Protestant martyrs laid down their lives rather than deny Christ or renounce their faith in Him. They would face even death rather than recant. So why did they all defy the authorities, and why will true Christians do the same today, even at the cost of being laughed at? Let the whole world mock and laugh and jeer, they will go on, even if death be involved. Why? The answer is quite simple. The apostles gave it: "We ought to obey God rather than men" (Acts 5:29).

Why were the apostles preaching? First, it was because our Lord had commanded them to preach. He had said to them, "Tarry ye in the city of Jerusalem, until ye be endued with power from on high" (Luke 24:49). Jesus also had said, "Ye shall receive power, after that the Holy Ghost is come upon you: and ye shall be witnesses unto me" (Acts 1:8). He had given them a commission; He had sent them out; He had commanded them to go. They obeyed a higher authority than these rulers. The rulers were important on earth, but here was the King of heaven commanding them, the one who says, "All power is given unto me in heaven and in earth" (Matt. 28:18).

We can sum it up in the words of the apostle Paul. In 2 Corinthians 5 he tells us why he preached: "The love of Christ constraineth us" (v. 14). That is wonderful. Again we see this same compassion for men and women in sin and shame and evil. The love of Christ constrains me. Look what He has done for me; He can do it for them, and I must tell them.

But there is another aspect. "We must all appear before the judgment seat of Christ; that every one may receive [give an account of] the things done in his body . . . whether it be good or bad. Knowing therefore the terror of the Lord, we persuade men" (2 Cor. 5:10-11). We have to give an account to God. Peter and John knew that. Could they listen to the rulers? Of course not. The risen Lord had commanded them, and they had to give an account to Him. How could they face Him and feel that they had been cads again, saving their lives by ceasing to speak? They could not. There was no choice; they had to obey God rather than men.

If you have not come to that, well, if you are a Christian at all, you are not much of a Christian. If you are putting the opinions of men and women before the opinion of God, if you are putting what people think of you and their praise before the praise of your Christ who has died for you and risen again, I say you do not know Him. You are saved to be a witness and to bear your testimony. I repeat that if you are animated by a fear of others, it means that somewhere or another you do not know Him, and you have not understood the Gospel, and you have not experienced its power in your own life.

But, second, they defied the authorities not only because Christ had commanded them to preach, but because not to do so would have made life not worth living. If they had to be silent about the most wonderful thing, the thing that had made life for them, then they did not want to go on living. Life without this would have been mere existence; it would have become empty. So they said, "We cannot but preach. We don't care what happens. We have life, we have new power, we have new understanding, we have new joy, and you are telling us to deny it. We cannot do it; it is impossible."

Once people become true Christians, then merely existing or prolonging their lives in this world is not the chief thing. They look out upon it all, and they say:

> *Fading is the worldling's pleasure,*
> *All his boasted pomp and show.*
> John Newton

The world is empty. So the disciples say that they must go on preaching. This Gospel is everything. In the words of the apostle Paul, "To me to live is Christ" (Phil. 1:21). Christ is the mainspring of my life, the center of my whole being. I think in Him and speak in Him, do everything in Him. If He is not there, there is nothing left; chaos is come again.

But the last reason for the apostles' defiance of the authorities, even at the risk of death, is this—and here is the glory of Christianity—they were no longer afraid of death. Death has no terror for the true Christian. "The sting of death is sin; and the strength of sin is the law. But thanks be to God, which giveth us the victory through our Lord Jesus Christ" (1 Cor. 15:56-57). The Christian is someone who can look at the grave and death and say, "O death, where is thy sting? O grave, where is thy victory?" (1 Cor. 15:55). "Put us to death," Peter and John said, in effect, "and you are not doing us any harm because we are no longer afraid to die. We were once, but not any longer. Death has lost its terror; death has lost its sting; the grave is not the end. Kill us," they said, "and you are simply sending us into the presence of Christ earlier than we thought." What is death? It is "to be with Christ; which is far better" (Phil. 1:23).

Peter and John had come to see that Christ is the conqueror of every enemy, including "the last enemy," which is death. "[He] hath brought life and immortality to light through the gospel" (2 Tim. 1:10). They had had glimpses of that "land of pure delight, where saints immortal reign"; they had seen the glory of God's kingdom and knew that they would be ushered into it by death. They had the faith that sees through death to the glory that awaits every true believer in the Lord Jesus Christ. And so they said:

> *Fear Him, ye saints, and you will then*
> *Have nothing else to fear.*
>> Nahum Tate and
>> Nicholas Brady

That is it! Our Lord once said it all: "Fear not them which kill the body, but are not able to kill the soul: but rather fear him which is able to destroy both soul and body in hell" (Matt. 10:28). So they could have said with Augustus Toplady:

> *The terrors of law and of God*
> *With me can have nothing to do,*
> *My Saviour's obedience and blood*
> *Hide all my transgressions from view.*
>> Augustus Toplady

And we, too, can look at the authorities, with all their pomp and show and defiance and edicts and laws, and say with a smile upon our faces:

> *Man may trouble and distress me,*
> *'Twill but drive me to Thy breast;*
> *Life with trials hard may press me,*
> *Heaven will give me sweeter rest.*
> *Oh, 'tis not in grief to harm me,*
> *While Thy love is left to me:*
> *Oh, 'twere not in joy to charm me,*
> *Were that joy unblest by Thee.*
>> Henry Francis Lyte

The only thing that mattered to Peter and John was their relationship to God, their knowledge of Him. Give them the world without Him, and it would be emptiness, tinsel, nothing but dung and refuse. They might have nothing in this world, but having Christ, they had everything. That is what true Christianity does to men and women. They do not just speculate about ideas; they do not spend the whole of their time in talking about political or international issues. That is not Christianity; in a sense, it has nothing to do with it. I say again that this is Christianity: "To me to live is Christ, and to die is gain . . . [for it means] to be with Christ; which is far better" (Phil. 1:21, 23).

Has what you regard as Christianity changed you? Does it master you? Do you feel you must tell everybody about it because of what it has done for you? Are you ready to die for it? That is true Christianity.

8

THE SPIRIT OF UNBELIEF

Now when they saw the boldness of Peter and John, and perceived that they were unlearned and ignorant men, they marvelled; and they took knowledge of them, that they had been with Jesus. And beholding the man which was healed standing with them, they could say nothing against it. But when they had commanded them to go aside out of the council, they conferred among themselves, saying, What shall we do to these men? for that indeed a notable miracle hath been done by them is manifest to all them that dwell in Jerusalem; and we cannot deny it. But that it spread no further among the people, let us straitly threaten them, that they speak henceforth to no man in this name. And they called them, and commanded them not to speak at all nor teach in the name of Jesus. But Peter and John answered and said unto them, Whether it be right in the sight of God to hearken unto you more than unto God, judge ye. For we cannot but speak the things which we have seen and heard. So when they had further threatened them, they let them go, finding nothing how they might punish them, because of the people: for all men glorified God for that which was done. For the man was above forty years old, on whom this miracle of healing was showed.
—Acts 4:13-22

The wonderful thing about the healing of the lame man and the events that followed is that we can look at the same truth from different angles and perspectives, all of which are equally valuable. I should now like to look at the reaction of the Sanhedrin to this truth committed by the Lord to the Christian church.

The message the Christian church preaches, we are reminded here, always calls for a decision. I go beyond that. It always produces a decision. Is that not obvious in verses 13 to 22? Have you noticed the division in the people here? Peter and John, the apostles, on one side and the rulers, the Sanhedrin, a collection of priests, the captain of the temple, and Annas the high priest, on the other side. But there was also another comparable division. In verse 21 we read: "When they had further threatened them, they let them go, finding nothing how they might punish them, because of the people: for all men glorified God for that which was done." The common people glorified God, but the Sanhedrin were annoyed and tried to put a stop to it. This message divides all humanity into two groups—those who are for it and those who are against it. We are, every one of us, in one of those groups.

The story here is dramatic. These rulers had a problem. They could not deny that the lame man had been healed. As we read in verse 14: "Beholding the man which was healed standing with them, they could say nothing against it." Their words betray their difficulty: "What shall we do to these men? for that indeed a notable miracle hath been done by them is manifest to all them that dwell in Jerusalem; and we cannot deny it." So they saw that they had to do something.

The apostle Peter told these leaders the same thing. Here they were, issuing their edict, prohibiting any further preaching or teaching in the name of Jesus, and Peter said, "Whether it be right in the sight of God to hearken unto you more than unto God, judge ye." He threw their problem back at them. "You must judge; you must decide." So the need for a decision, which they themselves had already seen, was pressed upon their minds and hearts and consciences.

Now this is always inevitable with regard to the gospel message. If you read the Gospels, you will find that our Lord Himself always had this effect upon people. He put it as a question: "What think ye of Christ?" (Matt. 22:42). His enemies asked themselves a similar question. We read: "They . . . communed one with another what they might do to Jesus" (Luke 6:11). They had to do something about Him; they could not evade Him. His presence demanded a decision.

And, of course, the message concerning Him still confronts us today. I suggest that if this message has not forced us to a decision, it means that we have never really heard it. We can be within earshot of it without hearing it. But when it truly comes, it always insists upon and always produces a decision. To do nothing about it is a decision—we reject it. If we are not for, we are automatically against the Gospel. There is no middle position. There is no "mean between two opposites," as Aristotle put it. Passive resistance is resistance. To do nothing is a form of resistance, sometimes the most effective of all. No one escapes. I repeat that we are all in one or the other of these two positions.

So I simply put this great question to you. You are in exactly the same position as the Sanhedrin. In my unworthy and small way—infinitesimally small by contrast with these apostles—I am holding the same message before you, and the question therefore comes to you: What will you do? What are you doing, and what have you done with this message? What is your judgment?

The great tragedy in the world is that the vast majority of our fellow human beings have come to the same decision as these rulers. "Nothing in it," they say. "Nonsense, rubbish!" And many are not saying anything at all. Our business is to discover the cause of this extraordinary rejection. How can unbelief be explained? That is what I am concerned about.

There is nothing under heaven more important than the decision you come to about the Gospel. As I shall show you, this is not only something that will affect you while you are in this world. It will affect you in the next, and you cannot say that about anything else. I am not here to say a word against political decisions; they are necessary; we must have government, but political decisions only last for this life. They will not be of the slightest interest or value when we leave this world. So it is with everything else. What is your opinion about a certain painting or piece of music? That topic is, indeed, full of interest. Let us indulge in it; it is all excellent. But it is only of interest and of value as long as we are in this world. The gospel message, on the other hand, will be of concern to us forever and forever and forever. There is no greater tragedy, I repeat, than to reject this message.

Am I addressing someone who up to now has rejected the Gospel? If so, have you realized what you are doing? It is because of my concern for your soul and your eternal destiny that I am pleading with you. Now I shall show you what unbelief is, in terms of the members of the Sanhedrin here at Jerusalem. I am taking this approach because I know myself, and I know human nature. I know that when we ourselves are involved in something, we tend to be prejudiced. We are always on the defensive. But as we have seen, when we look at something objectively, then we are more dispassionate and give a better judgment. As we consider, therefore, the tragedy of the members of the Sanhedrin so long ago, may God grant that someone today may recognize himself or herself and fall a willing captive to the pleadings of the Son of God.

Now the problem of unbelief is put before us here in this passage in a very clear and precise manner. I have tried to reduce it to a number of principles so that you may remember it more conveniently. The first, obviously, is the spirit that animated these people. We cannot read the account without seeing it—the prejudice, the bias against Peter and John. Have you noticed the way these rulers were fighting for their position? They had no reason for their opposition. Even they had to admit that, but they were still opposed. Now that is nothing but sheer prejudice. It was purely a matter of an antagonistic spirit.

The same spirit is to be seen in Luke 23. Can you not feel it as you read about that crowd calling for our Lord's death? Even Pilate, the Roman governor, was doing his best to disabuse their minds and to get them to see sense and behave with an element of justice. But no, the more he pleaded with them, the more they shouted, "Away with Him! Crucify Him!" They had given in to violent bias and unreasoning prejudice. This behavior is entirely a matter of one's spirit. And similarly here in Acts these members of the Sanhedrin were determined to stop Peter and John at all costs, without any reason.

Prejudice is ever a characteristic of unbelief. I have already given you the most tragic illustration of it. It passes my comprehension how anyone can read those last chapters of the four Gospels, with their accounts of the treatment meted out to our Lord, and not see at once that unbelief is purely a matter of prejudice. There it is, the utter unreason of it all, the bitterness and vehemence. The chief priests and scribes "vehemently accused him" (Luke 23:10). And, of course, unbelief always goes beyond prejudice. It does not stop merely at not accepting the message, but persecutes it and is determined to stamp it out. That is what these men did. They had the power to stop the message, and they exercised that power.

If you read the story of the Christian church throughout the centuries, you will find that this persecution has constantly been repeated. The story of persecutions is one whole aspect of the history of the Christian church. We frequently read of princes and powers and potentates persecuting God's simple, faithful people, using all the force of their authority to silence and destroy such people, to exterminate them completely. Such behavior is all the result of unreasoning, blind prejudice.

Somebody is probably saying, "That's the past, but there's nothing like that now."

Is there not? I suggest to you that there is a great deal of persecution at the present time, not merely among the common people who are outside the church, but also in some of the highest academic circles. A few months back I was reading an article by an American scientist who said that he was a teacher of science and he did not believe in the theory of evolution. He added that he knew numbers of professors and lecturers in various colleges who also did not accept this theory, but they dared not say so. Why not? Because if they did, they would be up against vested interests, against prejudice, and would never get a promotion. It did not matter how brilliant their academic qualifications, how excellent their work, or how impressive the results achieved by their students; if it became known that they did not subscribe to this shibboleth, they would suffer for it. It took exceptional courage to be prepared even to ask questions or raise any doubts about this controlling, prevailing theory.

There are many true Christian people today—and I have known many myself—who are being persecuted in this way. I have known people who have been denied office in political circles because they were Christians. I knew one man very well indeed, a schoolteacher, who was becoming a leader in political circles, but the moment that man became a Christian, he was a marked man. The powers that be kept him in the smallest and the least important school belonging to the entire Education Authority for no reason at all but that he had become a Christian. I could multiply examples and illustrations of the same spirit—the bias, the prejudice, the assertion of authority, the use of power, the bitterness against Christianity, and the determination to hold it down, come what may.

That is the truth about the spirit of unbelief. Of course, it represents itself to us as openness; it talks about "free thought" and "the freethinker." The person who rejects the Gospel is the freethinker; it is we Christians, we are told, who are biased. We are held in captivity by the same old tradition that we have inherited, but they have an open, detached, dispassionate, scientific outlook. I am sorry to have to put it like this, but there is only one thing to say about that kind of talk—it is a lie. There is as much bitterness and prejudice and bias in scientific circles as in any other circle. Prejudice and persecution are conditions of the spirit and are to be found in the highest circles as well as the lowest and equally among intellectuals and nonintellectuals.

Then there is something even more important, and that is the unreasonableness of unbelief. I want to establish this because people today are ever claiming that their use of reason prevents them from becoming Christians. We, the Christians, are just the unintelligent sentimentalists, the singers of hymns and choruses, the people who refuse to face the facts of life. But I want to show you that there is nothing in the world more unreasonable than the rejection of the Gospel. That is why I have selected this phrase in verse 14: "Beholding the man which was healed standing with them, they could say nothing against it." Yet they did say everything against it! They could not, but they did—that is unbelief; it is utterly unreasonable.

People who reject the Gospel are not rejecting opinions; they are rejecting facts, and that is what is so frequently forgotten. So often the Gospel is regarded as a point of view that can be accepted or rejected. But when you are dealing with the New Testament, as I constantly seek to point out, you are dealing with hard facts, with things that had been "seen and heard."

When you realize that the Bible is history, you see how completely unreasonable unbelief is. That truth is put here in a dramatic form: "Beholding the man which was healed standing with them, they could say nothing against it." If they could have, they would have. If they could only have made that man lame again, they would have done it. The wretched man was healed; they could not deny it. Facts are terrible things, are they not? If you are dealing with philosophies and theories and ideas, of course, you can go on arguing forever. However, a fact is a very stubborn thing, and there was the fact standing before them. And they were opposed. They tried to silence the apostles.

Is there anybody who would argue that this was a reasonable procedure? Is there anybody who would say that these members of the Sanhedrin were behaving in a rational manner? Was this a calm, detached consideration of the facts? It was the exact opposite, and they themselves had to admit it, but this is exactly how unbelief behaves.

Now let me take all this and put it in a different way. Have you ever approached the unreasonableness of unbelief by asking: What reasonably can be said against this message? What can you reasonably say against the person of the Lord Jesus Christ? What have you got against Him? Look at that young man working as a carpenter in Palestine. Look at Him at the age of thirty, beginning to preach. Follow Him along, look into His eyes, come near Him as the people did—what is your objection to Him? What is lacking in Him? What is wrong with Him? Did He come into the world to blast it and destroy it? He spent all His time healing people, talking to the outcasts, sitting down and eating and drinking with the tax collectors and sinners. Look at Him; read the record. Tell me, in the name of reason, what have you got against Him? Look at this unique personality who still dominates the whole world. Even the world that rejects Him cannot get rid of Him. Look at Him— what possible objection can there be to the Lord Jesus Christ? I would like to know on the grounds of reason what that objection is.

And then take His teaching. Read His Sermon on the Mount, as we call it. What is your objection to it? What is wrong with a sermon that tells you that you are to be "poor in spirit"? If everybody were poor in spirit, there would be no international problems. What is wrong with a teaching that says, "Blessed are the peacemakers"; "Blessed are they that mourn"; "Blessed are they which do hunger and thirst after righteousness"? Come along! If you reject this Gospel because you are a reasonable person, I want you to adduce your reasons. What is unreasonable about the Sermon on the Mount? Go right through it—His treatment of murder, of adultery, and of almsgiving. What is the objection? I urge you to produce your reasons.

Then go back to the Old Testament and read the Ten Commandments. What is wrong with them? Do you object to commandments that say, "Thou shalt not kill?" and "Thou shalt not steal"? What are your rational objections to the commandment that says, "Thou shalt not commit adultery"? Why is it unreasonable to put that commandment into practice? What is wrong with a commandment that tells you that you must not bring a false testimony against anybody? What is wrong with a commandment that tells you that you must not covet your neighbor's wife or any of his possessions? What, in the name of reason, is wrong with that?

Do you not realize that if the whole world and every individual in it were only living life according to the dictates of the Ten Commandments and the Sermon on the Mount, this world would be paradise? There would be no need to argue about whether we should have armies east of Suez or be making bombs. Can you not see that it is the opposite of reason to reject this teaching?

And then consider the great message of salvation that is the heart of the Gospel. Here is a word that tells you that God was sorry for men and women in a state of sin and with all the calamities that they had brought upon themselves. His love was so great that He sent his only Son into the world. We read: "God so loved the world, that he gave his only begotten Son, that whosoever believeth in him should not perish, but have everlasting life" (John 3:16). Here is a message that tells us that the world has brought all these calamities upon itself because of its arrogant rebellion against God and because of its fall from Him, but nevertheless God sent his only Son into the world. He did not only send prophets, though He did do that, but He sent His only begotten Son from the courts of heaven and the unmixed bliss of eternity. He told His Son to humble Himself and to be born as a man, to be born of the womb of a virgin.

And the Son said, "Here I am; send me." So "he humbled himself" and "took upon him the form of a servant" (Phil. 2:8, 7). Then He humbled Himself further. God had told His Son to start a new human race, to rescue them and deliver them. So Jesus said, "The Son of man is come to seek and to save that which was lost" (Luke 19:10). And "he stedfastly set his face to go to Jerusalem" (Luke 9:51). He deliberately went to death, because the only way He could save any one of us was to bear our punishment. The gospel message tells us that the Son of God "loved me, and gave himself for me" (Gal. 2:20). God took my sins and laid them on Him and punished Him with the punishment that I deserve.

That is the message—that He was the innocent, spotless Son of God, against whom nobody could bring any charge at all, for there was no charge to bring. Even the authorities had to admit that there was not a vestige of evidence against Him. Yet He went willingly to the cross to bear the punishment of my sins that I might be forgiven and reconciled to God, that I might become a child of God and an heir of eternal bliss. Here is a message that tells you all this. So what is your objection to the love of God, the love that is "so amazing, so divine," the love that "spared not his own Son, but delivered him up for us all" (Rom. 8:32)?

Reason? Unbelief is the antithesis of reason. You should surely admit that, especially when I remind you that this great message goes on to say that you have nothing to do but to believe the message, and you are immediately forgiven and accepted of God. You do not have to go and fast and sweat and pray. Salvation is a free gift from God; it is all of grace, and you can have it just as you are at this moment without any preparation at all, without your doing anything. You come as an empty-handed pauper. Just as you are, you can be forgiven, cleansed, renewed, made a new person, and given a blessed hope that can never fade away. So what is your objection in terms of reason?

And then think of the results of believing and accepting this message. Look at its effect on individuals. Look at them as you see them here in the Bible and as you see them in the history of the church throughout the centuries. Such reformation of character! Violent, vile, desperate people have been suddenly changed, suddenly delivered from all that had gotten them down, and have been made happy and joyful. This transformation has been one of the most amazing and romantic stories in the whole of history. Thank God, I have often been privileged to see it. I have known men who were the slaves of sin, hopeless drunkards and wife-beaters and adulterers, who stopped just short of murder. I have seen them become saints and great gentlemen. What produced the change? The probation officer? No, they had been in his hands for years. Psychological treatment? It did not touch them. The appeals of wife and children, fathers-in-law, mothers-in-law, fathers, brothers, sisters—nothing could touch them. But this message did, and it completely changed them, made them noble citizens, not only of the kingdom of God but even of the kingdom of this world.

And so this is the great story—the power of the Gospel unto salvation to change men and women and to set them free.

> *He breaks the power of cancelled sin,*
> *He sets the prisoner free;*
> *His blood can make the foulest clean,*
> *His blood availed for me.*
> Charles Wesley

Is not this the greatest need of the hour? We see the misery caused by drink and drugs, adultery and promiscuity. Oh, the unhappiness in the world because of these things! The men and women who are guilty of them are poor helpless victims. Many would give anything if they could only be freed, but they cannot. But here is a message that delivers. A lame man standing whole! And there standing before you are the saints of the centuries. So if you reject the Gospel, you are rejecting it in the face of that evidence.

Then take the story of the church. How has she persisted? Can you really dismiss the story of past revivals? No, you cannot explain the church. If people could have put an end to this institution, they would have. The church would have been killed off here in Acts at the very beginning. It would never have survived the first century. If it were but a human institution, it would long since have been finished. But it has gone on in spite of these powers, in spite of princes and kings, in spite of church councils, in spite of popes and bishops and archbishops. In spite of all their malignity and power and hatred, the church has gone on. Why? Because God is acting in her—that is the only adequate explanation, and you are running in the face of that.

And then think of what the Christian church has done in this world. I am simply presenting facts. I think any honest, dispassionate historian must admit that the Christian church has been the greatest civilizing force, the greatest benefactor, that the world has ever known. We boast so much of our education today and of all its advantages and thank God for them. But do you know who began educating poor people? Christians! The church! And look at the hospitals. Who began treating the sick and especially the poor sick? The answer is the same—the Christian church. The oldest hospital in

London, St Bartholomew's Hospital, was founded by a monk over eight centuries ago. Then who started Poor Law Relief? The Christian church!

That is what unbelievers are rejecting, those who think they are so clever. Why do they not face the facts? Nothing compares to what the church has achieved. Beyond any question, the saints of the Christian church stand out as the world's greatest benefactors.

So I repeat that to reject this message is to be utterly unreasonable. Nobody can say anything against our blessed Lord, against what He has done, against His teaching, against the people He has produced, or against the institution He has founded. So why not admit that? You are unreasonable. You are flying in the face of facts. You are guided by nothing but blind prejudice.

But, further, let me show you the bankruptcy of unbelief. By bankruptcy I mean that unbelief is entirely negative. Did you ever see a more negative attitude than that of this Sanhedrin or the attitude of the mob at the time of our Lord's crucifixion? They had nothing to say except no! The Jewish rulers could not explain the miracle of the lame man. They had to admit that it was beyond them, that it baffled and bewildered them. And yet they resisted the power that had done it and the message that had given rise to it.

The contemptible nature of this negative attitude shows in another way. If the rulers had been capable of doing something for a man like this, if it had been a question of one rival treatment against another, then there would have been some excuse for them. Two companies have two different products that can deal with the same problem. All right, it is fair competition. But here that was not the position at all. These authorities had not been able to do anything for the lame man. He was over forty years of age, and he had been lame almost since his birth. He had been carried to the Beautiful Gate and left there in his helplessness, and the Sanhedrin, with all its knowledge of the law and all its quoting of books and authorities, could not help him. They had left the moral problem unsolved. They did not understand; they could do nothing; they were entirely negative.

So this unbelief is not only unreasonable; it is also a confession of sheer bankruptcy. All the priests and scribes could do was go on repeating with a negative dogmatism that they would not believe. They had nothing themselves, but they would not accept this message. Our Lord said the truth about them: "For ye shut up the kingdom of heaven against men: for ye neither go in yourselves, neither suffer ye them that are entering to go in" (Matt. 23:13). What do you call people like that? What is to be said in their defense?

But that is the position of many who still reject the Gospel. Can you not hear it in the speech of these people in Acts? "Beholding the man which was healed standing with them, they could say nothing against it. But when they had commanded them to go aside out of the council . . ." They did not want to make fools of themselves in the presence of Peter and John and the healed man. ". . . they conferred among themselves, saying, What shall we do to these men? for that indeed a notable miracle hath been done by them is manifest to all them that dwell in Jerusalem; and we cannot deny it." And yet they wanted to stop it. But how? Well, they were just going to go on repeating dogmatically that they did not like it, that they did not believe it, and that they were not going to countenance it.

A modern quotation expresses that attitude better than I can ever hope to do. It comes from a learned book called *The Implications of Evolution*, published in an international series of monographs by Pergamon Press and entitled "Pure and Applied Biology, Zoology, Division number 4." At the time of writing, the author was in the Department of Physiology and Biochemistry of Southampton University. He does not say he is a Christian, and I have no reason to think that he is. He has written a purely scientific book, so scientific that much of it loses me, though there was a time when I had to study this sort of thing, and then I could have followed it. But now I want to give you the conclusion:

> It seems at times as if many of our modern writers on evolution have had their views by some sort of revelation, and they base their opinions on the evolution of life from the simplest form to the complex, entirely on the nature of specific and intra-specific evolution. It is possible that this type of evolution can explain many of the present-day phenomena, but it is possible, and indeed probable, that many as yet unknown systems remain to be discovered. *[Now listen:]* And it is premature, not to say arrogant, on our part if we make any dogmatic assertion as to the mode of evolution of the major branches of the animal kingdom.

There is a scientist accusing scientists of dogmatism and arrogance. Yet most people today are not Christians because of science, because of the theory of evolution that has knocked the bottom out of Christianity. Ever since Darwin, Christians have been regarded as fools. But here is the answer from a scientist. And then he finishes like this:

> The answer will be found by future experimental work and not by dogmatic assertions that the general theory of evolution must be correct because there is nothing else that will satisfactorily take its place.

But scientists are making this dogmatic assertion even though evolution cannot be proved and is nothing but a theory. No one can prove that what we are told about the creation of the world in Genesis is not the truth. Yet dogmatic assertions are made that evolution must be right and Christianity must not be believed at any cost. That is the position. And it is the old position of the Sanhedrin. It is an unreasonable and negative refusal to face facts and a determination to hold on in the interests of a particular little theory.

Finally, consider the desperate seriousness of all this. It is a defiance of God. That is the warning Peter gave. He was telling them: "You are not dealing with us. My companion and I are nobodies; we are only fishermen; we have never been to the schools; we cannot debate with you on your own level. We are, as you say, 'unlearned and ignorant men.' But we have not healed this man—how could we? We have no inherent power or goodness. Do you know what you are doing? You are not dealing with us. You are dealing with God." "Whether it be right in the sight of God to hearken unto you more than unto God, judge ye."

This is what makes unbelief so terrifying. If you do not believe, you are not merely rejecting what I say. You are not merely rejecting the testimony and the witness of the Christian church. What you are really doing is pitting yourself against the Lord of heaven. How can you explain Jesus of Nazareth in any terms except that He is the Son of God incarnate, the everlasting Son of God, the Word made flesh who has come out of the eternal? If you reject Him and His message, you are rejecting God, your Maker and Creator, the One before whom you will have to stand at the eternal bar of judgment.

If there were nothing beyond death, perhaps I would not be preaching at all. However, I know that there is something beyond death, and it is judgment. God is the Judge. The God who so loved the world that He sent His only Son into it and put our sins upon Him and smote Him for us—He will be the Judge. He has given you the way out, and your whole eternal destiny depends upon your response. As I said at the beginning, it is not a decision for time—it is a decision for eternity.

Let me, therefore, ask this question: What is the explanation? Why can men and women behave in such an utterly unreasonable manner? How can it happen that intelligent, able people can refuse to face the facts and just go on asserting their negative dogmatism? There is only one explanation—and we have already looked at it in detail in an earlier chapter. It is the explanation given in the Bible. When the first man and woman disobeyed God and rebelled against Him and fell, all their faculties became twisted. The supreme tragedy is that men and women can no longer think straight. They have become the slaves of the devil, the slaves of lusts and passions and desires. "If our gospel be hid," says Paul, "it is hid to them that are lost: in whom the god of this world hath blinded the minds of them which believe not, lest the light of the glorious gospel of Christ, who is the image of God, should shine unto them" (2 Cor. 4:3-4). This blindness is a most terrible thing.

Is there any hope for such creatures? Ah, it is still in this old Gospel. Though you may have rejected God and arrogantly dismissed Him, if you turn back to Him, He will still receive you. Let me put the appeal in the words of Peter and John. When the Sanhedrin said, "You must not preach," they replied, "Whether it be right in the sight of God to hearken unto you more than unto God, judge ye." Now I like another translation that puts it like this: "Whether it be right in the sight of God to hearken unto you more than unto God is your decision, and you will have to answer him, not us." Or another translation says, "Judge for yourselves, and take the consequences of your decision."

The apostles' position was clear: "As for us, we must obey God. We dare not do anything else. We have a message that has ravished our hearts and changed us, and we know it can do the same to others. We have made our decision, and we are prepared to abide by the consequences. If you put us to death, well, we are ready for it. But as for us, we are going on. We cannot stop speaking. And as for you, judge for yourselves and take the consequences of your decision."

And I say to you in the name of God—there is the lame man standing before you, whole. It is a fact. Look at the man; look at the one who put him on his feet; look at Peter and John. Judge for yourselves, and bear in mind the consequences of your decision. If you reject Jesus, you will probably be popular in the schoolroom tomorrow morning, or in the bar, or in the office, or in the factory. But people there are not your judges; God is your Judge, and you will have to explain to Him.

On the other hand, believe the fact; believe in the one who has done it; give yourself to Him. The world will probably laugh at you and deride you, perhaps pity you. It does not matter—you will already have "passed from death unto life" (John 5:24). You have no need to fear life; you will have no need to fear death; you will have no need to fear the judgment. You will become a child of God and an heir of eternal bliss, and you, like Peter and John, will want to live henceforth to the glory and the praise of this blessed Son of God who loved you and gave Himself for you. "Judge ye!"

9

KNOWING GOD

And being let go, they went to their own company, and reported
all that the chief priests and elders had said unto them. And when
they heard that, they lifted up their voice to God with one accord,
and said, Lord, thou art God, which hast made heaven, and
earth, and the sea, and all that in them is.

—Acts 4:23-24

These verses are, of course, a sequel to the events we have been considering in the last chapter. Peter and John had been arraigned before the great Jewish court, the Sanhedrin. They had been put on trial not only because of the miracle they had performed in the healing of a lame man, but more because of their preaching. And they had asserted themselves in the courtroom and had spoken their message with real boldness. Though they were ordinary men—fishermen, unlearned and ignorant—they had not been overawed or frightened by the great Sanhedrin and had said, "Whether it be right in the sight of God to hearken unto you more than unto God, judge ye. For we cannot but speak the things which we have seen and heard." The Sanhedrin was forced to let them go; so here were Peter and John sent out with a tremendous warning, a great threat, that if they persisted in speaking in the name of Jesus, they would not only be arrested again but would undoubtedly be put to death.

So what did Peter and John do? They went back to the other apostles and to the people who, having been converted on the day of Pentecost and afterwards, were now forming the Christian church. They went back to their own company and reported what had happened. We are interested in this not only because of its inherent interest and worth, not merely because it happens to be history, but because it is of vital concern to us. This, after all, is the authentic account of what the Christian church is. The mere fact that we may think we are Christians does not prove that we are Christians. People have curious ideas about what constitutes a Christian. So we must all examine ourselves in the light of all that we are told about these men. Here we have a very thorough and profound test, and in these verses we have still another test that we must of necessity apply to ourselves.

What would you say is an acid test to apply to one who makes a profession of being a Christian? Some people seem to think that being a Christian is merely a matter of tradition and upbringing, that if you happen to have been brought up in what is called a Christian country and have been taught to go to church and chapel and Sunday school, then that automatically makes you a Christian. Is that what Christianity means? Can you be a Christian without knowing anything of the Bible, without understanding its teachings, without being able to give any reason as to why you are a Christian? Is Christianity simply a matter of custom and habit? Now I do not say that there is no value in tradition, because there is—thank God for every good tradition—but if that is all you have, you are in a pathetic condition. That is not what makes a Christian.

Then there are people who seem to think that being a Christian means that one holds a given set of beliefs. Of course, you cannot be a Christian without believing in something. Christianity does constitute a body of belief. But there are some who think that that is all there is. However, I want to show you that while orthodoxy is essential—you have to believe the truth—a mere intellectual acceptance of the truth does not make anyone a Christian. It is possible for us to receive teaching with our minds only. A dry-as-dust theology is of no value. There have been men and women who have known the truth and believed it in their minds, but when they have come to die, they have felt bereft and lost and have had nothing to fall back upon. That is not Christianity.

Then there are others who think that what makes someone a Christian is living a good life, upholding moral values in a world where there is so much immorality. They say that Christians are people who do not do certain things, for example, who do not drink or commit adultery or gamble or smoke. That view is a purely negative approach. Others say that being a Christian is more positive. Christians set out to do good; they help their fellow men and women; they are concerned about life and the state of humanity at the present time, and that is what makes them Christians.

And then there are still others who would say that none of those things make someone a Christian. The test is whether there has been a dramatic, climactic experience. Has there been a vision, a ball of fire, as it were? It is sometimes put in these terms: "When people claim to be Christians, have their lives been changed? Has something happened to them that has turned them around and made them into different people? That is the essence of Christianity."

I am very ready to agree that you cannot really be a Christian without some experience. Christianity is not mere intellectualism or goodness; it is a living and vital experience. But many unbelievers have had experiences that have done them great good. Sometimes psychotherapy and psychology or following cults or other teachings can give people experiences. But that does not make people Christians.

So how do you know if you are a Christian or not? This is a vital question because Christianity is the only hope for the world. What is the acid test? I suggest the real and thoroughgoing test in this incident that we are now considering. It is this: How does one react to trying and testing circumstances? You may have been religious all your life, and as long as life is going fairly smoothly and evenly, all is well. But suddenly you find yourself in a great crisis, and you become aware for the first time that all your religion means nothing at all to you. It does not help you. So the way to test a profession of faith is the test of circumstances, trials, tribulations, troubles, or death staring you in the face.

Now this test is more thorough than all others. Many men and women who have been very orthodox have found that their orthodoxy did not help in their hour of need. When you are in some grievous trouble, your own goodness and morality do not help you or sustain you. The fact that you have done a lot of good to others does not somehow answer your problems. It is the same with some of those experiences that people talk about. The experiences really do not help them when they need the help most of all.

Now in saying all this, I have been giving you a summary of the whole of the Old Testament. In the Old Testament there is a great dispute between the true and the false prophets. The false prophets could always put up a very good show—indeed, such a good show that they were almost invariably more popular than the true prophets. They said what people wanted to hear. Their message was easier, and the crowd followed them. But when the testing time came, they had nothing to show. This is all summarized in one great incident in 1 Kings 18—Elijah on Mount Carmel. The false priests, when faced with a challenge, could do nothing. The true prophet, Elijah, the man of God, could turn to God, and the answer was given.

We have exactly the same situation here in the book of Acts. We say about a friend, "A friend in need is a friend indeed." A real friend is not one of your fair-weather friends who are all over you and will do anything for you as long as you have money and everything is going well, but the moment you get into trouble, they slink out and leave you alone. The ultimate test as to whether there is any value in our profession of the Christian faith is our response, our behavior, when everything is against us, when we seem to be bereft of all human aid, and we ourselves can do nothing.

What is the true Christian response in times of trial? We find it here. Here is genuine Christianity. When the two apostles went back to the believers and told them that they were prohibited from speaking or teaching in the name of Jesus, when they said that they thought that these authorities were about to exterminate the Christian church, what did the believers do? "They lifted up their voice to God with one accord . . ." In other words, they prayed. And that is the ultimate test. The ultimate test of our profession of faith is our prayer life.

What does prayer mean? Here again I am asking a fundamental question. What a lot of loose talk there is about prayer. What curious notions people have about it. It is almost incredible that people with an open Bible in front of them should hold the views of prayer that they do. Some people seem to think that prayer is entirely a matter of posture, that if you are on your knees, you are praying, and that if you are not on your knees, you cannot pray. That seems to them to be the essence of prayer—just a posture. Of course, the posture is important, but it does not constitute prayer. God knows, we have all of us probably spent much time on our knees and thought we were praying, but our minds were wandering all over the world, and so were our imaginations. We were not at all conscious of God and were only talking to ourselves. That is not prayer.

Then many seem to think that prayer is a kind of thoughtless repetition. Our Lord rebuked the Pharisees and scribes of his own day because they thought they would be heard "for their much speaking" (Matt. 6:7). You may have television shots of some of these poor people of other so-called religions with their prayer wheels or beads—vain, thoughtless repetition. Again let us be honest—have we not all of us many a time gotten on our knees and gabbled through the Lord's Prayer without thinking of the meaning of a single word we uttered? That is not prayer. "Saying your prayers" is not praying. It is easy to "say your prayers." When people use this phrase, how they give themselves away!

Not so long ago I heard a man describing a visit he had paid somewhere, and he said, "I was feeling somewhat exhausted, so I went into a cathedral, and I said a prayer." He dashed in, said a prayer, and dashed out. Is that praying? No, and, indeed, there are others a little nearer home to us, who rather frighten me sometimes when I hear them saying quite lightly and glibly, "Let us have a word of prayer about it." "A word of prayer" about it! Almost like sending a telegram! That is not prayer.

Again true prayer does not doubt. We have all known what it is to be on our knees when we are in trouble and do not know what we are to do. We say, "Is there really anything in Christianity? Is anybody there listening?" So we spend our time on our knees arguing with our own doubts and trying to persuade ourselves. That is not prayer. It may lead to prayer eventually, but it is not prayer. No, there is no uncertainty in true prayer.

Then there are some people—we have all read of this kind of thing and may have acted like this ourselves—whose notion of prayer is something like this: You are in a desperate position, and you do not know what to do. Then you suddenly remember God, and in a state of panic and desperation, you frantically begin to speak. You make a kind of experiment; you cry to "whatsoever gods there may be," hoping against hope. You do not know what you are doing; you are distracted and distraught and cry out into the void in the hope that something may happen. But that is not prayer.

No, the characteristics of true prayer are all put before us very simply here in Acts. Here were people who were threatened with extermination, with death, with the end of all things. Have you noticed their calmness, the quiet, assured, confident, certain manner in which they spoke? They were talking to God, and they had no doubt about it. "When they heard that, they lifted up their voice to God with one accord, and said, Lord, thou art God, which hast made heaven, and earth, and the sea, and all that in them is." And then they continued by quoting the second psalm. Now this is real prayer. They did not merely get on their knees and repeat some set prayers. They began to talk to God with confidence and absolute assurance.

Now this is of vital concern to us. You and I are living in a strange world, a world of crisis, a world in which we never know what is going to happen next, a difficult world, a passing world. Do we know what it is to pray? This is prayer—this talking to God, this speaking confidently to Him, this lifting up to Him the whole situation in which we are involved. This is what Christianity does, and that is why I call attention to it.

What was the explanation for the confidence of these early believers as they came to God in prayer? Their secret was that they knew God. The primary purpose of the Christian message is to bring us to a knowledge of God,

and for some extraordinary reason this truth has been forgotten. Some people think that the Christian faith should give some wonderful thrill and experience. It may or may not do that. Others say that the aim of Christianity is
to give me assurance that my sins are forgiven. I quite agree, but that is only
a step. The ultimate object of the Christian faith is to bring us all to a knowledge of God. If we have not come to this knowledge, then, to say the very
least, our Christianity is defective. These early Christians had a living, vital
knowledge of God. In their extremity they went to Him with an amazing
assurance. There was no panic, nothing frantic, nothing excitable about them;
they were as cool as could be, and in this quiet confidence they spoke to God
and knew Him.

Now the New Testament describes Christians as people who know God.
Listen to the apostle Paul putting it to the Galatians: "Howbeit then, when
ye knew not God, ye did service unto them which by nature are no gods. But
now, after that ye have known God, or rather are known of God, how turn
ye again to the weak and beggarly elements, whereunto ye desire again to be
in bondage?" (Gal. 4:8). In this significant statement Paul argues that though
there was a time when his readers did not know God, now they did. And that
is the very essence of the Christian position.

What characterizes this knowledge the Christian has of God? Well,
clearly, from this incident in Acts 4, we can see that these men and women
here in the early church knew God as the living God. They were talking to a
person, a living being. That is the essence of prayer, and it stands out on the
very surface of this record. These people were not crying out into the void;
they were going into the presence of someone they knew. And, oh, how vital
this is! A great contrast is drawn in both the Old Testament and the New. The
Galatian Christians (even some of these people here in Acts before they were
Christians) had worshiped idols. They had thought that this was right, and
they had built temples to them. They had made gods out of silver and wood
and stone and bowed down and sacrificed to them. They had been most regular in their worship, and their religion had meant a great deal to them. But
they were worshiping nothing. Their idols had no life and could not do anything; the worshipers had to do everything for these idols.

Now worshipping dead gods, lifeless gods, the projection of human
ideas—that is idolatry. Many people are still doing that. They do not know
the living God. This problem is not only true of people who are idolaters, but
it is also the whole trouble with the philosophers. Some of them say that they
believe in God, but what is their God? He is just some great idea. Look at the
very terms they use; see how they give themselves away. They talk about the

"absolute" or the "uncaused cause." But that is a concept, an idea. There is no person there; there is no life.

These people in Acts were, however, not praying to "the absolute" or to "the ultimate reality" or "the ground of our being." They were praying to a person, one they could address, a personal God. That is a complete contrast to idolatry, whether it be the vulgar idolatry of the populace or the refined, subtle, sophisticated idolatry of the philosophers. Nor did the Christians in Acts pray to some vague "something." To whom have you been speaking when you thought you were praying?

Some people tell us that the great value of prayer is that it enables us to think beautiful thoughts and that makes us feel better. I remember hearing a man once preaching on prayer, and that is how he put it: "Five minutes a day for health's sake." Others go further and say that when you are praying for other people, you are really transferring healing thoughts to them. But that has nothing to do with prayer. No, praying means speaking to the living God, the God who acts, the God who knows where we are and what our circumstances are and is able to do something about them.

Secondly, these Christians in Acts believed that this living God is all-powerful. We are told: "They lifted up their voice to God with one accord and said, Lord . . ." Now *Lord* is a tremendous word. The Greek word for it means that He is a sovereign Lord of absolute power. It is the word from which our word *despot* has come, though *despot*, of course, is a corruption of the idea. The term suggests illimitable might and authority. The one to whom these people were speaking is the sovereign Lord of the entire universe. It is of the very essence of true prayer that in one's terrifying and terrible circumstances one goes without hesitation immediately and directly, with confidence and assurance and boldness, to this sovereign Lord.

Do we know Him? Can we turn to Him in that way in our hour of need and trial? That is Christianity. There was a time when these early Christians could not have done that, but now they could, and this is the fact that made the early church what she was, that made her turn the world upside down. This dynamic message, which has always become manifest in every period of revival and of reformation, is the only hope for the world today. Here it is, a knowledge of the only true and living God, whose power is endless and eternal. It is knowing God in this way that makes the difference between religion and Christianity. Christianity is not religion. Religion is the counterfeit that has misled so many people and I believe is keeping thousands outside the Christian church. People look at our churches and chapels and see nothing but religion, and they do not want it. I agree with them. I do not want it either.

What we want, what we need, and what we commend is this—a knowledge of the Lord God of the universe. Is there anything comparable to this?

Do we have that knowledge? Are we able to rely upon it confidently, come what may? Let me put it like this: How does one come to such a knowledge? On what is it based? How may I get to know God so that I can turn to Him and pray as these people prayed in their hour of need? We are given the answer here very fully. This relationship is not only a matter of experience. Experiences can be treacherous. If you detach experience from the truth of the Bible, you are doing a very dangerous thing. The experience that is true and of value is an experience that results from the teaching of the Bible.

So how, according to the Scriptures, is God to be known? First, He is to be known through nature. Here the apostles were in crisis, and yet they did not think they were wasting either their words or their time in saying to God: "Lord, thou art God, which hast made heaven, and earth, and the sea, and all that in them is." Now we are living in an age when people think that it is clever to say that because they are Christians, they do not need the Old Testament. The early Christians did not think like that. God did not begin to live at the birth of Jesus Christ! God has always been and always will be; God is eternal. The Incarnation is merely a turning point. You do not start with Jesus Christ. I say that at the risk of being misunderstood, but I know so many people today who never talk about anybody except the Son, God the Son, the Lord Jesus Christ. They never mention God the Father. But that is not New Testament Christianity. The God I believe in is the God of Genesis: "In the beginning God created the heaven and the earth." New Testament Christianity starts with God the Creator.

Now this is the great emphasis of the Bible. God is the everlasting and eternal God. The apostles knew that they would not be alive but for Him; there would be no world for them to be alive in, were it not for Him; there would be nothing, were it not for God. The New Testament is full of this concept of God. Take the letter to the Hebrews. The author was writing to people in trouble, and this is what he says: "*Through faith* we understand that the worlds were framed by the word of God, so that things which are seen were not made of things which do appear" (Heb. 11:3, emphasis mine). Our whole position is that we are not in a world that has evolved by chance out of nothing. The New Testament teaches that we are in a world that has been made by an almighty Creator who is above all and through all and in all and to whom all glory must be ascribed.

If you go on through this book of Acts, you will find Paul arriving in a place called Lystra where, because he was enabled to work a miracle there, the people thought that he was a god and began to worship him. But he said, "Sirs, why do ye these things? We also are men of like passions with you, and preach unto you that ye should turn from these vanities unto the living God, which made heaven, and earth, and the sea, and all things that are therein" (Acts 14:15). And he preached exactly the same thing to the philosophers, Stoics, Epicureans, and others in the great city of Athens.

When Paul wrote his great letter to the Romans, he made the same point:

> *For I am not ashamed of the gospel of Christ: for it is the power of God unto salvation to every one that believeth; to the Jew first, and also to the Greek. For therein is the righteousness of God revealed from faith to faith: as it is written, The just shall live by faith. For the wrath of God is revealed from heaven against all ungodliness and unrighteousness of men, who hold the truth in unrighteousness; because that which may be known of God is manifest in them; for God hath showed it unto them. For the invisible things of him from the creation of the world are clearly seen, being understood by the things that are made, even his eternal power and Godhead; so that they are without excuse.*
>
> —Rom. 1:16-20

These men in Acts believed that the whole universe was made by God and that He controls it and sustains it. That is the God to whom they were speaking. Do you know this God? Well, if you do not, I invite you to look at nature and creation. Look at the order and the design and the arrangement. Is all this the result of chance? Look at the evidence, the intricacy and the delicacy and the balance in the whole of created life. Is all this fortuitous, contingent? Of course not! There is a mind behind it all, a great purpose and design. Or as James Jeans puts it: There is a great Mathematician at the back of it all. There is a living God, a God who could say, "Let there be light"; a God who brings into being things that were not, creating something out of nothing; God—the everlasting Creator.

Secondly, we are told that this God is to be known as the result of revelation. Having said, "Thou art God, which hast made heaven, and earth, and the sea, and all that in them is," the believers went on to add, "who by the mouth of thy servant David hast said . . ." A better translation is this: "who by the Holy Spirit through the mouth of thy servant David hast said . . ." And then they quoted the second psalm.

So if you want to know God, then consult nature and creation, and then, having begun to feel that there is something you do not understand—something immense, something profound, something beyond human computation and comprehension—come to the Bible. Here you will find extraordinary things and nothing perhaps more extraordinary than prophecy. Look at David, king of Israel, who lived about a thousand years before the birth of Christ. He wrote that second psalm and in it describes some great person, not himself, but one to whom God says, "Thou art my Son; this day have I begotten thee" (v. 7). This Son is someone who can rule kings and princes and nations with a rod of iron and to whom you say, "Kiss the Son" (v. 12). Do it while you can, for He is a mighty governor. With the insight given them by the Holy Spirit, the first believers saw, as David himself had seen, that this is a description of the coming Messiah, the Son of God. Now this is prophecy, and you will find it throughout the Old Testament.

If you want to know God, therefore, read this book. Note the prophecies, note the time they were given, note the details, and then notice the fulfillment in the New Testament. David was a very able man, but do you think that he could imagine a thousand years beforehand the precise details about the Son of God that are recorded in the Gospels? Take the great prophets of the eighth century B.C.—how did they arrive at their knowledge? How did they know that Jesus would be born in the little town of Bethlehem or ride into Jerusalem on the colt of an ass?

Here is the only answer: There is a living God—not a piece of wood or stone or metal—but a God who acts, and He has revealed truth. He has made himself known; He has given accounts of Himself to men and women. He is the one who gave Moses the Ten Commandments. He is the one who gave the revelation of Himself and His truth through the prophets. If I had no other reason for believing in God, this would be enough. The argument of prophecy is unanswerable.

The next element is history, which provides a great proof of the being of the living God. How often in times of crisis does one fall back on history? Thank God for it. Again we see the great message of the Old Testament. The story of God's salvation did not start, I repeat, with the birth of Jesus Christ in Bethlehem of Judea. It began in the Garden of Eden. Jesus Christ came "when the fulness of the time was come" (Gal. 4:4). The Old Testament is a book of history that just tells us what God had been doing before His Son ever came to this world. It is a proof of the fact that He is the Lord God Almighty, the Governor of the universe, and that He has all authority and power.

Read the Old Testament history, and you will find this: He is a God who not only can make a world, but He can also destroy it. He is a God who brought a nation into being—the children of Israel. He created them out of one man whose name was Abraham, and He led them, directed them, and delivered them. If you can explain the story of the Jews apart from the interventions of the living God, then you have an ability that I cannot even imagine, let alone attain unto. There is only one explanation for the existence of the children of Israel, an explanation the Old Testament writers constantly emphasize. The people of Israel were nobodies. How did they triumph? Oh, God acted on their behalf.

As the apostles in Jerusalem were praying, God gave a further proof that he is a living God and that with Him nothing is impossible. How did He do that? By shaking the place where they were praying (v. 31). That was just a proof of the fact that God is a living God and that these people were not talking into empty space, nor addressing gods of their own making, but were addressing the one who had made the universe, who was still controlling it and could shake buildings and men and empires and kingdoms whenever He chose. That was the God to whom they prayed; hence their calmness and their confidence.

And, I repeat, is that not the whole story of the Old Testament, too? The God who made the world destroyed it in the flood and then restored it. When in their folly the people tried to build a tower up into heaven, He destroyed their plans by confusing their languages so that they could no longer understand each other.

He is the God of the Exodus, do not forget. When Abraham's descendants were slaves in Egypt, they were completely helpless. Egypt was then the leading power in the world, and the pharaoh had armies and chariots and horsemen. The Hebrew people were a handful of ordinary agricultural, nomadic people, and they had nothing. They could do nothing, but God can do everything. Hearing their cry—like the cry of these people in Acts—He answered them. He sent them a deliverer. He led pharaoh's horsemen out into the Red Sea, and then He overwhelmed and destroyed them, delivering His people.

That is the God in whom these people believed and whom I commend to you. Read your Old Testament as well as the New, and you will find Him there. Look at the great scene on Mount Carmel—Elijah with the 850 false prophets against him. After they had scarified their flesh and had screeched at their gods, who could do nothing, Elijah very quietly said, "LORD"—the same kind of prayer offered by the believers in Acts— ". . . let it be known this day that thou art God in Israel" (1 Kings 18:36). Let it be known! And God did. He sent down the fire, and it consumed the offering and the wood and the stones and licked up the water in the ditch. The God of Elijah, the

God of Mount Carmel, the God who went on to destroy a Sennacherib and all his mighty hosts in a night—He can turn the tables. He shakes everything, as he shook this building here in Jerusalem when the believers were praying.

So history will tell you about this God. But above and beyond everything else, the ultimate proof is Jesus of Nazareth, referred to in the Acts passage as "thy holy child Jesus." Do you want absolute proof of the existence of the living, true, eternal God, the sovereign Lord of the universe? Here it is. He sent His only Son into the world. He had promised this gift throughout the centuries, and then He kept His promise exactly, in every detail, and the babe was born in Bethlehem—the Son of God, the proof of His eternal power.

Do you want to know whether God is a true and living God? Look at Jesus of Nazareth. He said, "He that hath seen me hath seen the Father" (John 14:9). What, then, do you see in Him? Well, you not only see holiness, but you see authority. You see power. There he is asleep in the boat. A storm has blown up, the billows are rolling, and the gale is howling. The disciples wake Him and say, "Master, carest thou not that we perish?" Then with calmness and the majesty of God, He says to the raging wind, "Peace, be still." And we are told, "There was a great calm" (Mark 4:37-41). That is living power; that is authority over the elements; that is authority over the universe.

He could heal the sick; He could raise the dead and give sight to the blind. There was nothing He could not do. Consider His miracles and His power. Ah, but they crucified Him, and He died in apparent weakness, and they laid Him in a tomb.

Was that the end of the story? Of course not! He burst asunder the bands of death and "arose triumphant o'er the grave." The last enemy had no power over Him. He has all power in heaven and on earth. He conquers everything and shakes every enemy to nothing. These believers had seen that power, and that is why they could pray to God. Our Lord had told them that He was going back to the Father, and if they ever wanted anything, they should pray to His Father, and He, the Son, would be there to represent them and to pass on their prayer. Their Father already knew all about them and all their needs, but they were to offer prayer in the Son's name, and He would be there and add the incense of His own person to their feeble petitions. They knew all that. They had seen the risen Christ; they knew the power of the living Christ; so they prayed with confidence.

Do not forget that these were the people who had passed through the day of Pentecost. When they were crestfallen and downhearted because of Jesus' forthcoming death, He had said, "Let not your heart be troubled" (John 14:1). He would not leave them as orphans. He said, "I will pray the Father, and he shall give you another Comforter, that he may abide with you for ever" (John 14:16). The Comforter would guide them and teach them everything they needed to know (v. 26). And when Jesus had gone back to heaven, He sent the Holy Spirit upon them, and they had seen the results on the day of Pentecost.

These are the proofs of the living God, the proofs that we do not pray to an abstraction or to "ultimate reality" or to "the ground of our being" but to the living, personal God who thinks, who acts, who sees us, who knows all about us, who can answer our prayer and is ready to do so. This is the confidence we have.

Finally, in order to be able to pray as these people did, you must not only believe in a living and powerful God, on the basis of the evidence that I have been putting before you, but you must have a personal experience of God, as these believers had. They had passed through Pentecost; they had undergone a change; their lives had been renewed; they were new men and women, and they knew that nothing and no one but an almighty God could have done it. Now they knew they had life, and they knew that God was their Father and that they were His children. Hence, threatened with death by the Sanhedrin, the supreme Jewish power, they were not terrified. They showed no sense of panic or excitement. With absolute calm and assurance they lifted up their voices to God with one accord, knowing that with Him nothing is impossible, that these authorities and powers were nothing to Him. The God who could deal with a pharaoh and a Sennacherib, a God who could drown the whole universe when it pleased Him to do so—who were these rulers to Him? So the apostles just quietly told Him all about it and besought Him for His own name's sake and glory's sake to vindicate His own truth, to vindicate His own Son, to let these people know that He is the living God and that Christ is His Son, who came into the world to save them.

And we have the same hope. Whatever happens to us, we can turn to Him and say:

> *O the all embracing mercy,*
> *Thou ever-open door,*
> *What should we do without thee*
> *When heart and eyes run o'er?*
> *When all things seem against us*
> *To drive us to despair,*
> *We know one gate is open,*
> *One ear will hear our prayer.*
> Oswald Allen

Do you know this living God? I press my question on you because I tell you again, as I told you at the beginning, that the whole world is being shaken, soon, perhaps for the very last time, for we have a prophecy about this also. This is how He has put it to us; it is quite plain: "Whose voice then shook the earth: but now he hath promised, saying, Yet once more I shake not the earth only, but also heaven. And this word, Yet once more, signifieth the removing of those things that are shaken, as of things that are made, that those things which cannot be shaken may remain" (Heb. 12:26-27). Your country will be shaken; your kings and queens and princes and emperors and presidents and prime ministers will all be shaken to nothing. The earth and the heavens will be shaken; the television sets will be smashed; there will be nothing left. Public houses will be rubble on the ground, and dance bands will be a tangle of nothing. All that men and women are living for and are living by will be shaken to oblivion.

But you will remain, and the question for you and for all of us is this: In that final cataclysm, will you be the possessor of the things that cannot be shaken? Will you know this true and living sovereign Lord of the universe through His blessed and dear Son and the power of the Holy Spirit? Christ came into the world to form a kingdom that cannot be shaken—the kingdom of God. The vital question for all of us is this: Are we in this kingdom that can never be shaken?

How do you enter it? Quite simply. Confess your sin; acknowledge your arrogance, your ridiculous impudence in disputing these matters; confess it and ask Him to receive you, and He will. "God so loved the world that he gave his only begotten Son, that whosoever believeth in him should not perish, but have everlasting life" (John 3:16). "Believe on the Lord Jesus Christ, and thou shalt be saved" (Acts 16:31). You shall then enter into His kingdom, the eternal kingdom, the everlasting kingdom, the kingdom of God and His glory.

10

THE ONLY ANSWER

Who by the mouth of thy servant David hast said, Why did the heathen rage, and the people imagine vain things? The kings of the earth stood up, and the rulers were gathered together against the Lord, and against his Christ.

—Acts 4:25-26

England has set aside November 11 as a special day to honor those who gave their lives fighting for their country. In a world of confusion and trouble, a world of pain and of unhappiness, the great questions that should be in the minds of all intelligent people, particularly when Remembrance Day comes around, are: What is the matter? Why are things as they are? Why are there wars? Why are the nations still piling up armaments? Why, indeed, is there such a thing as death? Why is there disease and pain? Why is there sorrow and unhappiness?

Now we do not just observe Remembrance Day sentimentally. Many of us have already passed through two world wars, and it is about time we all began to ask these questions in depth and with a new seriousness. Those of you who read the newspapers and listen to newscasts will agree that it is quite clear that nobody in the world can give us an answer; that is abundantly proved. But I want to make a positive statement—the Bible has the answer, and it has the only answer.

The Bible's answer, as we are reminded by Psalm 2 is, first of all, that there is nothing new about all this; such troubles are not peculiar to the twenty-first century. Our fellow men and women start with the fatal assumption that there is something special about us because we are living in this century. We have become drunk on our own knowledge and especially on science. Therefore, we think that all our problems are new problems, that nobody has ever had them before. Now the Bible, being such an old book, tells us immediately that that idea is altogether wrong. Today's problems are a manifestation of what has been going on in the world for a very, very long time. War and death, people being maimed, and jealousy and rivalry are all here in the Bible from the very beginning; it is the story of the human race. Here is the oldest book in the world, and I invite you to listen to what it has to tell us about our own immediate situation in this world.

Now I shall look at this in terms of the second psalm. This message is only one of many similar statements that are to be found right through the Bible, but we are studying it now because it was quoted by the early Christians in their prayer after the council had let Peter and John go. This is a fascinating psalm from every standpoint. In many ways it is the easiest psalm to divide up. It has twelve verses that can be divided into four groups of three. In the first three verses the psalmist states the position, and in the next three verses he tells us God's reaction. In verses 7, 8, and 9 we have the Lord Jesus Christ, the Son of God, speaking; and then in the last three verses the psalmist sums it all up and makes an appeal to men and women to listen to the message.

David is undoubtedly the author of this psalm, but he is not writing primarily about himself. He sees that he is only, as it were, a suggestion of what will be true of the great Deliverer, the future great King. Though the psalm does have an application to David, it is, as is generally agreed, a psalm that is prophetic of the coming of the Lord Jesus Christ. We see this in the terms used. The Lord is called the "anointed" and the Son of God: "Thou art my Son; this day have I begotten thee" (v. 7). And He is called God's King, whom God sets upon His holy hill of Zion.

The Jews themselves had always regarded Psalm 2 as a Messianic psalm—a psalm pointing to the coming of the great Deliverer. But you notice that in the prayer of the early church in Acts 4, these believers, filled with the Holy Spirit, had no doubt or hesitation in applying the psalm to the Lord Jesus Christ. In verse 27 we read: "For of a truth against thy holy child Jesus, whom thou hast anointed, both Herod, and Pontius Pilate, with the Gentiles, and the people of Israel, were gathered together." They gathered together to condemn Him and to sentence Him to death. In other words, the reaction described in this psalm has been the attitude of humanity to God throughout the running centuries, but it all came to a climax, a focus, in the crucifixion of Jesus of Nazareth, the Son of God.

Here, then, is the message of the Bible for us. We are dealing, remember, with the state of the world. Why is it as it is? Now that question is raised in the very first verse of the psalm: "Why do the heathen rage, and the people imagine a vain thing?" *Why?* The psalmist puts the question, and he uses an interesting word that is not only a question but is also an expression of horror and astonishment. The psalmist was a man of God, and he could see the behavior of the heathen, and not only of the heathen. The word *people* here means the people of Israel. The Bible divides humanity up into the heathen and the people, and the people always represent the children of Israel, God's chosen race. So the psalmist, looking out upon his world, as you and I look out upon a similar world today, asks: Why? Why are things as they are?

So let us listen to the answer, and as we do so, we are doing the most important thing a human being can do. Nowhere in the world today will you find any light on your present situation except here. I am not saying that we do not need statesmen. We do. We need governors and officials; we need law and order. Let us even grant that they are doing their best. But they are obviously in trouble, and they are in trouble because they are viewing the world solely upon the horizontal human level; they are not viewing it in the depth revealed to us by the Bible. So, then, listen to the message.

Let us start by looking at the psalmist's description of the state of the world. What was true of the world then is still true of the world today. The world is "raging." "Why do the heathen rage?" And the word *rage* means "make a tumult." Their raging is like the roaring and the raging of the sea. Now the Bible is very fond of describing life apart from God in those terms. The prophet Isaiah in a great statement puts it like this: "The wicked are like the troubled sea, when it cannot rest, whose waters cast up mire and dirt" (Isa. 57:20). That is a description of the human race apart from God. Have you seen the sea going backwards and forwards, rising, churning up mud and mire and dirt and refuse—"the troubled sea, when it cannot rest"? Can you imagine a more perfect description of the people of the world today than just that? We all see this restlessness, this trouble, this perplexity, this being carried backwards and forwards, victims of the latest news bulletin, never knowing what is going to happen, victims of circumstance and chance, tossed about hither and thither.

Is not that the great trouble in life? Men and women have lost all sense of direction. They are asking, "Is there anything in life? Is it worth living?" Many would be glad to be dead; many are committing suicide. I am not exaggerating. This is the world the papers tell us about. The world is like the troubled sea in a storm. The nations are raging. Can you not hear the sound, the rumbling? Look at Africa, that great continent—can you not see the waves beginning to surge, the raging that is commencing? Go to the Far East. Look anywhere you like, and you will see this tension, this striving, this restlessness, this confusion. Oh, it takes numerous forms. Racial hatred is only one of many problems. The Bible knows all about it, and that is why it gives this accurate description.

But look at the raging as it manifests itself in terms of the evils of living. Sin is always sin, but sometimes it appears to be fairly quiet and placid. We sometimes look at the sea and do not see any waves. We say, "It looks like silk, like velvet—there's scarcely any movement. On a glorious summer's afternoon, how smooth and calm the sea is." But the depths are there, the movement, and when a storm blows up, the waves gather and turn into billows that roll and rage, and there is confusion and crashing. You and I are living in an age like that. People have always sinned, but they have not always raged in their sin as they do now. There are no longer any limits; it is a riot, an abandon. Behavior that was once regarded as sinful is now not only justified but gloried in. Men and women have lost all sense of decency and control. Listen to them on the television or radio. Shame has gone, and sin is raging—drink, drugs, sex, the violence, the riot, the excess. "Why," says the psalmist, "do the heathen rage?"

Then take this further question: "Why do . . . the people imagine vain things?" A better translation might be: "Why do the people devise futile and empty schemes?" Oh, what a perfect summary of our day! That is what people are doing. The psalmist has chosen a word that perfectly describes the world's plans. They are "empty," "vain." Why is this? Because they are cut off from God. God *is*. God is being; God is the author of being and of life, and if you are not in connection with Him, then you really have nothing. Something may appear to be there for a while, but it is nothing.

Not only that, but anything done apart from God always ends in nothing. This is a conclusion reached by many profound thinkers, though they have not been Christians. Life! What is it? Shakespeare puts an answer in the mouth of one of his characters: It is "full of sound and fury, signifying nothing." "Nothing!" And is not that the simple truth about life apart from God in this world? All the excitement and all the sophistication and all that the world boasts and writes so much about—what does it come to? What does it lead to? "Full of sound and fury, signifying nothing."

But the world is very confident. It is quite sure that it can produce schemes to put things right. People "imagine" a "vain," a "futile," or an "empty" program, and they put it before us. The world is convinced—as it was in David's time and in the time of our Lord—that it can make a perfect world and that it can give us all peace and plenty and happiness and enjoyment. The world is quite sure that it is capable of making things just as it wants them to be.

Now that is nothing but a description of civilization. Civilization is the story of the great schemes and proposals of men and women. What do they propose? Well, away back in the time of the Greek philosophers, people began to dream of an ideal state. In 1516 Sir Thomas More wrote *Utopia*, describing such a state. There is nothing new about this longing; you see, "There is no new thing under the sun" (Eccles. 1:9). This idea that our problems and solutions are new is laughable! People have imagined utopias and have planned them out—how you divide up the people, how you apportion various tasks to them, how you govern them, how you teach people to conduct themselves. Utopia—solving the problems of the world!

Now as I said, this is the story of civilization; this is what the politicians have been doing throughout the centuries; this is what the philosophers and the believers in education have been doing; this is what science is claiming to be able to do at this present time. These men and women have abandoned God and are quite convinced that they can order a perfect society. They call themselves "classical humanists," "scientific humanists," but they are all *humanists*. God is not included. So they "imagine" their grandiose schemes. They will give us a life that is worth living; they will solve our problems.

Some of us are old enough to remember the speeches delivered during the First World War: We would have "a land fit for heroes to live in"; this was "the war to end all war." We remember the League of Nations and the Locarno Pact—all those brilliant ideas about what we were going to do after the war when there would never be any more trouble. We were quite certain of it. We were going to renounce war. There are some advantages in being old, my friends! We have so often heard all that we are now being told. This is not to be cynical; it is to be realistic. And now we have the United Nations! Look at the energy being put into this organization; look at the enthusiasm. "The people imagine"—schemes and proposals, blueprints of Utopia! But the Bible says that they are all "vain" things, empty; they come to nothing. Is it not about time that we became realists and really began to face these things? Are you content to have these grandiose proposals put before you that spring from human imaginings?

But now come to something much more serious. Many men and women who are not Christians would accept all that I have just said. Some of the greatest natural philosophers understand that people are fools, and they hold out no hope at all for the future. Read their works. They have great names—the Bertrand Russells and Julian Huxleys. They are observers of facts, and they can see the problems.

But here the Bible comes in with something that such people know nothing about. The Bible not only describes the condition, but it gives us the explanation. It opens our understanding to the causes of this condition. "Why do the heathen rage, and the people imagine vain things?" There is only one adequate answer. There is only one explanation of why we have a Remembrance Sunday, why such a day ever came into being, why there are wars and troubles and trials—it is all due to humanity's rebellion against God. Listen: "The kings of the earth set themselves, and the rulers take counsel together, against the LORD, and against his anointed, saying, Let us break their bands asunder, and cast away their cords from us."

Let me interpret. Notice that everyone is involved in this situation: "The kings of the earth," "the rulers," and the "judges of the earth" are all involved, and so are the philosophers, politicians, and the masses of the common people who listen to their teachers. No section of society is left out. But the psalm particularly describes the leaders, the great people of the earth. In every realm they stand up against God, or they ignore Him. But Tom, Dick, and Harry at the street corner are saying exactly the same thing: "Nothing in religion; tommyrot; played out, this idea of God." "There is none righteous, no, not one" (Rom. 3:10).

But notice the next point. Not only are all involved, but see the deliberation with which they rebel against God. "The kings of the earth set themselves, and the rulers take counsel together." This is the most terrible aspect of the leaders' behavior. What they are doing is not something unconscious. Men and women have deliberately rebelled against God; they have "set themselves." And they are still setting themselves. People meet in their humanistic societies and associations, take counsel together, write their books together, and praise one another. There is a deliberate organization of evil "against the LORD, and against his anointed"—against God and against His plans and purposes. This is the most appalling aspect of the situation. The trouble with the human race is not just that it is slack or indolent, but that it has deliberately and of set purpose, "with malice aforethought," organized itself in opposition to God. If you cannot see that in the world today, if you cannot see the powers organizing evil behind the newspaper stories, television documentaries, and all the modern displays of evil that lead to the muddle, you are very blind.

But let us go on. Why does humanity deliberately rebel against God?

Why do people say, "We don't want God; we don't believe in Him; God is a figment of our imaginations"? Why do they speak with such assiduity, zest, and enthusiasm? Why do men and women glory in their rebellion? Well, here is the amazing answer: They do it because of the enmity in their hearts against God. Their words betray their spirit: "Let us break their bands asunder, and cast away their cords from us." They are animated by enmity against God and His holy laws.

The apostle Paul has summed that up in a great statement in Romans 8: "The carnal [natural] mind is enmity against God: for it is not subject to the law of God, neither indeed can be" (Rom. 8:7). Enmity against God! Notice how God's holy laws are regarded as "restraints," as "cords," as "shackles." God made men and women and gave them laws by which to live. We all need teaching, and God in His love and kindness and compassion has given us this instruction. He has given us the Ten Commandments; He has given us the teaching of the great prophets; He has given us the Sermon on the Mount, and all this teaching is meant for our good.

To quote the apostle Paul again: "The kingdom of God is not meat and drink; but righteousness, and peace, and joy in the Holy Ghost" (Rom. 14:17). God did not make laws simply to keep us down and to fetter us. He made laws for our benefit, in order to help us, to teach us how to live and how to have a full and enjoyable life, a holy and peaceful life. But instead of thanking God for His teaching, people regard His laws as something intolerable. They say, "He's making slaves of us. We have it in us to be great, but here is God clamping down on us and making us slaves." That is why the world is as it is.

I have often said from my pulpit, and I say it again here, that if only every man and woman and every nation in this world today were living according to the Ten Commandments and the Sermon on the Mount, this world would be paradise. You would not need the United Nations. If only everybody lived according to God's laws, according to God's ways, according to God's view of life, the world's problems would disappear, nationally, internationally, individually, socially, and in every other respect. The world would become the paradise that it was when God originally made it. There are laws in paradise, and paradise is paradise because it observes the laws. The moment you break laws, you get chaos, confusion, and strife, and the world becomes like "the troubled sea when it cannot rest."

So people rebel against God first because of enmity, and the second reason is because of their self-confidence. They say, "Let us break their bands asunder, and cast their cords from us." Notice when that expression, "Let us," appears in the Bible. If you read the eleventh chapter of Genesis, you will find people again rebelling against God. This time they say, "Let us build us a city and a tower, whose top may reach unto heaven" (Gen. 11:4). "Let us"! This fatal self-confidence damns the human race. Human beings look at God and His holy laws and say, "Let us break them, let us smash them, let us do away with them, let us emancipate ourselves, let us be free. Let us rise up and get rid of this tyranny that God has imposed upon us." They think they can do it. They think they can succeed in making the kind of world they want and in enjoying themselves without any trouble or any interference. They believe that they can liberate themselves from God and from His holy laws.

But now, having considered the cause of the troubles in the world—the rebellion and enmity against God and the self-confidence—let us look at the folly of this condition. Oh, this is the tragedy of the human race! "He that sitteth in the heavens shall laugh: the LORD shall have them in derision. Then shall he speak unto them in his wrath, and vex them in his sore displeasure. Yet have I set my king upon my holy hill of Zion." This is God's response to human folly, to this raging, to this imagining of vain things, to this fatal self-confidence that believes it can defy God.

What is the trouble with men and women? It is their fatal ignorance of God. That is the theme of the whole Bible. At the end of His life our blessed Lord said in his great high-priestly prayer: "O righteous Father, the world hath not known thee: but I have known thee" (John 17:25). As we have already seen, the trouble with the world is always that it does not know God. The psalmists sometimes have a very graphic and dramatic way of putting this truth. One of them says that God looked upon humanity and said, "Thou thoughtest that I was altogether such an one as thyself" (Psa. 50:21). And that is what we all tend to do. We measure God by ourselves. We sit in judgment upon Him. Of course, we are modern people, are we not? We have such great knowledge. We turn God into a subject for analysis upon our laboratory table. We, the great ones! And so we stand up to God.

But listen again to the answer: "He that sitteth in the heavens shall laugh: the LORD shall have them in derision." It is terrifying to think that the great God is looking down upon our world, our "clever" world, the world that thought that Charles Darwin's one book, *On the Origin of Species,* was going to get rid of God. There is only one thing to do with people who can believe a thing like that. It is to laugh them out of court, to ridicule them out of the universe, and God is doing that. "He that sitteth in the heavens shall laugh: the LORD shall have them in derision." Why? Because of who He is and what He is. People say, "Let us break their bands asunder, and cast away their cords from us." They are saying that about the one who "sitteth in the heavens"!

We were so excited about sending astronauts up in rockets to orbit the earth. Heaven? They have not smelled it; they have not come anywhere near to seeing it; we are only children playing with toys. God sits upon the heavens. He suspends the earth from nothing. He dwells in eternity. He is the Creator of this universe. And He is not only its maker but its ruler. Whether we like it or not, He owns it and controls it. He sits on the throne of glory over the whole universe, seeing the end from the beginning.

Not only that, but let us never forget that He is the Judge. "Then shall he speak unto them in his wrath, and vex them in his sore displeasure." My dear friends, we are living in a moral universe. I know that all the immoral and amoral people today do not believe that, but we are. There are laws that cannot be tampered with. Put your finger in the fire, and it will be burned. You may wish you could change that, but you cannot. And if you try to play fast and loose with God's laws, you will soon find that they work inexorably.

Though the mills of God grind slowly, yet they grind exceeding small.
Friedrich von Logau

"There is no peace, saith the LORD, unto the wicked" (Isa. 48:22). That is why there have been two world wars; that is why we have Remembrance Day; that is why the world is in trouble. Do what you like, stand up against God, write blueprints for your utopias—which you will never achieve—and you will be in trouble and in misery. There will be "wars and rumors of wars" (Matt. 24:6). Why? Because you are defying the God who owns the universe and who "shall judge the ends of the earth" (1 Sam. 2:10). Oh, what folly to ignore His wrath, His indignation, His fury! How can anybody who has ever read the Bible or even read secular human history doubt this for a moment.

But beyond all this—and here we especially see the folly of the attitude I've been describing—men and women are standing up and trying to defy God's plan and purpose for this universe: "against the LORD, and his anointed." It is amazing that people do not realize that God has a plan, a great purpose. He began to reveal it away back at the beginning of the human race. Even when Adam and Eve fell, He began to reveal it. The man's sin brought chaos and judgment, but God had a plan: "I will put enmity between thee [the serpent] and the woman, and between thy seed and her seed; it shall bruise thy head, and thou shalt bruise his heel" (Gen. 3:15). There is the beginning, the outline. God carried out His plan. It runs through the whole of the Old Testament—God's increasing, certain, sure plan. Read the story of the children of Israel. God made them, but they got into trouble, and their enemies conquered them. Then God delivered them, and their enemies were defeated. But the same thing happened again, and again they were delivered— it is the whole story of the Old Testament.

But, as those early Christians realized so clearly in that upper room in Jerusalem, it is in the life and death and resurrection of the Lord Jesus Christ that God's plan is demonstrated most clearly. In the life of our Lord we see how "the kings of the earth set themselves, and the rulers take counsel together." We see King Herod and Pontius Pilate, the old enemies who became friends, joining together with the rulers. We see the heathen and the Jews, all conspiring together against this Christ. They said, "Away with Him! Crucify Him!" And they began to laugh in triumph.

Then God laughed! He laughed them to nothing in the fact of the Resurrection. He revealed their unutterable folly by raising His Son from the dead, revealing Him to chosen witnesses, and then taking Him back to Himself in the glory. This was a part of God's plan. Let people, and let the devil, and let hell all come out together with their last reserves against Him, but He will triumph over them all. In the Resurrection He put them to an open shame, triumphing over them in the very thing they had done to Him (Col. 2:15).

And this is only a prophecy, in a sense, of what is yet to happen. "Thou shalt break them with a rod of iron; thou shalt dash them in pieces like a potter's vessel." That is what the Father has said to the Son. And not only did He say, "I shall give thee the heathen for thine inheritance, and the uttermost parts of the earth for thy possession," but He has made His Son the Judge. That is what makes preaching and writing such a solemn responsibility. I have to tell you again that the Son of God will come back into this world "with a rod of iron." He will come back to "judge the world in righteousness" (Acts 17:31). This world will not be allowed to go on like this forever; it will not always be governed by the devil. No, it does not belong to him, for he is a usurper. The one to whom it belongs is coming back, and He will "break them with a rod of iron; and . . . dash them in pieces like a potter's vessel." He will come back again into this world, "and every eye shall see him, and they also which pierced him" (Rev. 1:7). They will try to hide from the terror of His face; they will cry out to the rocks, saying, "Hide us from the . . . wrath of the Lamb" (Rev. 6:16). But nothing will avail. Yet the world is ignorant of all this. They talk about their science, their learning, their utopias, and their schemes; they "imagine vain things"—vain things about themselves, vain things about God. But here is the answer.

I cannot finish on that note. This psalm not only shows human folly.

There is something even worse: It is the tragedy of humanity. Oh, that the world might have its eyes opened to its tragedy! Men and women are not merely defying the might, the power, and the righteousness of God. They are rejecting the love of God. Listen: "The rulers take counsel together, against the LORD, and against his anointed. . . ." What does this mean? Who is the "anointed" of God? He is the Lord Jesus Christ. He is "Jesus of Nazareth." He is God's Son.

In the light of such a message, it is almost impossible to understand men and women in sin. Though we have arrogantly rebelled against Him, defied Him, hated His laws and regarded them as "cords" and as "bands," though we have insulted Him to His face, God's gracious message is still: "God so loved the world"—God so loved this world as it is!—"that he gave his only begotten Son, that whosoever believeth in him should not perish, but have everlasting life" (John 3:16). God has sent His "anointed," His only begotten Son, out of the eternal glory into this world. Why did He ever send Him into this evil world to be mocked and laughed at, spat upon, to have a crown of thorns crushed upon His holy brow, to stagger under the weight of a cross at Golgotha, to be crucified upon it, to die, and to be buried? There is only one answer: The love of God! The gracious purpose of God! God anointed His own Son to be our Savior and our Deliverer, as our Lord Himself said in the synagogue in Nazareth (Luke 4:16-21).

Do you remember how the apostle Paul puts this in the fifth chapter of his letter to the Romans? Here is the message for us in the light of Remembrance Day:

> *For when we were yet without strength, in due time Christ died for the ungodly. For scarcely for a righteous man will one die: yet peradventure for a good man some would even dare to die. But God commendeth his love toward us, in that, while we were yet sinners, Christ died for us. Much more then, being now justified by his blood, we shall be saved from wrath through him. For if, when we were enemies, we were reconciled to God by the death of his Son, much more, being reconciled, we shall be saved by his life.*
>
> —Rom. 5:6-10

Yet the world still laughs at this message and will not even consider it. People regard it as insulting. Fancy being asked to listen to an old Gospel like this when we can be reading the Sunday newspapers and the views and the schemes and the proposals of the clever men and their brilliant ideas and the discoveries of science!

In a sense, I can understand men and women rebelling against God's law, though to do that is terrible, and I have denounced it. But what I cannot understand is that people should reject not only God's law and justice and righteousness, but that they should throw His love back into His face and ridicule His mercy, kindness, and compassion. Yet that is what the world is doing. In spite of this rejection, God has not abandoned the world. He sent His Son into the world to save it and to restore it. But the world rejects God's love in exactly the same way as it rejected the law. That is the final tragedy: "He is despised and rejected of men" (Isa. 53:3)

Let me conclude by holding before you the appeal of the psalmist. In the light of all this, he says, "Be wise now therefore, O ye kings: be instructed, ye judges of the earth. Serve the LORD with fear, and rejoice with trembling. Kiss the Son, lest he be angry, and ye perish from the way, when his wrath is kindled but a little. Blessed are all they that put their trust in him" (Psa. 2:10-12).

Listen to this appeal: "Be wise." Stop and think! Turn off the television for a moment, and the radio, and your music. Put aside the newspapers. Stop for a moment and listen and think about what this word from God has to say to you. And then "be instructed," be ready to be taught. Be honest and admit that you do not know where you are, that you do not understand life or death, that you do not understand why there is war and rumors of wars in this enlightened, intelligent, scientific century. Become as a little child and be ready to receive instruction.

Here is the instruction: Realize what is happening. Realize why the world is as it is today. And this is the answer: "Kiss the Son, lest he be angry, and ye perish from the way, when his wrath is kindled but a little." I believe that today we are seeing a little kindling of the wrath of the Son of God upon this world. He is withholding His gracious influences. He is withdrawing the restraints, and He is allowing us to reap the consequences of our own insane folly. This withdrawal, this abandoning of us to ourselves, is a part of His wrath upon sin. And if we at this moment are turning our world into a little hell, it is nothing in comparison with what hell itself will be like.

Do you think that this world is hell? Do you say, "Life is hell!" Many people are saying this. They have had their fill of pleasure, but they cannot find satisfaction. They get involved in complications until they do not know what to do with themselves. They are raging in a madness, not knowing what to do. They may kill the next man they see. They do not want to, but they do not know what they are doing; they are mad. That is hell, they say. Oh, no, it is not; it is only a glimpse of hell. Hell itself is all that multiplied by infinity, and going on to infinity forever and forever.

Be careful, says the psalmist. Be careful lest you lose your way. The world has lost its way, but come back, he says, to this way. Be wise. Listen, consider, receive instruction. See where you are. See the end of the road on which you are traveling. Stop while there is still time. Realize that you are defying the Lord God of the universe in whose hands you are and from whom you cannot escape. "It is a fearful thing to fall into the hands of the living God" (Heb. 10:31). You can say, "I'll never listen to such preaching again." But you still have to go on living, and you still have to die. After death you still have to stand in the Judgment. You think that by forgetting this word, or, at any rate, by refusing to allow it to enter too frequently into your consciousness, somehow you do away with it. But you do not! It remains, it stands, it is the word of the living God! Be wise, be instructed, be careful that you do not lose the way.

How can you make sure that you do not get lost? By repenting, by thinking again about all these things, by acknowledging your emptiness, your rebellion, your deliberate enmity, your folly, and the tragedy of your refusal to listen to God. Then what do you do? Here is the appeal: "Kiss the Son." The Son of God is invisible, but the psalmist is urging you—and I urge you in the same way—"Kiss the Son." When people go to Buckingham Palace and are given office by the queen, they kiss her hand. That is the sign that they are submitting to her and will carry out her laws to the best of their ability.

The Son of God is holding out His hand to you now. "Kiss the Son," my friend. Give up your rebellion, submit yourself to Him, take the oath of allegiance, and trust Him. In your bewilderment, in your confusion, in your unhappiness, simply believe that Jesus of Nazareth is the eternal Son of God and that He came into the world to save you. Accept His message, believe the Gospel as it is, become a little child, and surrender yourself to Him. Trust Him to save you, trust Him to keep you, trust Him to share His eternal glory with you. Then immediately begin to serve Him. "Serve the LORD with fear" and begin to "rejoice with trembling" (v. 11). Then you will agree with the last statement in this old psalm: "Blessed are all they that put their trust in him."

11

THE CROSS OF CHRIST

And being let go, they went to their own company, and reported all that the chief priests and elders had said unto them. And when they heard that, they lifted up their voice to God with one accord, and said, Lord, thou art God, which hast made heaven, and earth, and the sea, and all that in them is: who by the mouth of thy servant David hast said, Why did the heathen rage, and the people imagine vain things? The kings of the earth stood up, and the rulers were gathered together against the Lord, and against his Christ. For of a truth against thy holy child Jesus, whom thou hast anointed, both Herod, and Pontius Pilate, with the Gentiles, and the people of Israel, were gathered together, for to do whatsoever thy hand and thy counsel determined before to be done.

—Acts 4:23-28

By their use of the second psalm, the early Christians showed that they understood why they were being persecuted. But then in their prayer, they did a most extraordinary thing. They suddenly made a reference to the recent death of the Lord Jesus Christ in Jerusalem. This is what they said: ". . . against his Christ. For of a truth against thy holy child Jesus, whom thou hast anointed, both Herod, and Pontius Pilate, with the Gentiles, and the people of Israel, were gathered together, for to do whatsoever thy hand and thy counsel determined before to be done." The question before us is: Why did these people in their prayer suddenly refer to Christ? Now this is the prayer of the early church; this is true Christianity. There is nothing irrational about the prayer of the true Christian; it is not a mere shouting of something, anything, or nothing. This is prayer inspired by the Holy Spirit. There is nothing violent or riotous about this prayer; it is an orderly progression of thought. Yet suddenly there is a reference to our Lord's death—and there was a reason for it.

Now you may say that this reference came naturally, as an interpretation of the second psalm that has just been quoted. I quite agree. Christ did fulfill the second psalm, as we have seen, but there is more in it than that. The believers saw also that the crucifixion of our Lord threw light upon their own predicament. They were saying, in effect, "They are doing this to us, but they did exactly the same thing to Him. It is the same principle." But also, by this reference to our Lord's death, and especially by the way in which it is put, our eyes are opened to see the apostolic teaching concerning His death on the cross on Calvary's hill. Here in verse 28 especially we have the early church's view.

I call your attention to these words because they are crucial in connection with the Christian faith. The very center of Christian preaching is the preaching of the cross. We have already seen that. You remember that on the day of Pentecost Peter stood up and began to preach, and in his preaching he gave an exposition of the death of our Lord. The same is true in the incident of the healing of the lame man at the Beautiful Gate of the temple. The moment Peter began to preach and to explain that this man had not been healed by him and John but by this Lord, he brought in the cross. And again, standing before the Sanhedrin, he did exactly the same thing: "This is the stone which was set at naught of you builders, which is become the head of the corner. Neither is there salvation in any other: for there is none other name under heaven given among men, whereby we must be saved" (Acts. 4:11-12). That is the preaching of the cross. So the moment the Christian church began to preach and to teach, she preached Jesus Christ and Him crucified. The cross is the very heart of the message. And here in the apostles' prayer, we see this pattern again.

Then when we turn to the ministry of the great apostle Paul, we find that he also centered on the cross. If you read the report of his sermon in Antioch in Pisida (Acts 13), you find that he expounded the cross, and he always did so. We have a most memorable phrase in Paul's first letter to the Corinthians: "I determined not to know any thing among you, save Jesus Christ, and him crucified" (1 Cor. 2:2). Here Paul is outside Corinth. What is he going to preach about? What is the heart and center of the Gospel? It is "Jesus Christ, and him crucified." In chapter 15 of the same epistle, Paul again reminds the Christians at Corinth of the message he had preached to them first of all, "how that Christ died for our sins according to the scriptures" and so on (vv. 3-4).

And again in the second letter to the Corinthians, he says, "We are ambassadors for Christ . . . we pray you in Christ's stead, be ye reconciled to God." And then it comes: "For he hath made him to be sin for us, who knew no sin; that we might be made the righteousness of God in him" (2 Cor. 5:20-21).

It is this message of reconciliation, that "God was in Christ, reconciling the world unto himself, not imputing their trespasses unto them" (2 Cor. 5:19), that is the great central message of the Christian faith. This message is always crucial. The early church always put it in the place of greatest prominence. The apostle Paul, indeed, uses very bold imagery in which he compares himself to a poster. He says, "Jesus Christ hath been evidently set forth"— literally, "put on a placard"—"crucified among you" (Gal. 3:1). Paul has held it before them. What has he placarded? Always the death of the Lord Jesus Christ. And there has never yet been a period of revival and of reformation but that it has always preached the centrality and the crucial nature of the death of our Lord upon the cross.

Therefore, it follows, does it not, by a logical inevitability and necessity, that what ultimately tests whether or not you and I are Christian is our view of the cross. I am not interested in what you call yourself nor in the goodness or the badness of your life; I am not interested in any experiences you may have had. No, our view of the cross is the touchstone; it is the acid test; it is this that always proves beyond any doubt exactly where we stand. If we judge ourselves by any other test, we will go astray. The world can counterfeit most of what we claim and boast of, but there is one thing it can never counterfeit—the death upon the cross on Calvary's hill.

So what is the meaning of that death? Let us look at it together; let us "survey the wondrous cross." What happened there? Now there are many who think that the answer is quite simple: Our Lord's death was nothing but the action of ignorant and cruel men, blundering humanity. They killed Socrates; they killed the prophets; they have always killed the greatest benefactors, and this is just another illustration of that. But that view is not sufficient because it does not explain or deal with the question of the person of Christ. Here He is. He was able to work miracles; He could control the raging of the elements; He could give sight to the blind; He could make the deaf hear; He could make the lame walk; He could even raise the dead. So why did He die? If the crucifixion was merely the blundering of ignorant men, why did such a person ever allow it to happen?

Not only does this explanation not deal with the person of Christ, but it does not deal with the power of God either. In this prayer in Acts 4 we see a great emphasis upon the power of God, "which hast made heaven, and earth, and the sea, and all that in them is," and a reference to the wonderful history of God's activity in the Old Testament. So why did the cross ever happen if it was merely the activity of men? In addition, the Gospel records tell us that our Lord Himself said that He could have been saved quite easily. If an Elijah was taken up to heaven by God, why not the Son of God (Matt. 26:53)?

So the great question is: Where is God's part in this death on the cross? And where do human beings come in? How do you reconcile these two elements? You cannot explain the cross in merely human terms. But how are God and humanity both engaged in the cross? And that is the very problem that is solved in our text. That is why these early Christians prayed as they did at this point: "Herod, and Pontius Pilate, with the Gentiles, and the people of Israel, were gathered together for to do"—and they did it—". . . whatsoever thy hand and thy counsel determined before to be done"—God's part. Here in this one pregnant sentence, we are given a view of the cross that opens the whole situation before us—God's part and man's part stated plainly and clearly in a prayer. What a wonderful thing prayer is!

So let me show you how this sentence not only gives us a great and true exposition of the meaning of the death of Jesus Christ, but in doing so also deals with and completely confutes all the modern misunderstandings of the cross. This misunderstanding is the great tragedy of the world. The Scriptures tell us that this was the tragedy of tragedies; the Jews, of all people, misunderstanding and stumbling at it; the Greeks ridiculing it and laughing it out of court. And the world has gone on doing that ever since. The most amazing thing of all is that not only has the world always rejected the meaning of the cross, but the church herself, alas, has so often been utterly confused about it, representing it as being almost the exact opposite of what it really is.

Now here are some of the misconceptions dealt with by this great statement in prayer. First of all, the death of Jesus Christ upon the cross was not an accident. It is shown here to be inevitable: "For to do whatsoever thy hand and thy counsel determined before to be done." The cross was not something unexpected. It is commonly held today that our Lord was taken by surprise and was upset. I remember a man once interpreting those glorious words, "It is finished," as meaning, "It is all up. I'm a complete failure. I thought I could persuade them, but I couldn't." "He died of a broken heart," said the man. "Jesus had come to reform His own people first and through them all the world, but it had all gone wrong."

But surely you cannot hold that view for a second, and not only because of this prayer. Our Lord Himself told His own disciples many times that He was going to die. At Caesarea Philippi, after that great statement of the apostle Peter: "Thou art the Christ, the Son of the living God" (Matt. 16:16), Jesus immediately began to tell them that He was going to be handed over into the hands of cruel men and be put to death. Peter did not like it; he could not understand it. "Be it far from thee, Lord," he said. But our Lord said, "Get thee behind me, Satan" (Matt. 16:22-23). He taught them plainly that His death was coming. He said, "The Son of man came not to be ministered unto, but to minister, and to give his life a ransom for many" (Mark 10:45).

When Elijah and Moses appeared to our Lord on the mount of transfiguration, we are told that they "spake of his decease which he should accomplish at Jerusalem" (Luke 9:31). After this our Lord constantly spoke of His death. His followers could not take it in, but that does not mean He did not tell them. He was constantly preparing them: "Let not your heart be troubled," He said (John 14:1). The death of our Lord was not an accident; it was not unexpected; it did not take Him by surprise.

Or, to put it another way, the death of our Lord upon the cross was not something that could have been avoided or that might not have happened. People say, "Oh, what a mistake. If He hadn't insisted on going up to Jerusalem, if He had kept away for a while until the excitement had quieted down, it might never have happened. It was an avoidable tragedy."

Again, there is a complete answer to that. At His arrest, when one of His disciples pulled out his sword and was going to defend Him, our Lord rebuked the disciple. "Put up again thy sword into his place," he said. ". . . Thinkest thou that I cannot now pray to my Father, and he shall presently give me more than twelve legions of angels?" (Matt. 26:52-53). If He had chosen, He could quite easily have been carried off to heaven. But, no, His death had to happen. It was an absolute necessity. So we must get rid of this notion that the cross was in any sense an accident to be attributed only to the blundering and the blindness of fallen human nature.

Let me take a second group of people who completely misunderstand our Lord's death. They say that the cross is just meant to be an example to us. This idea is common at the present time, and again people put it in different ways. In the last chapter, we were thinking of the two world wars. I am old enough to remember what was said so often during the First World War (we did not hear much about it during the second war). The death of Christ was used in order to inculcate a spirit of patriotism. But at the opposite extreme, our Lord's death is misused in exactly the same way. The pacifist says, "Here is the supreme example of one who does nothing to defend Himself. He is absolutely in the right while His opponents are altogether in the wrong, but He does not fight; He does not move a finger. He lets them do whatever they like to Him. In complete passivity He submits without grumbling or complaining, and He prohibits anybody else from defending him with a sword." Pacifism maintains that our Lord is teaching us from the cross to follow His example. Is that not a very common view of the cross of Christ?

A third variation of the idea that the cross is an example claims for itself the greatest amount of intellectual understanding. It is said that on the cross our Lord was giving us the perfect and most glorious illustration of the way we should be ready to submit ourselves utterly and absolutely to God and His will, even though it may mean that we must die. Our Lord was ready to die, and He did, in obedience to the Father. He has set us the greatest example of all of utter submission to God.

The third group of people who misunderstand the cross say that the cross of Jesus Christ is something to which God responds and something God uses. The cross, we are told, was entirely the action of man, these cruel men, these members of the Sanhedrin, these subtle Pharisees and scribes and Sadducees, these political, theological ecclesiastics. They were entirely responsible; they should not have done it, but they did. But God saw an opportunity in what they had done and reacted by making use of it. You may hear this view from people who are regarded as evangelical. "God," they say, "looks at the world and says, 'Though you have done that to my only begotten, dearly beloved Son, I still love you. You should not have done it; you have killed My only Son, but I will forgive even that.'"

Do you see what they are saying? This view teaches that it is man who is acting, and God is merely reacting. God takes hold of a human action and uses it to reveal His great and eternal love. Others would add that our Lord Himself was doing the same thing on the cross. He was looking at us and saying: "Though you have done this to Me, I still love you." The cross, we are told, is just a great proclamation that God loves us all, every one of us, whether we know it or not. He is telling us through the cross that however much we may disobey Him, however much we may violate His laws and spit upon His sanctity, if we even murder His only begotten Son, He still loves us in spite of it all.

But that was not the meaning of the cross according to the apostles. Verse 28 shows that God did not react to what happened on the cross; God was the *author* of the cross. Here, in this one text, the whole thing is put absolutely perfectly. It was the action of God. That is how the early church explained it in the middle of a prayer.

I sometimes wonder whether we have ever prayed, my friends. This is praying! This is praying with understanding. This is praying as the result of the revelation of the great doctrine of salvation given by God to His people. Men actually crucified our Lord, but His death was determined by God; they were but fulfilling God's plan. That is what the apostles taught. Peter had already said all this in his sermon on the day of Pentecost. In Acts 2:23 we read, "Him, being delivered by the determinate counsel and foreknowledge of God, ye have taken, and by wicked hands have crucified and slain."

Oh, what a message to proclaim, what a privilege to be a little herald of such a message! What is the meaning of the cross? I will tell you. The cross is not the action of man. In a sense, these rulers were merely the mechanical instruments because they did not know what they were doing—as our Lord Himself said on the cross, "Father, forgive them; for they know not what they do" (Luke 23:34). But God knew, and the Son knew. It was because the Son knew that He had shed drops of blood in his agony in the garden of Gethsemane: "If it be possible let it pass, but if not I will go through with it."

The death of Jesus Christ on the cross on Calvary's hill was something that was planned before the foundation of the world. Peter said it on the day of Pentecost, and now listen to him years later when he writes his epistle as an old man:

> *Ye know that ye were not redeemed with corruptible things, as silver and gold, from your vain conversation received by tradition from your fathers; but with the precious blood of Christ, as of a lamb without blemish and without spot [notice this] who verily was foreordained before the foundation of the world, but was manifest in these last times for you, who by him do believe in God, that raised him up from the dead, and gave him glory; that your faith and hope might be in God.*
>
> *—1 Peter 1:18-21*

The cross an accident? The cross a surprise? The cross something that might not have happened and that need not have happened? The cross merely something that God uses? No, the cross was planned, foreordained, before the world was ever created. Before man was ever made, God had planned the death of Christ His Son. This is the explanation, and these first believers had seen it: "Whatsoever thy hand and thy counsel determined before to be done."

Indeed, I can prove this to you from the Old Testament. Why was Abel's offering more acceptable to God than Cain's? There is only one answer: It was a blood offering. It starts there, you see. Then go on reading the Old

Testament. Read the books of Exodus, Leviticus, and Numbers, and so on. All the burnt offerings and the sacrifices, the lamb that was slain and offered both morning and evening, the priest placing his hands upon the head of an animal, killing the animal, collecting the blood, presenting it—always this emphasis upon blood. What is it all about? It is about prophecy. God, who had planned the death of His Son upon the cross, was preparing humanity for it, especially His own people. These Old Testament sacrifices and offerings are types, shadows, prophecies—call them what you like. They are all nothing in themselves, as it were, but they point forward. God was telling people that He was going to sacrifice His Son.

Then come to the great prophetic books of the Old Testament. Take the fifty-third chapter of Isaiah. There in the plainest possible terms, Isaiah prophesied the death of the Son of God on the cross. Yet those clever people in the church are telling us that it was an accident, that it need never have happened and that God simply made use of it. God, I say, not only planned the cross, but He informed this race of people, and through them the world, that He had and that it was the center of all His great and glorious activity.

But then we come to the New Testament, and the first preacher we find is John the Baptist—extraordinary man! There I see him one day standing with two of his disciples. Suddenly he sees Jesus of Nazareth, and at once he says, "Behold the Lamb of God, which taketh away the sin of the world" (John 1:29). The Lamb, God's own Lamb, the Lamb that God Himself has provided—not the lamb provided by priests in the tabernacle and in the temple. Here is God's own Lamb that will take away the sin of the world. The first preacher, the forerunner, puts his finger on it; he points to it. This is the meaning—not an accident, not a human action, but God's determined plan. The hour has struck, and it is about to happen.

Then when we read our Lord's own teaching in the Gospels, we find Him saying, "As Moses lifted up the serpent in the wilderness, even so must the Son of man be lifted up: that whosoever believeth in him should not perish, but have eternal life" (John 3:14-15). He is saying the same thing. Again He says, "The hour is come, that the Son of man should be glorified" (John 12:23). The hour: Keep your eye on that expression, especially in John's Gospel. He had come for a given hour. And so we read that "He stedfastly set his face to go to Jerusalem" (Luke 9:51). His own friends tried to stop Him. When He received a report that Herod was plotting to kill Him, he said, "Go ye, and tell that fox, Behold, I cast out devils, and I do cures to day and to morrow, and the third day I shall be perfected" (Luke 13:32). He knew exactly. And as we have seen, there He was in agony in the garden. He knew what was coming. He asked the Father if this was the only way. Then He said, "Not my will, but thine, be done" (Luke 22:42).

His last words on the cross were, "It is finished" (John 19:30). The thing He had to do had been done. Then He died, and they buried Him, but He rose, and here He is, suddenly appearing to two men on the road to Emmaus. They are depressed and say, "We trusted that it had been he which should have redeemed Israel" (Luke 24:21).

"O fools, and slow of heart," he says, "to believe all that the prophets have spoken: ought not Christ to have suffered these things, and to enter into his glory?" (Luke 24:25-26) Then He explains it all to them. The death—ought He not to have died? He must! It had been prophesied. Read that last chapter of Luke's Gospel and see how He put it all to them again in the Upper Room. He took them through the books of Moses and the Psalms and the prophets and showed Himself in all of them. He showed that He had to die and rise again and that it was all a part of this great and eternal plan of God.

When you read the rest of the New Testament and the epistles, you find that they are all saying exactly the same thing: "[God] hath made him to be sin for us, who knew no sin; that we might be made the righteousness of God in him" (2 Cor. 5:21). We have already looked at Peter's words. Peter said that the prophets had looked into this, but they did not understand it when they wrote about the sufferings of Christ and the glory that was to follow. They did not understand it, but they wrote it and were looking into it, the angels, too—God's greatest act (see 1 Pet. 1:10-12).

The author of the epistle to the Hebrews puts it in his own way: "Now we see not yet all things put under him [man]. But we see Jesus, who was made a little lower than the angels"—made a man; what for?—"for the suffering of death" (Heb. 2:8-9). That is why He was born. That is why He came to this world. Jesus Christ the Son of God was born in Bethlehem in order that He might taste death for everyone. Far from it being an accident, He came into the world in order that He might die. The whole of the biblical teaching is to this effect—and that is the very thing that these men summed up in one sentence in the midst of their prayer when they were hard-pressed by the verdict of the Sanhedrin. Men do the deeds, but it is God's purpose. It is God who brought Jesus there; it is God who planned it all—before the foundation of the world.

But why did God send His only begotten Son to die? This is the profoundest truth in the universe and ever will be. Yet there is a sense in which it is quite simple. There is only one answer: It is because He is God! We must always start with God. As we have seen, most of our troubles are due to the fact that we do not know God or the truth about Him, and we think He "was altogether such an one as [ourselves]" (Psa. 50:21), but He is not. The cross happened because God is God. That means that He is just. He is holy. He is righteous. It means that He is true, that He is truth.

The sin of man confronts the everlasting and eternal God with a problem. How can a holy, just, and righteous God ever forgive sinful human beings? God's nature demands that sin should be punished, and God has said that many times over. He revealed this truth constantly in the Old Testament in explicit language, in all the burnt offerings and the sacrifices. It is summed up in Hebrews in a great phrase: "without shedding of blood is no remission [of sins]" (Heb. 9:22). Sin must be punished. God has said it, and unlike politicians, He does not change His laws. He is "the Father of lights, with whom is no variableness, neither shadow of turning" (James 1:17). God is, and what God says is eternal. He cannot modify His law; He cannot change it. God cannot lie. His own nature abhors sin, and sin cannot live in His presence. He is "a consuming fire" (Heb. 12:29). "The wages of sin is death" (Rom. 6:23); every person who has ever sinned deserves to die. It is inevitable. God's just, righteous, holy nature demands it.

So here is the problem. Does that mean, then, that the whole of humanity is to be consigned to death? No, that would have meant the triumph of the devil. God, for the sake of His own glory, must save His people. But how can He? The law is useless because it is "weak through the flesh" (Rom. 8:3). What, then, could God do?

There is only one thing, and I say it with reverence, that God could do, and He has done it. He sent His only Son into this world "for the suffering of death . . . that he by the grace of God should taste death for every man" (Heb. 2:9). God's Son took our sins upon Himself: "The LORD hath laid on him the iniquity of us all" (Isa. 53:6). God must punish sin, and God has punished sin in Him. Therefore, God remains righteous and true and holy and can give me a free pardon. It was the only way whereby a single individual could ever be forgiven his sins.

If there had been another way, God would have adopted it. But there was not. Our forgiveness necessitated the Incarnation, the Word being made flesh, and His going to the cross. He could have escaped, of course, but if He had, He would not have fulfilled all righteousness. He had to bear the wages of sin; He had to receive the punishment. Men killed Him, yes, but in doing so, they were carrying out this eternal purpose of God. The death of the Son of God is the means of our salvation.

He died that we might be forgiven,
He died to make us good.
                              Cecil Frances Alexander

"Who his own self bare our sins in his own body on the tree, that we, being dead to sins, should live unto righteousness: by whose stripes ye were healed" (1 Pet. 2:24).

Our Lord's death is the only way of salvation, the only way that even God can forgive us. It is the only way "that he [God] might be just, and [at the same time] the justifier of him which believeth in Jesus" (Rom. 3:26). This is what makes men and women Christians: They realize that the Son of God died, and had to die, for their sins, in order that they might be forgiven. Christians say with the apostle Paul, ". . . the Son of God, who loved me, and gave himself for me" (Gal. 2:20). So you do not really pray unless you go through Christ's death; this must come into your prayer. There is no access to God apart from this. By means of this, by the blood of Jesus, you are reconciled to God, and you go into the holiest of all knowing your sins are forgiven, knowing that you are a child of God, knowing that you are an heir of the glory that awaits all God's people.

12

JESUS AND THE RESURRECTION

And now, Lord, behold their threatenings: and grant unto thy servants, that with all boldness they may speak thy word, by stretching forth thine hand to heal; and that signs and wonders may be done by the name of thy holy child Jesus. And when they had prayed, the place was shaken where they were assembled together; and they were all filled with the Holy Ghost, and they spake the word of God with boldness. And the multitude of them that believed were of one heart and of one soul: neither said any of them that ought of the things which he possessed was his own; but they had all things common. And with great power gave the apostles witness of the resurrection of the Lord Jesus: and great grace was upon them all.

—Acts 4:29-33

We have been considering the reaction of the early Christians to persecution. Now we have arrived at the point in their prayer when they mention themselves. So far they had been doing nothing but worshiping and adoring God in spite of their trouble, in spite of the fact that they were, in a sense, face to face with death. They were worshiping God in His greatness and glory. They realized that He was still the God who inspired the second psalm, the God of the psalmists and the prophets. Then we saw that they were reminded of the death of the Lord on the cross.

Then, at last they came to themselves and their own trouble. But notice what they prayed for—not that they might be set at liberty or that they might be given an easy or happy time or that God would deliver them out of a predicament. "Lord," they said, "behold their threatenings: and grant unto thy servants, that with all boldness they may speak thy word." They wanted to go on preaching the Word of God. Again in verse 31 we read, "When they had prayed, the place was shaken where they were assembled together; and they were all filled with the Holy Ghost, and they spake the word of God with boldness." And in verse 33, "And with great power gave the apostles witness of the resurrection of the Lord Jesus."

Now they had already spoken of our Lord as "thy holy child Jesus" and as the one anointed by God. They had already referred to Him in His glorious person and had referred to His death upon the cross, and now they came to this other mighty fact—the Resurrection. Now this is Christianity, this blessed person—His birth, His teaching, His miracles, His death, His burial, His resurrection. These are the things that the apostles preached. They did not preach about themselves. Later the apostle Paul makes a never-to-be-forgotten statement when he says, "We preach not ourselves, but Christ Jesus the Lord" (2 Cor. 4:5). That is apostolic preaching. As you go through these early chapters of Acts, you will find that every time these men had an opportunity to preach, they preached facts; they preached historic events and happenings, their meaning and significance. They were witnesses to the Resurrection; they were talking about the things that they had seen and heard.

The disciples preached in this way, of course, because it was crucial to their whole position as Christians. These were not merely people who had had an experience. They had had an experience, thank God. This is *the* experience, but they did not preach that. No, they preached the one who had given them the experience; they preached the events that had made the experience possible. They were bound to preach that way because they would never have been apostles at all but for this person, Jesus Christ. They would never have been Christians, and there would never have been a Christian church, were it not for these events, and in particular were it not for the Resurrection.

Take the two men on the road to Emmaus, cast down, commiserating with one another, or the disciples in the Upper Room after the Resurrection. They were all utterly despondent. That would have been the end of the story were it not for this tremendous event that had happened—the Resurrection. Now I am making such a point of this because of the modern confusion. People are telling us today that the facts do not matter at all. Unfortunately, these people receive great publicity on television and everywhere else; their books are popular, and they are controlling theological thinking, particularly on the continent and in other parts of the world. Indeed, they do not hesitate to say that you can be sure of almost none of the facts.

The popular teaching is that you cannot believe all these records we are given here, but that does not matter at all as long as you get the "religious value" of the stories. It does not matter whether or not Jesus was born of a virgin; it does not really matter whether or not He worked miracles or atoned for our sins by His death. It certainly does not matter whether He arose in the body from the tomb. The facts do not matter, they say, as long as you have the religious value of Jesus and His teaching. Now it is because of this teaching that I am emphasizing this passage. In a sense, these apostles preached nothing but the facts, which to them were all-important. They kept on talking about "the things which we have seen and heard." The experience of these men came directly out of the facts about which they were constantly speaking. If your experience does not result from the facts of Christ's life and death, it is not a Christian experience.

In their prayer the disciples emphasized the great fact of the Resurrection. Now I wonder if I am addressing somebody calling himself or herself a Christian who may be adopting the modern idea that it does not matter whether you believe in the Resurrection or not. The answer to this view is found in the fifteenth chapter of 1 Corinthians, one of the longest chapters in the New Testament. Paul wrote this chapter to show that belief in the Resurrection is absolutely essential. Just as in the church today, so there were people in the early church who said that the Resurrection was past already, that the Resurrection never took place in a literal manner, or that it did not matter. "It doesn't matter?" says Paul, in effect. "I have nothing if this does not matter; all my preaching has been a lie and is of no value at all."

If ever there was a time when we need to emphasize the facts, these great foundational facts on which the whole of our faith is based, it is this present moment. The world is as it is because it does not believe these facts. If you give your experience to the world, it will say, "All right, if that's the sort of thing that pleases you, get on with it. I'm not interested; it has nothing to do with me." On top of that, you can hear proponents of the cults saying, "Believe us, and you will get happiness. Though you have not slept for years, you will be able to sleep peacefully." But we preach facts, and we preach the apostolic witness to the facts, including this tremendous, glorious fact of the Resurrection of the Lord Jesus Christ.

So, then, what does it mean? Well, let me first of all emphasize that the Resurrection is indeed a fact. These apostles did not merely preach that Jesus—the one whom they had all known and listened to, the one who had been crucified and who had died and was buried—was still alive in the other spiritual realm. They did preach that, but the Resurrection does not merely mean that Jesus is still in existence in the spiritual realm; it means much more than that, and this is what we must be clear about. These men preached the empty tomb. They said: "We were witnesses, we saw Him crucified, we heard His cry of dereliction, we heard Him saying at the end, 'Father, into thy hands I commend my spirit' (Luke 23:46). We saw them taking down His body; we saw them laying it in a tomb, rolling a stone in front of the entrance, sealing it, ordering Roman soldiers to guard it. We saw that, but we also saw the empty tomb on the morning of the third day."

That is what they were witnesses to, and that is what they preached— not merely that Jesus can still help us from the unseen realm, but that Jesus literally rose, leaving nothing behind except the grave clothes. He arose in the body; it was a changed body, but it was essentially the same body, His body. He was able to show them His hands and side. You remember the incident in connection with Thomas, who was very slow to believe and stumbled at it. "Reach hither thy finger," said our Lord, "and behold my hands; and reach hither thy hand, and thrust it into my side" (John 20:27) It was the same body, but changed.

Also take the argument that our Lord Himself implied there in the Upper Room, as it is recorded in that last chapter of Luke's Gospel. He asked if there was anything to eat. They gave Him a bit of broiled fish and a piece of honeycomb, and He ate it before them. Why? Because they thought He was a ghost, a spirit. He said, "A spirit hath not flesh and bones, as you see me have" (Luke 24:39). A spirit does not eat; it is immaterial, but our Lord was proving that He was material, though different. He could come through a closed door. The doors were all shut because the disciples were afraid of the Jews. Then He suddenly appeared. Yet He had essentially the same body. He was not a spirit, not an apparition, or ghost. He literally rose out of the tomb in the body that He had had before and was appearing to them. That is what is meant by resurrection.

Now, of course, our scientific age cannot believe anything like that, but they could not believe things like that in the first century either. In the last chapter of Matthew we read that the clever people at that time invented a story and bribed the Roman soldiers to tell a lie in order to disprove the Resurrection. They went as far as that, and people are doing similar things today. That is the dishonesty of unbelief. The idea that it is unbelief alone that is honest and that believers juggle the facts is the reverse of the truth! Unbelief is in such a hopeless position that it has to bribe people and utter deliberate lies, as these authorities in the Sanhedrin did. We are familiar with all the proffered explanations that attempt to refute the Resurrection, but they contradict one another, and they are all dealt with, in a sense, in the Scriptures.

But the final argument for the truth of the physical Resurrection is surely just this—the apostles themselves. We have already seen that when the authorities perceived the boldness of Peter and John, these unlearned and ignorant men, they marveled. Quite so, and well they might! So how do you explain these apostles? How did the Christian church ever come into being? We have seen that before the Resurrection these men were utterly cast down and completely hopeless. Left to themselves, they would never have done anything at all. But actually they did tremendous things. They were the men on whom the church was founded. It spread throughout the world; it turned the old world upside down; eventually it conquered the Roman Empire and has gone on ever since.

This change in the disciples has to be explained, but there is no explanation apart from the literal fact of the Resurrection. Not only that, but people who are not even Christians have always had to admit that the teaching of these apostles in the New Testament epistles is the most glorious literature we have. How did they do it if they were frauds, if they invented facts, if they pretended that their Lord had risen from the dead when it was not true? Yet the author of a recent foolish book has been trying to say that they had concocted their teaching, and the Resurrection was a clever invention to impose this teaching upon people! But how could such frauds ever have produced such literature? How could they ever have had the beneficent influence that the Christian church has had in this world? The idea is ridiculous; good does not come of evil. There is only one explanation: The resurrection is a fact. That is why these apostles held on to it, and that is why they continued to preach it. That is why they were even ready to die rather than deny it.

Why, then, did they think the Resurrection was so vital? First of all, the Resurrection is what finally proves to us who Christ is. If you read the Gospels again, you will find that at times these disciples did see something. Peter at Caesarea Philippi said, "Thou art the Christ, the Son of the living God" (Matt. 16:16). On another occasion when Jesus said, "Will ye also go away?" Peter, speaking for all of them, said, "Lord, to whom shall we go? thou hast the words of eternal life" (John 6:68). They had had flashes, glimpses, of the reality of who He was and His glory. But it was not clear to them, and, of course, when He died, they were shattered. That is not too strong a term to use. They could not take it; they could not understand it. The glimpses had not been sufficient. It was the Resurrection that gave the disciples absolute proof.

But why? Because here was one who had literally risen from the dead. As Paul puts it later on in preaching to Agrippa and Festus, "He should be the first that should rise from the dead" (Acts 26:23). What happened with Lazarus had not been a resurrection; that had merely been a resuscitation. Lazarus had simply been brought back to life for a while before dying again. But here was the first to rise literally in the body from the dead: "the first begotten of the dead" (Rev. 1:5); "the firstfruits of them that slept" (1 Cor. 15:20); "the firstborn among many brethren" (Rom. 8:29). This is the striking, tremendous event that finally convinced these apostles. He had literally risen. He had given them proof beyond any doubt or question, repeated a number of times during forty days.

Furthermore, our Lord also gave His followers instruction from the Scriptures, as we see in Luke 24. They now saw the whole thing. There were prophecies in the Old Testament not only of His death but also of His resurrection, prophecies that showed that He was sure to be put to death but also that He would rise on the morning of the third day. He took the two disciples on the road to Emmaus through the Scriptures. He showed them that Moses, the Psalms, and the prophets had foretold the very things that had happened to Him. That is why He said to the two disciples, "O fools, and slow of heart to believe all that the prophets have spoken" (Luke 24:25). He gave the same teaching in the Upper Room, showing the disciples from all the Scriptures the things concerning Himself. So if you want to be certain about these things, get to know the Bible; that is the foundation.

Those first disciples not only had visual evidence of our Lord's resurrection, but they also saw that this was a fulfillment of all the great prophecies. As Peter puts it in that last letter of his, "We have also a more sure word of prophecy" (2 Pet. 1:19). Peter is advising Christian people to pay attention to the prophets who give us a "sure" prophecy.

Then there were our Lord's own prophecies. He said to the disciples in the Upper Room, "These are the words which I spake unto you, while I was yet with you, that all things must be fulfilled" (Luke 24:44). If you read the Gospels, you will find that He constantly told them that He was going to rise on the third day. He used the illustration of Jonah more than once. Yet they could not see it. But now they saw that His prophecy had been verified.

Who was this who had risen from the dead and who was able to prophesy that He would? There is only one answer. This is the eternal Son of God. This is why the Resurrection was so vital; it was this event that finally gave the disciples assurance. Paul puts it in his own inimitable manner in Romans 1:3-4: "Christ Jesus our Lord, which was made of the seed of David according to the flesh; and declared to be the Son of God with power, according to the spirit of holiness, by the resurrection from the dead." People needed to know that Jesus of Nazareth was the only begotten Son of God—and it was the Resurrection that proved this.

The Resurrection was thus absolutely vital, and that is why the apostles went on preaching it. As we are told: "With great power gave the apostles witness of the resurrection" (v. 33). The enemy was threatening, but it did not matter; they went on saying it. "The things which we have seen and heard." They saw Him crucified, they saw Him dead, they saw Him buried, and they saw Him risen. They were not talking about themselves but about Him. And this is what matters in the world today, that the *Son of God* has visited it.

Then, secondly, it is the Resurrection that finally proves that our Lord's death accomplished everything He claimed for it. The Resurrection proclaims that the death of Christ has given complete satisfaction to the holy God and His holy law. Oh, how vital this is! It is not surprising that Paul should say, "Who was delivered for our offences, and was raised again for our justification" (Rom. 4:25). Have you ever realized this truth? What is the argument of 1 Corinthians 15? You have often heard that chapter read, have you not? We often hear it at funerals—and what a chapter it is. When a saint has died, how these words transform the funeral into a moment of rejoicing, praise, and thanksgiving.

But what is the argument of this chapter? It is this: "If Christ be not risen, then is our preaching vain, and your faith is also vain . . . ye are yet in your sins . . . If in this life only we have hope in Christ, we are of all men most miserable" (vv. 14, 17, 19). Let us assume that Jesus Christ did not rise from the dead. Let us assume that when they laid Him in the tomb, He remained there. Or let us take one of the clever theories. One is that somebody stole the body. Another, still more fatuous, is that somehow or another the conditions in the tomb were such that the moisture was extracted out of the body, and there was nothing to be seen because it had become dust.

People keep on repeating these old fairy tales, and that is the kind of story they have to resort to when they deny the facts! But let us assume that He never did rise in the body from the dead. What is our position? It is this: "The wages of sin is death" (Rom. 6:23). God has made that perfectly clear. "The soul that sinneth, it shall die" (Ezek. 18:4, 20). You cannot play with the laws of God; they are absolute. We have all sinned, every one of us, and, therefore, we are all faced with death, and eternal death at that.

Now there is only one way of salvation. Christ offered Himself; God took

Him as His own lamb, put our sins upon Him, and punished them in Him. What was the punishment? Death. So here is the question: Can our Lord save us? He can only save us if He can prove that He was big enough and great enough to take this punishment, which is death. He could only prove that by coming out on the other side, which is resurrection. And that is precisely what He did. The Resurrection of the Lord Jesus Christ is the proclamation of God to the whole universe that His Son bore the punishment for the sins of His people, that He received all the vials of God's wrath upon Himself, and completed it all and rose on the other side of it—"Who was delivered for our offences, and was raised again for our justification" (Rom. 4:25). "We are fooling you," says Paul, in effect, in 1 Corinthians 15. "We are deluding you, and you are deluding yourselves. You are yet in your sins, and you have to die for them, and you will die eternally if He has not completed the work. But He has completed the work; He has given proof of it. He has risen." That is why the apostles with great power gave witness to the Resurrection of the Lord Jesus.

Then the next thing proved by the Resurrection is that Christ is able to save us from all our enemies. I proclaim to you that Jesus of Nazareth is the Son of God and the Savior of the world. Savior? What does He save us from? He saves us from the world, the flesh, the devil, and the law of God. Yes, the law of God is against us, and the law in that sense is our enemy. "By the law is the knowledge of sin" (Rom. 3:20), and the law condemns us; "By the works of the law shall no flesh be justified" (Gal. 2:16). The law of God accuses us, and we cannot escape it. It stands over and against us.

World, flesh, devil, law. At the back of them all is the most terrifying of them all—death, the last enemy, the enemy that the modern world is trying to fight with all its ingenuity and cleverness and science. We are all struggling to keep ourselves young and to fight off old age and death. You can postpone it for a year or two, but you cannot evade it. There he is with his scythe, advancing nearer and nearer and nearer, and the day—we all know it—must inevitably come when he will hammer at your door and say to you, "Move on." You will have to go. The last enemy. And he is not only the last enemy chronologically, but he is the last enemy in the sense that he is the one who faces us with the judgment, the law, the holiness of God, and possibly an eternal destiny of misery and wretchedness and unhappiness—the last enemy.

Now our Lord claims to be the Savior, but if He cannot save us from all our enemies, He does not merit the designation of Savior. Thank God, He can meet the challenge. He dealt with the devil many times when He was here in the flesh and conquered Him with ease. He lived untouched by the world, separate from it. The sins of the flesh He never knew. He was tempted externally in all points like as we are, yet was without sin; and He was never tempted from sin within. As for the law of God, we have already seen how He met its every demand. He never broke His Father's law, and there on the cross He gave a complete and perfect satisfaction for all its demands.

Yes, but that obedience involved His death. Has the last enemy got Him? It is one thing to beat the world, the flesh, the devil, and the law of God, but what about the last enemy? Has it not conquered Him; has it not succeeded? The world said, "Yes, it has!" They were beginning to triumph, but their triumph was short-lived, shattered by the Resurrection. Christ conquered our last enemy, enabling His people to look in the face of death and say, "O death, where is thy sting? O grave, where is thy victory?" (1 Cor. 15:55). Paul continued, "The sting of death is sin; and the strength of sin is the law. But thanks be to God, which giveth us the victory through our Lord Jesus Christ" (vv. 56-57). He has conquered the last enemy. He is a complete, a perfect, Savior. I would not be able to say that if He had not risen literally in the body from the tomb. But I can say it because the Resurrection is a fact. "And with great power gave the apostles witness of the resurrection of the Lord Jesus." This is what a man or woman does who is filled with the Spirit as these people were. The Resurrection is the fact on which everything is based, and this is what the world needs to know.

Shall I ask an unusual question at this point? Are you enjoying the power of the Resurrection? If you are not, you are outside; you are under the wrath of God; you are under the condemnation of the law. Jesus and the Resurrection are meat and drink to the Christian, the wine of heaven to the true believer. The Resurrection is a proof to those who believe in Him, in what has happened to Him, and in what He has done; it is a proof that our redemption will be complete.

When man fell, he fell as a whole. He did not merely fall in his will, or in his heart, or in his mind; the whole of him fell; his very body fell. The apostle Paul uses an extraordinary term in respect to our bodies; the Authorized Version puts it like this in Philippians 3:21: "our *vile* body." The Revised Version has improved the translation somewhat by saying, "the body of our humiliation," and yet the old translators have a point. The human body is vile; it is a body with corruption in it: "If Christ be in you, the body is dead because of sin; but the Spirit is life because of righteousness" (Rom. 8:10). That is why we get aches and pains; that is why we get diseases and illnesses; that is why the body is running down—there is corruption in the body. You remember

Paul's argument again in 1 Corinthians 15: "Neither doth corruption inherit incorruption" (v. 50). This present body is a body of humiliation.

Our human corruption is the result of the Fall. If we had never fallen, our bodies would not be corrupt. These are the bodies of sinful flesh, and Paul tells us that Christ came "in the likeness of sinful flesh" (Rom. 8:3). His body was not sinful, but it was like sinful flesh, and so He looked very much as we do. My redemption will not be complete until my body is delivered, and the Resurrection tells me that it will be delivered. Christ not only redeemed the spirit, but He also redeemed the body. When He came into the world, He took on a human body because He came to redeem men and women in their entirety. John tells us in his first epistle that our Lord came into this world to undo the works of the devil. If He did not undo them all, He is not a perfect Savior. But you and I have a perfect Savior. He came to bring to nothing, to nullify, all the works of the devil, and the final thing, therefore, is the redemption of the body.

So Paul writes to the Christians in Philippi, "We look for the Savior, the Lord Jesus Christ: who shall change our vile body, that it may be fashioned like unto his glorious body, according to the working whereby he is able even to subdue all things unto himself" (Phil. 3:20-21). Or again Paul writes to the Romans, "Ourselves also, which have the firstfruits of the Spirit, even we ourselves groan within ourselves, waiting for the adoption, to wit, the redemption of our body" (Rom. 8:23). This is what the apostle Paul says at the height of his spiritual experience.

A day is coming when those who believe in Him, as John reminds us, shall see Him as He is and be made like Him (1 John 3:2). When He rose from the dead, His body was glorified; that is why the disciples on the road to Emmaus did not recognize Him. He came among the disciples, and they were terrified. Why? It was because, though His body was the same, yet it was different—a glorified body. Thank God, you and I can look forward to glorified bodies. Our spirits, immortal and free from all sin and every spot and wrinkle, shall be clothed in glorified bodies—the body will be redeemed.

Jesus Christ delivers us completely, and the Resurrection alone proves that. He is, as we have seen, "the firstborn among many brethren" (Rom. 8:29), "the firstfruits of them that slept" (1 Cor. 15:20). When He comes back, those who died in Christ will rise. "And the dead shall be raised incorruptible, and we shall be changed" (1 Cor. 15:52). We shall be given glorified bodies and shall spend eternity with Him in those bodies.

Lastly, the Resurrection is absolutely vital to us because it is proof that Christ will be the Judge of all. You remember how Paul put it in Athens?

When he spoke to the Stoics and Epicureans, the clever philosophers of Athens, they referred to him as "a babbler," but he preached to them and said, "The times of this ignorance God winked at; but now commandeth all men every where to repent"—why?—"because he hath appointed a day, in the which he will judge the world in righteousness by that man whom he hath ordained; whereof he hath given assurance unto all men, in that he hath raised him from the dead" (Acts 17:30-31).

Now it is a principle of justice in this land that you are judged by your peers, and all humanity will be judged by a man, the man Christ Jesus. He is the "ordained." God has given notice to the universe that there is to be a final judgment of the whole world, and the Judge will be the one who was born as a babe in Bethlehem and put in a manger, the little boy who could confound the doctors of the law at the age of twelve, the carpenter of Nazareth, the Jesus who began to preach at the age of thirty, the miracle-worker, the one who taught as no man had ever spoken hitherto. The Judge will be the one who died in apparent weakness and helplessness upon a cross and whose body they took down and laid in a tomb. But He rose again because He could not be held by death, because He is God as well as man. After He had shown Himself to His chosen witnesses, He ascended into heaven while they looked at Him—that is another fact. Then He gave final proof that He was who He said He was by sending the promised Spirit upon them. And now, filled with the Spirit, they gave with great power witness to Him, to His life, His death, His resurrection, His present activity, and His coming in glory to judge the universe in righteousness and to execute that judgment.

That is what the apostles preached, and I am preaching it now for the same reason. Can you not see the significance of all this? Why did the Son of God ever come into this world? Why did He ever die that death? Why was He ever buried? Why did He rise again? There is only one answer: It is the only way any one of us can ever be saved and avoid the condemnation of the law and the punishment of eternal death. The apostles constantly preached these things because they knew that men and women were going to hell. Death was nothing to these apostles. They had already passed from death to life. Having passed from judgment to life in Him, they were not afraid of death. They knew where they were going—they were going "to be with Christ; which is far better" (Phil. 1:23).

The disciples were not worrying about their own lives, and so in their prayer they did not ask that they might be relieved or released. No, they asked for power to go on preaching this message. These Jewish leaders were ignorant. They had crucified Christ in ignorance; they were still rejecting Him in ignorance. They did not know that they were under the condemnation of the law; they did not know that they were going to meet God in judgment. So the apostles prayed for power to tell them of their awful predicament and of what God Himself had done in His only begotten Son to save them. The apostles knew that the need of men and women was not primarily for happiness or health. Their need was to be saved, saved from the wrath to come, reconciled to God, made fit to meet Him at His coming and to enter with Him into the joys of eternity. Read again, I beseech you, the preaching of these apostles. Read these early chapters of Acts, and you will find that all along they went on preaching "Jesus and the resurrection" and the meaning of that.

So I am not asking you whether you are happy or miserable; I am not asking whether you are suffering from insomnia or whether you are the victim of various phobias. I am not asking you about your health problems. I have one great question to ask you because this is the question raised by these facts: Are you ready to meet God in the judgment? Do you know where you are going to spend eternity? That is the real meaning and significance of these facts.

"With great power gave the apostles witness to the resurrection of the Lord Jesus." Have you heard this witness? Have you believed it and accepted it? Have you submitted yourself completely to Him? If you have never done so before, do it now, and you will know that your sins are forgiven, that you are a child of God and a joint heir with Him of all the glories of God.

13

GOD THE HOLY SPIRIT

And when they had prayed, the place was shaken where they were assembled together; and they were all filled with the Holy Ghost, and they spake the word of God with boldness.

—Acts 4:31

Most people almost by instinct think of the Christian church as some tremendous institution that has existed in the world for a long time, with magnificent buildings, a powerful hierarchy, different orders—popes, bishops, archbishops, deacons—a great system that the state recognizes and uses when it suits her. That is what people think of Christianity; it is virtually a branch of the state, and it is characterized by considerable pomp and ceremony.

Then there are those within this great institution who seem to be spending most of their time in refined philosophical and theological disputations. Ordinary men and women do not know what they are talking about, and yet the theologians go on doing it; they live in some rarefied atmosphere. They bring out wonderful terms and concepts, and you are given the privilege sometimes of watching them on the television, and there is all this—something—but what?

Now all this has happened before under the old dispensation, the Old Testament. There had been a religion, and we can trace its origin, but the record shows us how it turned into something that was the exact opposite of what it had been at the beginning. When our Lord came, His greatest fight was with the religious authorities. The people who should have been foremost in giving Him a welcome, believing His message, surrendering themselves to Him, and following Him were the very people who rejected Him and incited others to do so. The religion of the Jews had become so hardened, fossilized, and institutionalized that it became the greatest enemy of the Christian faith.

This rejection by institutionalized religion still goes on, and I suggest that what is known as "Christendom," what the average person thinks of as the Christian church, is about as far removed from the church of the New Testament as can possibly be imagined. But why is all this important? It is because, according to the New Testament record, in the teaching of the apostles we are given the only truth that can save a man or woman. It does not make much difference what view you take of many of the things that are in the world. I am one of those who happens to think that it does not matter very much how you vote in a general election—it comes to much the same thing in the end. We make a great deal of fuss about such issues, but they are not vital.

But the claim that the Christian message makes is that our reaction to it not only determines what happens to us in this world, but it determines our eternal destiny. Our attitude to the Gospel leads to consequences that we will never be able to undo. This Gospel claims to be a message from God, not from man, and it is not, therefore, a matter for our opinion but for listening to what the almighty God Himself has said to us. It is indeed most urgent that we should be clear about this message that the world needs today above everything else.

Now we have seen that Christianity is not just a system of philosophy or a point of view. Nor is it a matter of moral behavior or one's view of ethics. No, Christianity is supernatural; it is miraculous; it is the action of the living God among men and women. Furthermore, Christianity is not merely an experience. There are many people today who say that it does not matter very much what people think as long as they have had an experience that does them good and makes better people of them. But we cannot accept that. Now I do agree that experience is essential: It must be since, by definition, Christianity is the action of God upon us. There is an important subjective element in the Christian faith, and, I repeat, if you and I have no experience— I do not care how slight it is—if we have no experience at all of God dealing with us, then we are not Christians. Christianity is the activity, the power, of God. We must have some experience. It may be inchoate; it may be partial and very small, but it must be there. Otherwise our faith is merely some arid, intellectual belief that is of no value.

But I am equally concerned that we do not take up the position of saying that it does not matter what leads to the experience as long as we have it. The amazing thing about this record in the Bible is that there are two sides to it. There is the subjective, the experimental, the experiential side, but there is also the objective side. It is this grand objective emphasis that I am anxious to hold before you now.

I have been emphasizing the historicity of what happened, and I am compelled to do this because that is the emphasis we find here in these early chapters of the book of Acts. Further, historicity is the answer to the psychological attack upon the Christian faith. The way you test the validity of an experience is to ask on what the experience is based. There are many agencies that can do people a lot of good; it is no use denying that. Many of the popular cults can do people good. Otherwise they would never succeed. Psychotherapists and doctors can help people by suggesting various causes and remedies for their troubles. There are many agencies that make people feel much happier, including drugs.

The charge is that we Christians emphasize experience. "You are just fooling yourselves," people say. "You've merely experienced some kind of autosuggestion, and it makes you feel happier and brighter. You sing and enjoy yourself. You work yourself up into some happy mood, avoiding the facts, running away from them, giving yourselves a psychological boost, and then go home feeling a little bit happier. But the problems come back, and you are in trouble again. So you return for another dose. The church is a dispensary giving out soothing drugs. It's all right," they continue. "We don't want to be critical. As long as your religion makes you better and happier, carry on, but don't expect us to join in with you." That is their argument. Religion is all right for people who have a temperamental or psychological makeup that is susceptible to religion, people with a religious complex.

But we deny that because Christianity is not merely subjective; it is equally objective, and the subjective element arises out of the objective. The answer to the psychological charge is these historical facts and events. This truth has already been brought out by the astonishing prayer offered by the early church, and it is brought out equally by the answer given to that prayer.

Notice these apostles. The proof that they did not merely have some subjective experience is that in their trouble they did not try to comfort themselves by some sort of autosuggestion;[3] they did not merely utter pious hopes and aspirations. No, they started with great objective facts—God the Father, God the Creator. They did not look in upon themselves and their own experience; they looked out. "They lifted up their voice to God with one accord, and said, Lord, thou art God, which hast made heaven, and earth, and the sea, and all that in them is . . ." We have considered that prayer. Like the psalmists, they started with God the Creator, and then they reminded themselves that God is the one who controls history.

In trouble, the people of God, even in the Old Testament, recapitulated their history: "God of Abraham, God of Isaac, God of Jacob, God of Moses, God of the children of Israel, God of the Red Sea." History! Events! This is the only basis for faith. They were not fooling themselves. They said, "We believe in this living God who has given proof that He is a living God; our history is full of this story."

The element of prophecy, too, was always important. In their very prayer here in Acts 4, the believers realized that David was prophesying the coming of the Messiah. They attached great significance to prophecy because it can be checked. Here were men writing eight hundred years earlier, and what they said would happen did happen. That is not persuading yourself; that is not autosuggestion. That is objective record, written down in considerable detail.

Then the believers talked about God the Son and about the things that they had seen and heard (Acts 4:20). They did not have a magical formula to make people happy. They just reported. They were witnesses to this person, and we have considered the great importance they placed on "Jesus and the resurrection." We have seen that "with great power gave the apostles witness of the resurrection." All these things accounted for the faith and assurance of the believers.

Yes, but I have still one more fact to put before you. These verses speak of God the Father, God the Son—and also of God the Holy Spirit. "When they had prayed, the place was shaken where they were assembled together; and they were all filled with the Holy Ghost." Now this is not the first time we have come across the power of the Holy Spirit as we have studied these early chapters of the book of Acts, but here it is again in the very context of this prayer. The Holy Spirit is a vital and an essential part of Christian preaching. Christianity is Trinitarian through and through. That sounds strange, does it not? But the way we differentiate between Christianity and every other religion or cult, or anything that pretends to be Christian, is by asking: Is it or is it not Trinitarian?

Now all this is not something that can be understood. If Christianity is miraculous and supernatural, by definition, it cannot be understood. I am sorry, Mr. Modern Man, even your great brain cannot understand miracles, and the sooner you realize that, the better. If the Gospel were something that you and I could understand, it would not be "the blessed gospel of the glorious God"; it would be a philosophy that we dissect and apprehend. This Gospel meets you at the very beginning by saying, "Take off your shoes!" That command came to Moses at the burning bush, and the same command was given to Joshua (Josh. 5:15).

We are all so clever; we see a phenomenon, and we bring our great minds to bear upon it: "I will now turn aside for a moment and examine this great phenomenon," said Moses. Modern men and women want to do that. They want to analyze God and understand Him, and they say, "I'm not going to believe a thing unless I can understand it." All right, my friend, you are not saying anything very original; people have said that from the very beginning, and that is why the world is as it is today. Men and women cannot understand themselves, but they are still foolish enough to say that they want to understand God and the miraculous and the supernatural! Because they cannot, they reject it, and their world becomes an increasing hell. Oh, the folly of modern humanity's confidence in its own intellect! I am here to preach to you a miraculous and supernatural Gospel, a Trinitarian message. Understand it? Of course not. Neither can I. I simply stand back with the apostle Paul and say, as I have said so many times before, "Great is the mystery of godliness: God was manifest in the flesh . . ." (1 Tim. 3:16). And I say the same about this great doctrine of the blessed holy Trinity.

What does this doctrine mean? It asserts a triune God; it asserts that there are three blessed persons in the Godhead—God the Father, God the Son, God the Holy Spirit. My business now is not to give you a nice comfortable feeling; it is not to enable you to forget your problems and troubles and trials for an hour or so. No, my business is to declare to you the truth, to declare what has been revealed. The three persons of the Trinity are coequal and coeternal; they are from everlasting to everlasting. But I want to emphasize as simply as I can that you and I are not just asked to believe this from the mouth of a preacher; we are asked to believe it because of the way in which these persons of the Godhead have manifested themselves in history. The Trinity is not known in experience only, but it is an objective revelation that took place in history. The three persons have made themselves known.

This revelation is to be seen first of all in the Old Testament. The Old Testament mainly, though not exclusively, reveals the activity of God the Father. As we read of the Creation, the Flood, the new race in Abraham—all their vicissitudes and everything that happened to them and to the other nations with respect to them—we see that God is all the time bringing His great purpose to pass.

Then we come to the four Gospels, and we look mainly at God the Son. "When the fullness of the time was come, God sent forth his Son, made of a woman, made under the law, to redeem them that were under the law" (Gal. 4:4-5). In the pages of the four Gospels we are not confronted by a theory but by a person, a concrete person who has entered into history. This is God the Son manifesting God in the flesh. "The Word was made flesh, and dwelt among us" (John 1:14). Our Lord said, "He that hath seen me hath seen the Father" (John 14:9). The invisible became visible.

Then here in the "Acts of the Apostles," as it is called, we are mainly looking at the activity of God the Holy Spirit. His work is as essential to the Christian message as the activity of the Father and of the Son. What is the teaching concerning the Holy Spirit? Let me summarize it. The Holy Spirit had acted in the Old Testament. We cannot read the first verses in Genesis without coming upon Him and something of His activity. "In the beginning God created the heaven and the earth. And the earth was without form, and void; and darkness was upon the face of the deep. And the Spirit of God moved upon the face of the waters" (Gen.1:1-2). The three blessed persons are involved in the whole story of the earth and the human race. The Holy Spirit was there taking His part in creation.

But the Holy Spirit's other great activity in the old dispensation was leading men to write the holy Scriptures. "All scripture is given by inspiration of God"—is God-breathed (2 Tim. 3:16). Read the accounts these Old Testament prophets give of how they received their message and how they came to write it, and you will find that they always say that "the burden of the Lord," "the Spirit of the Lord," came upon them. They were taken up. A divine afflatus took hold of them and possessed them, gave them a message, gave them understanding, and gave them the ability to write. They all disclaim that they were the authors of their messages. The great teaching is that it was the Holy Spirit, and He alone, who was the author of the holy Scriptures. They are the Word of God, and He is the agent in inspiration. This truth, of course, comes out particularly in the question of prophecy. The apostle Peter, in writing his second epistle, his last letter to the churches, puts this idea into those well-known words:

We have also a more sure word of prophecy; whereunto ye do well that ye take heed, as unto a light that shineth in a dark place, until the day dawn, and the day star arise in your hearts: knowing this first, that no prophecy of the scripture is of any private interpretation.
—2 Pet. 1:19-20

"You know," said Peter, in effect, "those men who wrote the prophecies, those prophets, were not just clever, able men." They were not the sort of people who write these special comments and articles in the Sunday press, the great thinkers who compose their weekly columns and give their understanding of events and times and make suggestions to governments, while the ordinary journalist is rushing backwards and forwards reporting the decisions of the courts. It was not like that. "No prophecy of the scripture is of any private interpretation." The Scripture does not originate from human understanding. So what was it? "For the prophecy came not in old time by the will of man: but holy men of God spake as they were moved [carried along] by the Holy Ghost" (v. 21). That is the Spirit's action in the Old Testament.

Now there is a great prophecy running right through the Old Testament that a day was coming when the Spirit of God would be poured out upon all flesh. We read it in the prophecy of Joel, and Peter quotes those very verses, you remember, in his sermon in Jerusalem on the day of Pentecost. People came crowding together asking, "What's happened?" Some said, "These men are drunk with new wine." But Peter, standing up with the eleven, said:

> *Ye men of Judaea, and all ye that dwell at Jerusalem, be this known unto you, and hearken to my words: for these are not drunken, as ye suppose, seeing it is but the third hour of the day. But this is that which was spoken by the prophet Joel; and it shall come to pass in the last days, saith God, I will pour out of my Spirit upon all flesh: and your sons and your daughters shall prophesy, and your young men shall see visions, and your old men shall dream dreams: and on my servants and on my handmaidens [fishermen and the like] I will pour out in those days of my Spirit; and they shall prophesy.*
> *—Acts 2:14-18*

The day would come when the activity of the Holy Spirit would not be partial as it had been in the time of the Old Testament, with an occasional person given a word of prophecy or a gift in connection with the building of the temple or something like that. The work of the Holy Spirit was to be no longer unusual and exceptional, but general, a profusion.

And Ezekiel 36 teaches exactly the same thing. The Old Testament prophets prophesied that a day would come when some mighty event would take place; a day would come when the Spirit of the living God would fall upon a body of people and revolutionize them, making them capable of doing things impossible by human strength. This outpouring would be a phenomenon, an amazing phenomenon. God would "take the stony heart out of their flesh" and "give them an heart of flesh" (Ezek. 11:19). He would fill them with the Spirit.

Then our Lord Himself promised the same thing. You can read this in the Gospels. On one occasion, the "great day of the feast" at Jerusalem, He said, "If any man thirst, let him come unto me and drink" (John 7:37). He said, "He that believeth on me, as the scripture hath said, out of his belly shall flow rivers of living water" (v. 38). He was talking there, says John, about the Spirit yet to be given—for the Spirit had not yet been given—"which they that believe on him should receive" (v. 39).

But not only that, in John 14 you will find Him saying, "Let not your heart be troubled. . . . I will not leave you comfortless" (John 14:1, 18). He would not leave them as orphans. He was going away, but He would send another Comforter; He would send the Spirit. Then in chapter 16, He says, "It is expedient for you that I go away: for if I go not away, the Comforter will not come unto you; but if I depart, I will send him unto you" (John 16:7). Can we believe Him? Is this the Son of God? How can I know that He is the Son of God? Well, by His resurrection. Yes, but not only that—by the sending of the Holy Spirit.

Later He again specifically promised the Holy Spirit. In Acts 1:7-8 we read, "He said unto them, It is not for you to know the times or the seasons, which the Father hath put in his own power. But ye shall receive power, after that the Holy Ghost is come upon you: and ye shall be witnesses unto me both in Jerusalem, and in all Judaea, and in Samaria, and unto the uttermost part of the earth." So, "Tarry ye in the city of Jerusalem," He said, "until ye be endued with power from on high" (Luke 24:49).

Now these are definite statements. This is not psychotherapy, not auto-suggestion, not some slogan that will make people feel a little bit happier. Here is a definite promise, a definite prophecy. It was as actual and as concrete as anything can be. You see the importance of this? The apostles were not men who had had a psychological experience. They were men who were comparing promise and fulfillment, prophecy and fact. These were men who were down to earth, men who were shattered when Jesus died but who were now rejoicing. Why? Because what He had said had come to pass.

And so the day of Pentecost is of vital importance in Christian preaching. Pentecost is one of the great acts of God—equally as important as the Incarnation, the death, the Resurrection, and the Ascension. These are the marvelous, wonderful works of God, and this day is one of the most marvelous of them all. You see, I am once more describing events to you. I am telling you something that happened in history. Here were a number of people, about 120, meeting together in a room where they had been praying for ten days. And then I read:

When the day of Pentecost was fully come, they were all with one accord in one place. And suddenly there came a sound from heaven as of a rushing mighty wind, and it filled all the house where they were sitting. And there appeared unto them cloven tongues like as of fire, and it sat upon each of them. And they were all filled with the Holy Ghost, and began to speak with other tongues, as the Spirit gave them utterance.

—Acts 2:1-4

Pentecost is a fact, an event.

Then later there they were, looking at one another, these poor Christian people. They were nobodies—no learning, no importance, no influence, no significance. Peter and John had been threatened and forbidden to preach and teach in the name of Jesus. If they disobeyed, they knew they faced extermination. Back they went to the others to give their report, and they began to pray, as we have seen. Suddenly we come across this sentence: "And when they had prayed, the place was shaken where they were assembled together."

Now that is another fact, an event. I am not just told that these people felt better and happier. They did—that is quite true. They were all filled with great joy, with great boldness. But the first thing we are told is that "the place was shaken." This is what I call divine humor, because modern people consider the idea of God shaking a building quite ridiculous. "Buildings don't shake," they say. They may say that, even though they know that buildings do shake, but, like the Sanhedrin, they try to explain facts away.

One of the most ludicrous attempts at an explanation is that what really happened was that these people were so terrified and were shaking so much that they thought the building was shaking. That theory is put forward quite seriously!

Unbelief is nothing but sheer nonsense. The Sanhedrin had not a leg to stand on. The healed beggar was staring them in the face, but they tried to wriggle out of accepting the miracle, and they made themselves ridiculous fools. The theory that the disciples were trembling does exactly the same thing. Peter and John, immediately after being threatened and warned in the most solemn manner, could look into the eyes of the members of the Sanhedrin and say to them, in effect, "You decide for yourselves whether we should listen to you or to God. We are telling you that we cannot but speak, and we shall continue to speak of the things that we have seen and heard." We are asked to believe that a few moments later these men had become so filled with craven fear and were shaking so much that they thought the building was shaking around them, and the others trembled with them! But these apostles were not concerned about themselves. They had not offered a single petition with regard to themselves and their own safety. All they had asked for was this: "Lord, behold their threatenings: and grant unto thy servants, that with all boldness they may speak thy word." God answered their prayer by shaking the building.

I repeat, this is one of the acts of God. It is objective and external, in series with the dividing of the Red Sea. God wanted His people to know that their faith was not reposed in Him in vain; it did not fall into some empty void. He said, as it were, "You are speaking to Me, making requests of Me, assuring Me that you believe that I am the living God, the creator of the ends of the earth and the sustainer of the universe, and that with Me nothing is impossible. I want to let you know that you are right, and here is the manifestation of My power." That is why the building shook. That is the objective side of our faith. The subjective aspect we shall deal with later, but I am holding before you now this great, grand objectivity—the acts, the facts, the happenings, the events! On these our faith is based.

These events are also a part of the proof of the living God. The message of Christianity is that the blessed holy Trinity is concerned about this old world in which you and I are living, this tragic world, this shameful world, this unhappy world of ours, this world that is hurtling, it knows not where, to some final cataclysmic destruction. Oh, what a message, and how we should thank God for it—that the blessed holy Trinity is concerned about our world, that They have a plan of redemption, and that They are cooperating in it! The Father produced His plan before the foundation of the world. He thought it out; it was the only way. And then the Son volunteered and came and carried out the plan. There is no hope for any of us apart from the Incarnation. As we have seen, if the Son of God had not come into this world, there would be no hope for anybody. Sin must be dealt with, and the Son did the work that was absolutely essential to our knowing God, being blessed of Him and delivered out of the destruction that is coming to this world. That is the Son's part.

Then the blessed Holy Spirit's part is to apply all that to us. All that is necessary has been done, but it must be applied. If the work of God on our behalf is not taken, if it is not applied, it cannot do any good. The astounding thing, we are told, is that the third person in the blessed Trinity, none other than the Holy Spirit, has been sent to apply to you and to me the great salvation achieved by the Son according to the dictates of the Father. This part is absolutely vital. The Spirit came on the day of Pentecost and began to act, and He has been acting ever since.

The Holy Spirit's activity can be divided into two main sections. He has a *regular* work, and, thank God, He is still doing it in the Christian church—convicting, converting, bringing to a rebirth, and sanctifying. This is His continuous work, and it is subjective, more or less. But now I am emphasizing the grand objectivity, and I want to hold something before you that I trust will be a great help to any weak Christian who may be almost frightened by the criticism of the world. Consider the objectivity of the action of the Holy Spirit! Where do I see it? Well, I have given you the great biblical evidence, but His activity does not stop there. You know, if I had no other reason for believing this Gospel, I sometimes think that my next point would be more than enough for me. Indeed, it played a great part in my coming to the Christian faith.

I had the privilege of being brought up in a country that has been known as "the land of revivals." Revivals! What am I talking about? I will tell you, and if you want to know whether or not there is a Holy Spirit, listen to the evidence of revivals and of reformation. They are what I call His *exceptional* work. He has His ordinary work, but He also has His exceptional work, and it stands out in the history of the church.

As you read history, you read about the dark Middle Ages when the church became not only institutionalized but even fossilized. It became something almost exactly opposite of all we read about in the book of Acts. The wealthy, arrogant, worldly Roman Catholic Church of the Middle Ages held everybody down in a condition of serfdom and in the darkness of spiritual ignorance, with a priestly tyranny worse even than a political tyranny. How utterly hopeless it all was.

But then came the Protestant Reformation. Martin Luther was able to stand up against that great institution and all its pomp and authority and power and its fifteen centuries of tradition. He shook it to its foundations, and the great Reformation came to pass. How did it happen? Was this the brilliance of Martin Luther? He was a very able man, quite a genius, but so was John Hus before him, so was John Wycliffe in England, and many another. But they could not do what Martin Luther was able to do—why not? Oh, this was the work of the Holy Spirit. It was not man; it was the Holy Spirit of God acting. No man, no body of men, could ever have shaken the Roman Catholic Church of the medieval period. But God the Holy Spirit through one man can do the impossible, and He did it.

We find exactly the same thing in the eighteenth century, two hundred years after the Reformation. England was in a most deplorable condition. In many ways she was as bad as she is today, if not worse. The moral condition was appalling. It was as if Christianity was finished. Churches were empty. People were scoffing. The rationalists, the deists, as they were called, were denying the miraculous and supernatural, denying the being of the Holy Spirit, and reducing Christianity to a bit of morality. There seemed no hope. But suddenly a boy called George Whitefield, brought up in a public house in Gloucester, began to preach in a manner that shook congregations, shook churches, and eventually shook England! This youth, this stripling, this mere nobody suddenly preached in a dynamic manner. He was later followed by the brothers Wesley, and the whole face of Britain was changed.

What is this? Oh, this is the Holy Spirit! He is living, He is vital, He is not a theory, He is not a force, He is not a suggestion. He is a living person, the third person of the blessed holy Trinity. And the same thing has happened in every other revival in the long course of the Christian church. The message of Christianity tells us what God has done—the God who made everything, the God who has not abandoned the world but is still acting. You have facts, you have evidence, you have objective events. These are as real as 55 B.C., or whenever it was that Julius Caesar first went to England and conquered it. The acts of the Holy Spirit belong to the very warp and woof of history—God's intervention.

But you ask why you should pay any attention to it.

I have already given the answer. One day you will be confronted by these facts, these events from history, and confronted by God the Father, God the Son, and God the Holy Spirit. The question the holy Trinity will ask each of us is this: "Why do you come to this last judgment in the state you are in, with your sins heavy upon you? Why do you come out of a life that has been one of entire carnality, living only to the flesh and the world and the devil, knowing nothing about Us and about the glorious possibilities We have offered? Why do you come like this?"

And you may try to say, "I didn't have the type of temperament that was interested in religion; I'm not an emotional type of person." You may say a thousand and one other things, but you will be silenced. You will just be asked: "What about the facts? What about the historical events? What about the 'wonderful works of God'? What about the babe lying in the manger in Bethlehem? What about the man on the cross? What about the empty tomb? What about Mount Olivet? What about the day of Pentecost at Jerusalem? What about the building shaking in Jerusalem? What about

Martin Luther, George Whitefield, and the Wesleys? What about men and women living in the same world as you, who once were exactly as you are? There they are. Look at them, shining bright, with the righteousness of the Son upon them, shining as the stars in the firmament. How have they become what they are?"

There is only one answer: They believed the facts and submitted to them. They repented and acknowledged and confessed their sins and believed on the Lord Jesus Christ as their Savior. Beloved people, face the facts of history, the facts concerning the Father, the facts concerning the Son, the facts concerning the Holy Spirit, and believe.

14

THE WORK OF THE HOLY SPIRIT

*And now, Lord, behold their threatenings: and grant unto thy
servants, that with all boldness they may speak thy word, by
stretching forth thine hand to heal; and that signs and wonders
may be done by the name of thy holy child Jesus. And when they
had prayed, the place was shaken where they were assembled
together; and they were all filled with the Holy Ghost, and they
spake the word of God with boldness. And the multitude of them
that believed were of one heart and of one soul: neither said any
of them that ought of the things which he possessed was his own;
but they had all things common. And with great power gave the
apostles witness of the resurrection of the Lord Jesus: and great
grace was upon them all.*

—Acts 4:29-33

The church consists of people who have believed the apostolic message and
who regard as facts the "wonderful works of God" culminating in the descent
of the Holy Spirit on the day of Pentecost and in His subsequent activities in
the church.

But how is all that related to us? We start by seeking the content of this
great message. Then we ask how this message comes to men and women. The
answer to the question is that the proclamation of the message was the very
thing about which the disciples prayed; that is why they prayed at all. They
were not praying, as you notice from the very terms of the prayer, about
themselves; they were not praying that they might be delivered or that these
opponents, these authorities, might be silenced. No, the prayer of the

Christian church at the beginning was for one thing. Peter and John had been told to go back and tell all their friends and helpers that they must no longer preach or teach or do anything "in the name of Jesus" (Acts 4:18). That is what made them pray.

The disciples prayed because the one thing they wanted to do was to go on preaching and teaching and working in the name of Jesus, and they realized that there was only one way they could do that—with God enabling them. They knew that they could not do it. Who were they? There was not a well-known man or woman among them—no influence, no authority, no money, no power, nothing. They were nobodies, and they were against the great authorities—the Sanhedrin, the Roman power behind that, and philosophers of Greece behind them. What could they do? They were helpless. There was only one thing to do, and that was to turn to God and ask Him to enable them.

So they did, and when they came to the application, this was how they put it: "Now, Lord, behold their threatenings: and grant unto thy servants, that with all boldness they may speak thy word, by stretching forth thine hand to heal; and that signs and wonders may be done by the name of thy holy child Jesus." It was a request for enabling to tell everybody about the things that they had seen and heard, these "wonderful works of God." The only deduction we can make is that this enabling is the special work of the Holy Spirit. We began in the last chapter to deal with the doctrine of the Holy Spirit as it is taught here, and we looked at the objective historical evidence of the working of the Holy Spirit. We are now looking at the same theme in a more subjective manner. The special work of the Holy Spirit is to make it possible for this message to be proclaimed and preached with holy boldness.

It is perfectly clear from the record here, as everywhere else in the New Testament, that the Holy Spirit enables Christians in two main ways. First, of course, He enables the preacher to preach the message. Now when I say "preacher," I do not only mean a man like myself standing in a pulpit. Anyone who tells someone else about these things is preaching. You will find that people preached in the early days, and have done so ever since, by talking to one another. In Acts 8 we read that there was a great persecution in Jerusalem, and the believers "were all scattered abroad throughout the regions of Judaea and Samaria, except the apostles" (v. 1). Then in verse 4 we read, "Therefore they that were scattered abroad went every where preaching the word." The Greek word used there for preaching means "speaking it." A good translation would be this: "they went everywhere gossiping the word," talking the word, explaining it to different people with whom they came in contact. The Holy Spirit enables Christians by giving them what is called in the New

Testament "unction"; He gives "anointing," understanding, freedom and clarity of speech, an authority.

Many terms can be used with respect to this God-given ability to preach. One quotation seems to me to sum it all up very well. Probably the first letter that Paul ever wrote was to the church at Thessalonica, and in the first chapter of the first epistle, he reminds the believers of how the Gospel had come to them: "Our gospel came not unto you in word only, but also in power, and in the Holy Ghost, and in much assurance" (1 Thess. 1:5). Paul was saying: "I did the speaking, but it was not I. I was used." As he was speaking, he knew that he was merely the vehicle, the channel, the instrument that the Holy Spirit was using. He was taken up; he was out of himself; he was, as it were, possessed by the Spirit, and he knew that he was preaching with "much assurance." Everything was against him. Thessalonica was a pagan city, part of Macedonia. The people did not have a Jewish background or the Old Testament Scriptures; they did not know the prophets; they knew nothing. They were living a life of sin and degradation in utter ignorance, and yet when the apostle appeared among them, he was able to speak with assurance. Why? Because it was not his word only, but he spoke "in power, and in the Holy Ghost."

Peter and all the apostles said exactly the same thing. Their experience was the same, and they had to describe it in the same way. Peter says:

Of which salvation the prophets have inquired and searched diligently, who prophesied of the grace that should come unto you: searching what, or what manner of time the Spirit of Christ which was in them did signify, when it testified beforehand the sufferings of Christ, and the glory that should follow. [Then notice:] Unto whom it was revealed, that not unto themselves, but unto us they did minister the things, which are now reported unto you by them that have preached the gospel unto you with the Holy Ghost sent down from heaven; which things the angels desire to look into.
—1 Pet. 1:10-12

The point Peter is making is that the Gospel, "these things," had been reported to them "by the Holy Ghost sent down from heaven." The Holy Spirit was using the preacher. That is what I mean by "unction" and by "power." That is how this "good news" and these "wonderful works of God" have been made known. The Holy Spirit takes people and helps them to speak in a clear manner.

In addition, from time to time signs are given of this great power of the Spirit. The people actually prayed for them here. They were not only asking "that with all boldness they may speak the word," but they also prayed, "by stretching forth thine hand to heal; and that signs and wonders may be done by the name of thy holy child Jesus." The apostles had seen our Lord working His miracles, and He had told them that He would enable them to do the same. They had had the experience of Pentecost; they had been speaking in tongues, and they had seen miracles. Peter and John had worked a miracle, and they knew that this gave authority and authentication. The miracle is not greater than the power of the Word; it is an accompanying demonstration. Indeed, in a sense, it is on a lower level because it is visual, and the visual often appeals to people very much more than the purely spoken. So at the beginning these signs did accompany the preaching of the Gospel.

You find the same thing stated in the epistle to the Hebrews: "How shall we escape, if we neglect so great salvation; which at the first began to be spoken by the Lord, and was confirmed unto us by them that heard him; God also bearing them witness, both with signs and wonders, and with divers miracles, and gifts of the Holy Ghost, according to his own will" (Heb. 2:3-4). Now notice these words. They could not perform these miracles whenever they wanted to. It was "according to his will." At times the preaching was accompanied by visible manifestations. If you read the accounts of the great revivals throughout the long history of the Christian church, you will find that in times of revival phenomena do occur, as if in a time of unusual difficulty God were saying, "I must now manifest this power in a visible manner as well as in the power of the preacher." But the ability to preach and to do miracles both constitute the enabling.

Now that is the balance in these matters. There may be signs, or there may not be signs, and the power of the Spirit is as manifest in authoritative, converting preaching, such as you get in great revivals, as in the most spectacular miracles. It is the same authority, the same Holy Spirit, at work in both.

That is the way the Holy Spirit works, but there is another—His action upon the listeners. If the Holy Spirit only acted on the preacher, there would be no conversions. The supreme example of the Spirit's action on the hearers is what happened when Peter was preaching in Jerusalem on the day of Pentecost. In Acts 2 we read that halfway through his sermon, as he was expounding the Scriptures, the people "were pricked in their heart, and said unto Peter and to the rest of the apostles, Men and brethren, what shall we do?" (v. 37). The Holy Spirit did the pricking. It was not Peter's sermon, which was a straightforward exposition of Scripture. The power, the convicting power of the Holy Spirit, was there working in the listeners. On that day three thousand were added to the church. The beginning of chapter 4 tells us that in the next day or so another two thousand were added.

This, then, is the dual action of the Spirit. He takes the preacher, the speaker, whether in a pulpit or in private, and gives this enabling. Then the Holy Spirit acts upon the ones who are listening and deals with their minds and hearts and wills. Both things happen at the same time.

Next I want to emphasize the way in which the Holy Spirit acts. It is all put here before us in a most remarkable manner. The believers prayed, "Now, Lord, behold their threatenings: and grant unto thy servants, that with all boldness they may speak thy word." They always put first "thy word." Then they asked for "signs and wonders." Why? That the word may be confirmed and demonstrated. Then we read, "When they had prayed, the place was shaken where they were assembled together; and they were all filled with the Holy Ghost." What did that lead to? "They spake the word of God with boldness." We must never separate these two: "the Holy Spirit," "the word of God." If we ever do, we shall go astray.

Some people put their emphasis only on the "word." These are the intellectuals. "Ah," they say, "nothing matters but the word." They spend their time reading and studying, and they become authorities on theology. As a result, they may become proud of their own great knowledge, and they may get the admiration of others who join in with them, but this is nothing but a little mutual admiration society. Nobody is converted; nobody is convicted. Heads packed with knowledge and understanding only—useless! "Word only," you see.

And there are people who put the whole of their emphasis on the Holy Spirit. They are not interested in the Word. They say, "It doesn't matter what a person believes." I heard of a man recently who shouted out in a great meeting, "Let yourselves go! Let yourselves go!" And they did let themselves go, I am told. But the New Testament has never told anybody to let himself go. Never! The Holy Spirit does not merely produce an experience; the Holy Spirit uses the Word. He is the Spirit of truth, the Spirit of enlightenment. He is the Spirit who leads to understanding. We must never jettison the intellect God has given us. The Holy Spirit can deal with our brains as well as with any other part of us. It is a false teaching that urges people to let themselves go. If you do that, you are letting yourself go to a riot of the imagination and of the feelings. You are letting yourself go to evil spirits and powers that are around and about you and ever ready to possess you and to use you and to fool you. The Spirit and the Word! "They spake the word of God." I repeat, the Word and the Spirit must never be separated.

Here is the work and the function of the Holy Spirit. He takes these facts—the wonderful works of God, the things that the apostles had seen and heard—and then shows their meaning. Christian preaching is not merely exhortation; it is not merely appeal; it is the recital of facts. The Holy Spirit enables people to bear witness to the facts, and then He shows their meaning and their significance to those listening.

So the early Christians prayed, "Lord, behold their threatenings: and grant unto thy servants, that with all boldness they may speak thy word." They did not merely ask for signs and miracles; they asked that these might accompany the preaching in order that the Word might be demonstrated. The Word is vital, and it is always the Word concerning the Lord Jesus Christ. The Holy Spirit is sent to glorify Him. Our Lord Himself said, "He shall glorify me" (John 16:14), and He always does. In this book of Acts, which some people say should be called the Acts of the Holy Spirit, what does the Holy Spirit do? The answer is: He always glorifies the Lord Jesus Christ. That is the prayer here: ". . . that signs and wonders may be done by the name of thy holy child Jesus."

So how exactly does the Spirit do this work of bringing glory to Jesus? I suggest that the best exposition of this section of Acts 4 is to be found in our Lord's own words. When He was talking to the disciples about the Holy Spirit, He said, "And when he is come, he will reprove the world of sin, and of righteousness, and of judgment: of sin, because they believe not on me; of righteousness, because I go to my Father, and ye see me no more; of judgment, because the prince of this world is judged" (John 16:8-11).

Let me start with this word *reprove*. "When he is come, he will reprove the world of sin . . ." It is generally agreed—and I concur with the commentators—that *reprove* is not a very good translation here in the Authorized Version. You will find, as you look up the various translations, that they vary between two words. About half use the word *convict*, and the other half use the word *convince*. I suggest that both are right and that both together are much better than the word *reprove*.

The element of reproof comes in, of course, but the Holy Spirit does more than that. There is an element of conviction and also of convincing. There is a vital difference between conviction and convincing. To convict is to establish a charge—to bring a charge home. But here is an important distinction. Take the example of a man in court on a criminal charge, a prisoner in the dock on trial. Now that man can be convicted though he may protest his innocence to the end. The fact that he is convicted of the crime does not mean that he admits that he has done it and pleads guilty. The jury may bring in a verdict of guilty; they may convict the man of the crime while he violently disagrees with the verdict. However, the fact that the prisoner does not agree with the verdict does not make the slightest difference; it is the court that convicts him. He is a convicted prisoner and is condemned as a result.

Now when we consider our standing before God, this distinction is of tremendous importance. The Holy Spirit always convicts—always. But He does not always convince, and in this book of Acts you will find many instances of people convicted without being convinced. The story of Stephen in Acts 7 is an illustration. Stephen the evangelist has been preaching, and in the application of his sermon he says, "Ye stiffnecked and uncircumcised in heart and ears, ye do always resist the Holy Ghost" (Acts 7:51). Now you cannot "resist the Holy Ghost" without feeling something of his convicting power. Only those who have felt something of the power of the Spirit resist the Spirit. But Stephen says, ". . . as your fathers did, so do ye. Which of the prophets have not your fathers persecuted? and they have slain them which showed before of the coming of the Just One . . ." Then notice: "When they heard these things, they were cut to the heart, and they gnashed on him with their teeth" (vv. 51-52, 54).

What made them do that? When you disagree with something, you do not "gnash your teeth," do you? You just say, "I don't agree." You may get a bit heated about it, and you may begin to shout, but you do not gnash your teeth! Why not? Because you are not "cut to the heart." What cuts to the heart? That was the Holy Spirit convicting and bringing the message home, and they hated it. They gnashed their teeth and murdered Stephen. That is a case of being convicted without being convinced.

There is another example in the famous case at the end of Acts 24 where the apostle Paul, the prisoner, addresses Felix and Drusilla. This is what we read: "And as he [Paul] reasoned of righteousness, temperance, and judgment to come, Felix trembled." Then he stopped Paul and said, "Go thy way for this time; when I have a convenient season, I will call for thee" (Acts 24:25). What was happening there? You have often listened to things you do not agree with, but they do not make you tremble. Here was a man trembling. He was a great Roman governor, but he trembled; his knees knocked. Why? Oh, it was the conviction of the Holy Spirit, but he resisted.

The Greek word translated *reprove* also carries the notion of convincing. Now here is a man who agrees with the sentence and who pleads guilty. He is not only convicted, but he is convinced. In the great story in Acts, that was what happened to the three thousand on the day of Pentecost—they were convicted and also convinced. Having cried out in agony saying, "Men and brethren, what shall we do?" they repented and believed and were baptized; they joined the apostles.

We also find this happening under the preaching of Philip in Samaria (Acts 8:12) and when he preached to just one man, the Ethiopian eunuch (Acts 8:36-38). And there are other examples—Cornelius and his household (Acts 10), Lydia in Philippi (Acts 16:14-15); the examples are endless. Paul talked about this convincing in so many of his epistles. To the Thessalonians he said: "For our gospel came not unto you in word only, but also in power, and in the Holy Ghost, and in much assurance. . . . And ye became followers of us, and of the Lord, having received the word in much affliction. . . . ye turned to God from idols to serve the living and true God" (1 Thess. 1:5-6, 9). These people were not only convicted, but they were convinced. So in John 16 our Lord is saying that when the Spirit comes, He will convict and convince. I repeat that both aspects are of tremendous importance.

Here in John 16 our Lord says that the Holy Spirit will convict the whole world, and by His very coming on the day of Pentecost, that is what He did. The coming of the Holy Spirit was a vindication and proof of the prophecies and a fulfillment of the promises given by the Lord Jesus Christ Himself (John 14:16, 26; 16:7). So the coming of the Holy Spirit is a proof of who our Lord is, and that is how He convicts all who do not believe.

The Holy Spirit convinces by enabling men and women to believe—as we have seen. I want to impress upon you that it is He alone who can do that. Nobody can convince anybody about the truth of these things apart from the Holy Spirit. That is why our Lord said to the apostles, "Tarry ye in the city of Jerusalem, until ye be endued with power from on high" (Luke 24:49). They knew all the facts; they had been eyewitnesses of them. But it was not enough; they would never convince anybody until the power of the Spirit was upon them. He alone can enlighten and convince.

The Holy Spirit divides humanity into two groups—those who are only convicted and those who are also convinced. In 1 Corinthians 2 Paul puts this before us with unusual clarity: "Which none of the princes of this world knew" (v. 8). The princes of this world—the great men, the philosophers, members of royal families, leaders in science and in thought—they do not know Christ. They are blind. "The natural man receiveth not the things of the Spirit of God: for they are foolishness unto him" (v. 14). There is all your human wisdom.

But, thank God, there is another group of people:

But God hath revealed them unto us by his Spirit: for the Spirit searcheth all things, yea, the deep things of God. . . . Now we have received, not the spirit of the world, but the spirit which is of God; that we might know the things that are freely given to us of God. Which things also we speak, not in the words which man's wisdom teacheth, but which the Holy Ghost teacheth; comparing spiritual things with spiritual. . . . But he that is spiritual judgeth all things, yet he himself is judged of no man.
—1 Corinthians 2:10, 12, 13, 15

The "wonderful works of God" have happened. But the majority of people do not believe them because these people have never been convinced by the Holy Spirit. Again in 1 Corinthians 2, the apostle says, "I was with you in weakness, and in fear, and in much trembling. And my speech and my preaching was not with enticing words of man's wisdom" (vv. 3-4). "Man's wisdom" includes all methods. There is to be no playing about with lights and putting on a show, no entertaining people in order to get at them and win them, no psychological treatment. The Lord abhors any such things. "Not with enticing words of man's wisdom, but in demonstration of the Spirit and of power" (v. 4). There were no tricks in the work of the apostle Paul. He goes on: "That your faith should not stand in the wisdom of men"—in human cleverness and tricks and games—"but in the power of God" (v. 5). You can get adherents. You can get people to join your church, but you do not thereby make them Christians. The Holy Spirit alone can convince.

Then in John 16 our Lord goes on to tell us how the Holy Spirit convicts and convinces. It is always in terms of the truth. Men and women who do not know what they believe cannot, by definition, be Christians. The Holy Spirit always uses the truth, the Word of God, "thy word." And our Lord tells us what truths are involved: "When he is come, he will reprove [convict and convince] the world of sin, and of righteousness, and of judgment." Those were His themes, and they are still His themes today. This is still the message of Christianity—the Word of God, the word that the authorities do not like and try to prohibit. It is a word about sin, about disobedience to God, about self-will, about going our own way, about turning our backs upon Him and refusing what He tells us.

But our Lord particularizes, you notice. He says, "He will convict the world of sin"—in this way—"because they believe not in me." He means that there is nothing that so demonstrates and proves human sinfulness and blindness as the failure to recognize the Son of God. As Paul has reminded us, this blindness is as true of "the princes of this world" as it is of the common peo-ple. The fact that you have read a number of books does not help you at all to become a Christian. You are in the same position as the person who has read nothing. Christianity does not depend in any shape or form upon human wisdom.

"Oh," you say, "but I thought you told us just now not to let our-selves go."

I am still saying that. But I am saying that through your reading, the wis-dom that you garner from books will not help you. The Holy Spirit addresses the truth to your mind, and He wants you to use your mind. You must know what you believe.

In the blindness that fails to recognize Him, the world is convicted of its sin. It is the blindness that did not recognize the baby in the manger. Charles Wesley looks at Him and says:

> *Veiled in flesh, the Godhead see;*
> *Hail the incarnate Deity.*

The wise men recognized Him; they brought their gifts of gold, frankin-cense, and myrrh. They were coming to acknowledge a King! *They* saw Him, but the world did not. It was the world that would not make room in the inn for His mother about to give birth to Him, so that the baby had to be born in a stable with the cattle and the straw.

The world did not recognize the boy in the temple or the carpenter, this unusual man, or the young man bursting forth to preach at the age of thirty. They had to admit that they had never heard such gracious words falling from anybody's lips, and yet they did not recognize Him. At last they crucified Him, rejecting Him. The blindness that failed to recognize Him is due to sin. The Holy Spirit convicts people of sin "because they believe not on me."

And, secondly, there is the blindness that prevents the people from see-ing their need of Him. They looked Him in the face. They questioned Him. They even tried to beat Him in argument, to trap Him and weave a web around Him. They thought they were clever, but it was the Son of God they were opposing. Are you? If you are, you are the biggest fool in the universe and at the same time the biggest sinner. Sin fails to recognize Him because it has never seen its need of Him. The self-sufficient men and women judge God and Christ and everything else. They cannot live their own lives, of course, but they do not hesitate to express their great opinions! Oh, the blindness, the sinfulness of humanity that has not seen its need and is in such darkness that when He comes, it fails to fall at His feet and say, "Thank God, He has come. The Savior has arrived!" "Of sin, because they believe not on me."

And then "of righteousness." "Of righteousness," said our Lord, "because I go to my Father, and ye see me no more." He claimed to be "the righteous one." He said, "I and my Father are one" (John 10:30). The clever world looked at Him and said, "This man is a blasphemer. He says he's equal with God. He claims he has come from God. He has said, 'Before Abraham was, I am'; 'I and my Father are one'; 'He who hath seen me hath seen the Father.' This man is an imposter, a liar! Away with him!"

But our Lord said that when the Holy Spirit came, He would prove that Christ was the righteous one He claimed to be.

And, of course, the Holy Spirit did. The Resurrection in itself proved His claims. But then Christ sent the Holy Spirit, as He had said He would, and, as we have seen, this is the final and the absolute proof that He is the Son of God. He had been given this gift by His Father, and He showered it upon His people. The Holy Spirit would "convince the world of righteousness."

But there is a second meaning to these words in John 16:8-11. Our Lord is saying that the Holy Spirit teaches us and convinces us that He alone can make us righteous. That is what we need, is it not? "How should a man be just with God?" asked Job (Job 9:2). What can I do about my sins? How can I get rid of them? How can I stand before God in the judgment? How can I pray to God while I am still in this world? Can I live a good and a clean and a pure life—is it possible? Is any righteousness possible to a mortal human being? I know failure, sin, and degradation. Is it possible for me to approach God without terror and alarm? Is it possible for me to pray with a holy boldness to the holy one seated upon the throne of the universe? And our Lord assures us that when the Holy Spirit comes, He will convince people that there is only one way whereby they can ever be made righteous, and that is by believing in Christ.

Paul wrote, "For he [God] hath made him to be sin for us, who knew no sin; that we might be made the righteousness of God in him" (2 Cor. 5:21). The Holy Spirit alone enables us to see that. A man stands up and says, "Right; I'm ready to meet God. I've lived a good life. I've never gotten drunk, never committed adultery. I'm not guilty of murder. I've always lived to do good and have never done anybody any harm." He stands on his own feet, and he will be blown away like the chaff, as the first psalm puts it. Righteousness! "All our righteousnesses," as the Old Testament says, "are as filthy rags" (Isa. 64:6). "Ye are they," said our Lord to the Pharisees, "which justify yourselves before men; but God knoweth your hearts: for that which is highly esteemed among men is abomination in the sight of God" (Luke 16:15).

Let Saul of Tarsus have the last word. He had gloried in his righteousness as a Pharisee. He was, he says, "circumcised the eighth day, of the stock of Israel, of the tribe of Benjamin, an Hebrew of the Hebrews . . . touching the righteousness which is in the law, blameless." But then he continues, "But what things were gain to me, those I counted loss for Christ. Yea doubtless, and I count all things but loss"—as dung and refuse—". . . [that I might know] the righteousness which is of God by faith"—the righteousness of Christ (Phil. 3:5-9). What brought him to see that? The Holy Spirit. The proud Pharisee had to be convicted and convinced and smashed. On the road to Damascus he cried out, "Lord, what wilt thou have me to do?" (Acts 9:6). He surrendered to the righteousness of the righteous one, the one who died that his sins might be blotted out, who offered him His own righteousness for clothing and enabled him to know what Count Zinzendorf and John Wesley would know centuries later:

> *Jesus, Thy blood and righteousness*
> *My beauty are, my glorious dress;*
> *'Midst flaming worlds, in these arrayed,*
> *With joy shall I lift up my head.*
> Nicholas Ludwig von Zinzendorf
> Translated by John Wesley

The Holy Spirit would convince of righteousness because our Lord was going to the Father, there ever to live and to intercede on behalf of those who believed in Him and to guarantee their righteousness to all eternity.

Lastly, the Holy Spirit "will convince the world . . . of judgment, because the prince of this world is judged." "The prince of this world" is the devil, and our Lord is saying here that the Holy Spirit, using the Word, will convict and convince concerning the final judgment. The Spirit will do that, our Lord says, by demonstrating that the devil is already judged. How? Well, if you know the facts, if you know the "wonderful works of God," if you know the things that Peter and John and the other apostles had seen and had heard, you know the answer. The cross and the Resurrection were a complete defeat of the devil. Our Lord had said this before He died: "Now is the judgment of this world: now shall the prince of this world be cast out" (John 12:31). As Paul puts it to the Colossians: "And having spoiled principalities and powers, he made a show of them openly, triumphing over them in it [the cross]"

(Col. 2:15). These evil powers thought they had gotten Him—this was their ultimate achievement. They were going to kill Him, and that would be the end. They thought they had succeeded.

But He arose, and He sent the Spirit, and thereby He routed them completely, proving that they were all wrong and that He is completely right. Furthermore, His vindication is seen not only in the cross and the Resurrection, but the very fact that one single person has ever believed this Gospel is a proof that "the prince of this world" has been defeated and cast out and judged.

"How can you say that?" asks someone.

It is very simple. Why do men and women not believe this Gospel? The apostle Paul gives one of the answers. He says, "But if our gospel be hid, it is hid to them that are lost: in whom the god of this world hath blinded the minds of them which believe not, lest the light of the glorious gospel of Christ, who is the image of God, should shine unto them" (2 Cor. 4:3-4). People are unbelievers for one reason only. They are not prevented by learning or academic qualifications or by the great science of the twentieth century. No, "the god of the world" has blinded their eyes and minds. He holds everyone in captivity. The fact that one soul has ever believed this Gospel is an absolute proof in itself of the judgment and downfall of the devil.

This is why the angels in heaven are singing. You remember the parable of the lost coin? Our Lord said, "There is joy in the presence of the angels of God over one sinner that repenteth" (Luke 15:10). Why? Oh, they know, they understand. They see this fiend that has dominated the world, "the god of this world" that has turned men and women away from God, ruined the creation, and brought disaster upon all the progeny of Adam. They know how he has held people captive. But here is a man or woman believing, and that proves that the devil has been absolutely defeated.

Finally, the Holy Spirit proves that the devil is defeated by delivering us from his power. As we have seen, from birth we are all the slaves of sin and of Satan. Only one thing can ever deliver us, and that is the Gospel preached with the unction and authority and power of the Holy Spirit. Our Lord Himself told Saul of Tarsus when He apprehended him on the road to Damascus: "Rise, and stand upon thy feet: for I have appeared unto thee for this purpose, to make thee a minister and a witness both of these things which thou hast seen, and of those things in the which I will appear unto thee"— listen—"delivering thee from the people, and from the Gentiles, unto whom now I send thee"—what for?—"to open their eyes, and to turn them from darkness to light, and from the power of Satan unto God" (Acts 26:16-18).

That is the work of the Holy Spirit, and whenever a man or woman is delivered from the power of the world, the flesh, and the devil, the power of sin and evil, it is a victory for Christ. The Holy Spirit had done it, and in this way He shows how Christ has defeated Satan with all his wiles and power.

But listen once more to Paul. He is thanking God for the Colossians, and he says, "Giving thanks unto the Father, which hath made us meet [fit to be] partakers of the inheritance of the saints in light: who hath delivered us from the power of darkness, and hath translated us into the kingdom of his dear Son" (Col. 1:12-13). That transaction involves the defeat of the devil every time. He does not want to lose a single citizen; he will hold on to you; he will ridicule this Gospel; he will ridicule preaching; he will make you read articles that say it is all rubbish; he will put scientists before you on your television screen; he will give you great names who are against it. There is nothing he will not do just to hold you in captivity.

But, thank God, "Greater is he that is in you, than he that is in the world" (1 John 4:4). The Holy Spirit can open blind eyes. He is God, remember. He can give life anew. He regenerates as well as convicts. He can give power and understanding. He can give you "the mind of Christ." He can reveal the hidden things to you, and you will see them and believe them, and you will begin to rejoice in them. "When a strong man armed keepeth his palace, his goods are in peace: but when a stronger than he shall come upon him, and overcome him, he taketh from him all his armour wherein he trusted, and divideth his spoils" (Luke 11:21-22).

Here is the message: The Holy Spirit will do this. He will convince and convict the world of sin and of righteousness and of judgment. The devil is judged! The Spirit proves it. And you and I can be free—free to believe God, free to enjoy God, free to worship God, free to pray to God, free to live in a manner worthy of the glorious liberty of the children of God. That is the Spirit's work.

15

PEACE ON EARTH

*And the multitude of them that believed were of one heart and of
one soul: neither said any of them that ought of the things which
he possessed was his own; but they had all things common. . . .
Neither was there any among them that lacked: for as many as
were possessors of lands or houses sold them, and brought the
prices of the things that were sold, and laid them down at the
apostles' feet: and distribution was made unto every man
according as he had need.*

—Acts 4:32, 34-35

We have seen that the church came into being as the result of the apostolic
message preached and delivered in the power of the Holy Spirit. We saw that
this message had a mighty influence upon men and women. We have read of
the three thousand saved on the day of Pentecost and the two thousand probably converted on the next day, and we are told that the church continued to
grow from day to day: "And the Lord added to the church daily such as
should be saved" (Acts 2:47). That is how Luke sums it up in his history. But
now we must look at this society, the community of people, that thus came
into being.

We have already been told in the second chapter that ". . . they continued stedfastly in the apostles' doctrine and fellowship, and in breaking of
bread, and in prayers" (Acts 2:42). They met together in one another's
houses, eating bread, talking about these things, praying together, and, above
all, rejoicing together and praising God. That is the Christian church. Not
some mighty institution with potentates and powers and great ecclesiastics.

Those are the accretions of men and women and of the centuries. No, here in Acts we see the Christian church.

And now in this passage, we are reminded particularly of the character of this community, and what we are told is that they had "all things common." It is a picture of wonderful peace, a picture of unity, a picture of brotherhood, of fellowship. I want to try to show you how this fellowship was, in and of itself, a proof of the Gospel, because nothing but the Gospel of Christ ever will produce the state of affairs described in these verses.

"But," says someone, "this is a kind of primitive communism. That is what communism produces. It makes all people equal so that they share all their goods. In Acts 4 we see nothing but an example of a failed experiment at communism. People have repeated this experiment from time to time; some people, the Levellers and others, tried it in the seventeenth century, and the only hope for this world today is that we accept this principle of communism and share everything in this way."

But was this communism? I would suggest that it was not and that it is amazing that anybody should have imagined that it was. I want to try to show you that it was the exact opposite of communism or of any other human effort to produce that kind of community. What is the difference between the two? Well, there is one difference in this account that is enough in and of itself to prove my point. You notice that what happened here was entirely voluntary. How much of the voluntary principle is there in Russia[4] or in any other Communist country? Nothing is voluntary where there is communism. This system carries out its purposes by the power of the sword, by force. If you defy it, you are eliminated. Communism has eliminated (to use that terrible term) probably more people than even Nazism did. No, this Christian community was the antithesis of communism. Communism imposes an equality. In the early church there was a voluntary equality and a rejoicing in that. Nothing was done in a spirit of fear because the secret police were watching and you had no choice. It was the exact opposite of some imposed system.

As Christmas comes around year by year, men and women talk of peace, but the world remains torn and in trouble. We see problems in countries, nations breaking up, diplomatic relations severed, and fighting in various places. I need not remind you of the sorry catalogue. The world is sick and wretched, torn by strife and war and bloodshed.

Throughout its long history, humanity has been seeking peace, unity, fellowship, and brotherhood. There is a great deal of talk about peace, and institutions are set up one after another. They are given different names—the League of Nations at one time, the United Nations at another—but they amount to the same thing. The world has always been dreaming this dream and has done its utmost to produce some kind of organization that will really deal with the problem of humanity at strife. The world is seeking peace today as much as it has ever done, but it is obvious that the world can never produce it. If it could, it would have done so, but it has failed, and it is failing now.

It is against that background that we shall consider together this description of the early church. Here is the very thing that the world has been looking for and cannot find. Yet this is what you always have among true Christian people. Let us, then, ask the first obvious question: Why is it that the world lacks peace? Why do nations persist in their policies of bloodshed, division, and building these terrible armaments? We are especially compelled to ask that question at the present time because men and women, in particular at the end of the nineteenth century, were so confident that they were going to produce a state of peace. All those poets of the mid and late Victorian era simply expressed what everybody thought. I do not think that in the whole of human history there has ever been anything more pathetic than the confidence of that era—belief in the parliament of man, the federation of the world, and the Golden Age to come.

Now until you answer that first question, you have no right to go any further. I once more suggest to you that there is only one answer to the problem— the answer you find in this book called the Bible. If I had no other reason for believing this book, I would believe it because it is the only book that I know of that makes an accurate diagnosis. It is because the world has never really discovered its ultimate problem that all its efforts at amelioration fail. They are bound to fail. If your diagnosis is wrong, your treatment must be wrong.

So we must start with the Bible's explanation of these problems, and it can be put as simply as this: All humanity's problems are due to a wrong relationship with God. That is the whole of the trouble. The statesmen, the delegates in the United Nations, are looking, as somebody put it, "horizontally." They are looking at one another, forgetting God, and that is why all their efforts are futile. The problem is not primarily between one person and another. It is between humanity and God. The prophet Isaiah makes a great statement, which he repeats, and it is the key to the modern problem: "There is no peace, saith the LORD, unto the wicked" (Isa. 48:22; 57:21). That is a terrible statement, but it is true. However advanced, however developed, however learned, however wealthy, however important nations may be, they will never know peace while they are wicked, and "wicked" means, of course, in a wrong relationship with God. All the troubles of men and women result from the fact that they are in a state of sin and rebellion against God.

If you look at any other proffered explanation of the state of the world, you will find that the biblical explanation is never mentioned, and that is why all attempts to deal with the problem come to nothing. The truth about men and women is that they were made to be God-centered in their very nature and being. They did not make themselves; they have not just happened; they are not the result of an accident. They were created by God, and they were made in such a way that they can only function truly and successfully and happily as long as they obey God's laws, the laws of their nature.

Now there is no use in objecting to that, any more than there is any point in objecting to the way a watch is made. My watch functions by being wound up. It works according to the laws of its manufacture. Human beings are exactly the same, but they object to this and consequently get into trouble. They are fighting against their own constitution; they are fighting against the laws of their own being and of their own creation, and hence all their trouble. The happiness of men and women always depends upon their relationship to God. How anybody who has ever read the Bible can dispute that passes my comprehension.

You find great people in the Bible. You see them in despair, and then you see them rejoicing and happy. What accounts for the change? It is invariably a question of their relationship to God. Look at a man like David. You read some of his great psalms, and you find him rejoicing. He cries out to God, "The LORD is my shepherd; I shall not want" (Psa. 23:1). But then in Psalm 51 you see him in a condition of wretchedness and misery. He cries out, "Create in me a clean heart, O God; and renew a right spirit within me" (Psa. 51:10). What is wrong? Why the difference? Oh, it is always explained by his relationship to God. When he obeys God, he sings the Twenty-third Psalm. When he disobeys and rebels, he is down in the depths of Psalm 51. This universal law runs through the whole of the history of the Old Testament. It is the same with the New and in the story of humanity everywhere.

Man was never meant to be the master but the obedient servant. God is the Lord, the Master, the Governor of the universe, and man was made to obey His laws. If the man and woman had obeyed, the world would have continued to be paradise and at peace. But they rebelled, thinking that they were being robbed of something of their greatness. That was the original sin, the original Fall, with people beginning to assert themselves, claiming for themselves the right of government and of judgment and the power to order their own affairs. They set themselves up as autonomous beings, no longer recognizing the supreme Governor of the final law. Every person made himself a governor and law-giver. In other words, the world is in trouble because people, instead of being God-centered, have become self-centered. The moment that happened, they lost their happiness; they lost everything.

Men and women object to belief in God; they object to the law of God. They do not like the very term "law," and today they object more than ever to discipline. They want to be free, they say, to live their own lives in their own way. Yes, but unfortunately for the individual, every other individual is exactly the same. We have all become little gods. We are all by nature saying, "Why shouldn't I? I have a right to do what I like and what I think is best." We are all selfish; we all consider ourselves and nobody else. That is why there are so many divorces with little children suffering, and why there is so much agony and pain in the world today. These problems are inevitable. People are only thinking of what is going to make them happy and give them pleasure. I repeat, we were never meant to govern ourselves; we are not fit to; we are not big enough; we do not know enough; we cannot see enough. We are in a universe that baffles us. Yet we are always claiming that we can govern ourselves. We become irritable and quarrel with others because where everybody is irritable, there are bound to be clashes.

Of course, in setting ourselves up, we look at others and judge them. If we think they are higher up than we are, we are jealous of them and want to pull them down. We say, "What right have they got to be there?" But if we happen to be up, we despise the others and say that their place is down there, that they have no right to be up here because they are not equal to us! The whole world is divided up like this. Men and women divide themselves up according to their ability, the color of their skin, the amount of money they possess, their position—a thousand and one things. Sometimes historians put all the trouble in the world down to the problem of the haves and the have-nots, but that is just one manifestation of the problem. Inequality is the result of men and women not seeing themselves truly, setting themselves up and therefore looking at others in terms of their own supposed greatness. So the world is full of jealousy and envy, full of malice and spite and bitterness and hatred.

The politicians and the statesmen, the philosophers and others never start with the fundamental question of men and women in their relationship to God. That is why there is no peace, no fellowship, no unity. That is why there is such a contrast between the world and the early church.

But let me now go on to a second principle. I have already shown that humanity fails because it does not understand why the world is as it is, but let us look at the problem in another way. Has it not struck you that the world in all its efforts to produce peace is tragically superficial? People seem to think achieving peace is so easy, and they are surprised and disappointed when they fail. They think you only have to call a conference. Neville Chamberlain thought that he had only to visit Hitler and talk to him as a businessman across the table. People seem to think that strife and bloodshed is only a problem for the mind. They say, "If only you can get people to come to a conference, then when you put your cards on the table or when you put your case forward well, every reasonable person must surely agree to your proposals." Poor old H. G. Wells believed that education could do away with war. It is only primitive people who fight, he maintained. Educated people have too much sense. They can think and see what they are doing. We only need to apply sweet reason to our problems and perplexities.

Another characteristic of the non-Christian way of trying to find peace is that it is always so negative. Peace is thought to be cessation from war. It is said that if only all the nations would destroy their armaments, then there would be peace. But the destruction of all weapons—which is impossible while people remain as they are—would in any case never produce peace in homes or in families or between classes in society.

To me, there are no people in the world whose teaching is so opposed to the Christian faith as pacifists—the people who say that you really can stop wars by applying reason and teaching. Why are they so wrong? Because they have never realized that the cause of every kind of warfare, whether it be a quarrel between a husband and wife or between two other people, every quarrel, every fight, every lack of peace and fellowship, is always due, not to a wrong mind, but to a wrong heart. Ultimately, the whole problem lies in the heart.

Now I am not depreciating the mind when I say that. I am simply saying that a true psychology of the person realizes that the mind is not the controlling factor in the personality; people are ruled by their hearts. Someone may have great knowledge and wisdom and understanding, but does that of necessity mean that that person lives a great life? Of course not! There is something deeper, something elemental within each of us. We do ourselves what we condemn in others. If we are asked to give an opinion on an objective case, we may give a perfect judgment, but we do not apply the same wisdom to our own lives. Why? Because each of us is governed by the heart. As James puts it, "From whence come wars and fightings among you?" And he answers his own question: "Come they not hence, even of your lusts that war in your members?" (James 4:1). The war within you—desire, lust. The heart is the cause of the trouble.

Or to put it another way—and this again is of supreme importance— non-Christian thinking can never see that peace is not something that should be aimed at directly. Peace always comes indirectly. We can say the same thing about peace as we say about happiness. The last person to be really happy is the person who is living for happiness. If you set out to look for happiness, you will never find it; happiness must never be sought directly. If you do not realize that, you will go wrong about happiness and about peace. Set up happiness or peace as the goal, and you will never get there.

So peace is a by-product of something else, and that, according to the Bible, is righteousness. Here again is one of the fundamental propositions of the whole of the Scriptures. James has put this matter very clearly, it seems to me. Dealing with the whole question of warfare, he says:

Who is a wise man and endued with knowledge among you? let him show out of a good conversation [behavior] his works with meekness of wisdom.
—*James 3:13*

That is it—meekness of wisdom.

But if ye have bitter envying and strife in your hearts, glory not, and lie not against the truth. This wisdom descendeth not from above, but is earthly, sensual, devilish. For where envying and strife is, there is confusion and every evil work. But the wisdom that is from above is first pure [pure, notice, is what he puts first; it is clean, righteous] then peaceable, gentle, and easy to be entreated, full of mercy and good fruits, without partiality, and without hypocrisy. And the fruit of righteousness is sown in peace of them that make peace.
—*James 3:14-18*

James is saying that if men and women sow righteousness, they will have peace, because peace is the fruit of righteousness, purity, holiness, a right relationship to God, and obedience to His holy laws and commands. The tragedy of the statesman and the world apart from Christ is that they are always trying to sow peace, but they never produce it. If they began to sow righteousness, then they would have a hope of peace.

So the great central message of the Bible is that men and women are not at peace because they are not righteous. They can be clever, learned, wise, and they can advance in scientific knowledge, but there is no peace. Peace is always the result of righteousness. The world has forgotten God, and so, though it is trying to produce peace, it never will. The leaders of the world are trying to patch up quarrels; they are trying to find a formula, a compromise. They take their officials with them and spend their time attempting to produce a form of words that pleases everybody, but at best they only achieve a sort of armistice, a temporary cessation of warfare. What we are out for is fellowship and fraternity, and this is a matter of the heart, something elemental and fundamental, based always upon righteousness and truth and the holiness of God.

There is a peace that is possible, and it is described here at the end of Acts 4. How, then, is it obtained? How does it come into being? Christ alone can give peace. He alone produces fellowship and all the things for which the world is longing in vain. Christ came into the world in order to make and to give us this peace. He is the Prince of Peace, but that is not His only title. He is also King of Righteousness. He is always there—as the psalmist, acting as a prophet, discovered long ago. He said, "Righteousness and peace have kissed each other" (Psa. 85:10). They have met together in this one blessed person, Jesus of Nazareth, who was born in the stable in Bethlehem. His little body was placed in the manger, and Charles Wesley is right when he heralds Him in these words:

> Hail, the heaven-born Prince of Peace,
> Hail, the Son of Righteousness.

The two always go together.

The whole purpose of the Incarnation of the Son of God was to bring in this reign of peace of which He is the Prince. He brought peace by His teaching, and, as no one else had ever done, He taught men and women to love one another. But He did not stop at teaching, and we must never forget that His teaching alone will never produce peace because, as we have seen, the trouble is not in the mind but in the heart. No person in his right mind can love war, and yet people go to war against their reason, against their own wisdom and understanding. No, something further is needed. How, then, does the Prince of Peace make peace? The answer is given throughout the New Testament. He makes peace by His death and resurrection. That is the only way to peace. Human nature and our relationship to God are wrong; that is why there is no peace, and Christ came to deal with that fundamental problem. Paul describes it in this way:

> But now in Christ Jesus ye who sometimes were far off are made nigh
> by the blood of Christ. For he is our peace, who hath made both one,
> and hath broken down the middle wall of partition between us; hav-

ing abolished in his flesh the enmity, even the law of commandments
contained in ordinances; for to make in himself of twain one new
man, so making peace; and that he might reconcile both unto God
in one body by the cross, having slain the enmity thereby: and came
and preached peace to you which were afar off, and to them that
were nigh.

—*Eph. 2:13-17*

Christ made peace through the blood of His cross. Only as we look at this blessed person, as we watch His miracles and listen to His superb teaching, and, above all, as we look at the cross, do we find the solution to our problems. What is He doing on the cross if He is the Son of God? The only answer is that He is there because of our utter sinfulness, because we are alienated from a holy and righteous God. He is there because of our complete helplessness. He is there because men and women are guilty before God and are under His curse instead of His blessing. They are ill at ease and restless and fighting, trying to find something they cannot find. He has come to put that relationship right. There on the cross, and there alone, He puts it right. It is there that we see what we are and our plight and our need, and there we see that He reconciles us and restores us to God and procures our pardon.

Men and women must be at peace with God before they can be at peace with themselves or with anybody else and, says Paul, "being justified by faith, we have peace with God through our Lord Jesus Christ" (Rom. 5:1). Peace with God in itself is wonderful, but He not only procures the pardon of my sin and clears my guilt, but He gives me a new life and a new nature. And, as I have been showing you, this is our fundamental need. We do not need instruction. We have had enough of that throughout the centuries; the Greek philosophers had tried it as well as the biblical writers, but people do not listen to it, and they do not put it into practice. "This is the condemnation, that light is come into the world, and men loved darkness rather than light, because their deeds were evil" (John 3:19). Do you think the only thing the world needs is light and instruction? Well, here it is. If only the world applied these truths, it would be paradise again. Here is the way of life, the way to live.

But the world is as it is because it does not like this message. It prefers to be drinking and indulging in sex rather than studying the New Testament. The world really despises Jesus of Nazareth and the way He lived. The clever men on the television cater to the public palate, which wants a little bit of spice, something it thinks is missing in the Christian life. The public wants none of this straight-laced, narrow Christianity. The world is not interested in purity, in righteousness, and decency. Yet it is surprised that it is fighting and does not have peace and rest and fellowship. My dear friends, you have to obey the laws. If you love these evil things, you will reap the consequences: "Whatsoever a man soweth, that shall he also reap" (Gal. 6:7). That is an absolute law.

Men and women need new hearts, hearts that will love the light and hate the darkness. Until then they will never have peace. In Christ Jesus new hearts are possible. Christ knew that we need to be renewed; He knew that we need new hearts, new natures, new lives. So He came down and took on human nature in order that, by linking it to Himself and purifying it and by joining it to the divine, He might give it back to us and so start a new, a cleansed, and a purified humanity.

In addition Christ gives us the Holy Spirit. These people here in Acts were all filled with the Spirit, and they began to behave as they did because the Spirit produces a certain type of fruit. The apostle Paul describes that fruit in his epistle to the Galatians: "The fruit of the Spirit is love, joy, peace, long-suffering, gentleness, goodness, faith, meekness, temperance" (Gal. 5:22-23). This old warring world in its unhappiness, strife, trouble, and agony needs this fruit today. It is not instruction, not enlightenment, not education, not conferences, not consultations, not compromises that the world needs. Men and women need to have natures out of which will grow the fruit of the Spirit and the ability to bear with others—here is peace.

When these people in Acts began to believe the message, they received new hearts. "The multitude of them that believed were of one heart and of one soul." They had not always been like that—they had been quarrelsome and envious. But now, though they belonged to different nations and though by nature they were like all the rest of humanity, they were welded into one. They had now an amazing understanding and generosity and love and desire to help. There was self-giving and self-sacrifice. There was peace and fellowship. Why? Because they were new people. They were not people who had merely decided to take up and apply the teaching of Jesus. They were born again; they were filled with the Spirit; they had new natures, new hearts, and they were amazed at themselves. This is Christianity! This does what the world is vainly trying to do, and it is all in this blessed person, the Lord Jesus Christ.

What happens is this: The moment men and women are born again, because they are all born of the same Spirit and inherit the same nature, they all become one in a new and strange sense. When people are born again, they first see themselves in a new way. They used to think a great deal of themselves and were very proud of themselves, but when they are born again, all that changes. They see that they were blind and ignorant fools, their own worst enemy. They only get to know this as they confront this blessed person who was born as a babe in the manger in Bethlehem. Standing face to face with Him, they are humbled and ashamed. Like Saul of Tarsus, they see that they are the greatest of all sinners. They are knocked down. They become nothing. They see their selfishness and self-centeredness. They know the truth about themselves for the first time in their lives.

But they not only have a new view of themselves; they have a new view of others also. They see that all other people are just like themselves. They used to think that they themselves were right while everybody else was wrong! But Christians see now that everybody is wrong! We are all fools together; we are all lying helpless in the dust of hopelessness. They see that we are all creatures made by God, meant to be like that young man in Palestine. That was true life, and Christians see that they are meant to live like that. That life is big and great and glorious, not something just to get through, grabbing the best you can and forgetting everybody else. No, their views are revolutionized. Christians look at their fellow men and women here with them in the company, and they see that now all of them are what they are, not because of anything in themselves, but because of the grace of God. "By the grace of God I am what I am," wrote Paul (1 Cor. 15:10).

So there is nothing to boast about, is there? We used to look at one another and think, "Has he got more brains than I have? Is she better than I am? Have they got more money? How am I going to get the better of them?" But now we see that we are all paupers with nothing to boast about at all, and we are Christians together. Why? Because of the life we have lived? Not at all! Because we are all receivers of the grace of God. So boasting is dismissed. We have been given the same fortune, and we are all one, and we rejoice in the same Savior. We like to sing about the same Savior. We like to sing the same carols, the same hymns. We like to read the same Scriptures. We like to meditate about Him, the one who came out of the glory and humbled Himself even to death on the cross in order that we might be made rich. "Ye know the grace of the Lord Jesus Christ," said Paul, "that, though he was rich, yet for your sakes he became poor" (2 Cor. 8:9). When you are singing the same songs with people, you are one with them, and you begin to love them, and you rejoice together with them in the same Savior.

But above all, these people have now come to see that the whole of life is entirely different from what they had thought. They used to think that life was just a place in which to eat and drink and make and spend money. Money may be able to buy things, but it can never buy happiness or peace. Now they begin to see that we are not animals but pilgrims of eternity. Christians have all come to see that this life is but a journey, a pilgrimage, and we are all strangers and pilgrims, travelers and journeymen. We see that this is a passing world and also an evil world, a world of which you can always say, "Change and decay in all around I see." We are slipping out of it, and it is passing away—the world and its kingdoms and its glory. They are all vanishing, and anyone who lives for this world is a fool.

As our Lord came into the world from the glory, passed through it, and went back to the glory, so we are all sent into this world by God, but not to stay here. We are meant for a glorious heritage; we are traveling the same journey together. Christians are people who say together, "Here have we no continuing city, but we seek one to come" (Heb. 13:14). He has gone before us; He has gone to prepare a place for us. He has told us, "In my Father's house are many mansions: if it were not so, I would have told you" (John 14:2). We look at this world as simply a place of transition. Why should I parade my wealth? Why should I have many possessions and other people very few? This life is only temporary. We are all one, and we are all making for the same eternal home and looking forward to the same glorious inheritance.

These Christians in Acts were enlightened, and their attention was fixed on the glory to which they were going and for which He, by the Spirit, was preparing them. And so it was inevitable that "the multitude of them that believed were of one heart and of one soul: neither said any of them that ought of the things which he possessed was his own; but they had all things common." They knew that He was preparing a place for them. And so, instead of looking at one another and being filled with jealousy and envy or contempt, they looked at one another and loved one another. They belonged to the same God, the same Father, the same Savior, and they were making for the same country and would be joint heirs and participators in the great same inheritance. As it was true to say of those believers at the beginning, so it is true now:

> *Through the night of doubt and sorrow.*
> *Onward goes the pilgrim band,*
> *Singing songs of expectation,*
> *Marching to the promised land.*
> Bernhardt Ingemann
> Translated by Sabine Baring-Gould

They had one thought, one belief, one rejoicing, and one glorious, blessed eternal hope that can never fail.

When will this sad, old world begin to listen to this message? Listen:

> *Yet, with the woes of sin and strife,*
> *The world has suffered long;*
> *Beneath the angel-strain have rolled*
> *Two thousand years of wrong;*
>
> *And man, at war with man, hears not*
> *The love-song which they bring:*
> *O hush the noise, ye men of strife,*
> *And hear the angels sing.*

What are they singing? "Glory to God in the highest, and on earth peace, good will toward men" (Luke 2:14).

> *For lo! the days are hastening on,*
> *By prophet-bards foretold,*
> *When with the ever-circling years*
> *Comes round the age of gold:*
>
> *When peace shall over all the earth*
> *Its ancient splendors fling,*
> *And the whole world send back the song*
> *Which now the angels sing.*
> Edmund Hamilton Sears

Let us begin to sing, let us prepare, let us have a rehearsal. Let all who believe in Him join together and begin to sing it now.

16

POWER AND GRACE

And when they had prayed, the place was shaken where they were assembled together . . . and great grace was upon them all.
—Acts 4:31, 33

I am holding these two phrases before you because I want to try to show you that in a very wonderful way they tell us what might be described as the two focal points of the message of the whole of the Bible and of the Christian Gospel. At the time of this writing, the old year is passing into the new. In a sense, that does not matter, but in a sense it does. There is some purpose in this transition, as there is in a birthday. Every birthday is a time of rejoicing, yes, but if you have any sense, it will also tell you that you are older than you were a year ago and that, therefore, you have that much less time to spend in this world. The year's end brings the same message. So the end of a year is a good opportunity for us to examine ourselves in the light of this Christian Gospel and in the light of destiny to see where we stand in life.

Now there are many who have been hearing this Gospel for some time. How have you reacted to it? What difference, if any, has it made to you? Does it govern your thinking? Does it govern your thinking, in particular, about the end of the year and the beginning of another, about the whole of life, death, and what lies beyond it? That is what the Gospel is for. You and I will be held responsible for what we have done with our lives and with the time that we have spent in this world.

Christianity is primarily a very personal message, and the tragedy of the times in which we live is that people have forgotten this, or dislike it, and think of Christianity and its message only in some vague, general terms that have nothing to do with their own lives. That is why it is possible to have statesmen—and we have heard them so often—who can talk very eloquently about the sanctity of international contracts but who are not so careful about observing the terms of their own marriage contracts. That is why you get national as well as personal hypocrisy.

So the business of this message is to deal with us individually and personally. You will never get a good nation until you get good people in it. The word *nation* is, in a sense, an abstraction; the nation is a collection of individuals, and we must always start with the individual. So now we will look at the individual and at the two focal points that constitute the Christian message, the Christian proclamation. These are both seen in the passage we are studying. They are, first, "the place was shaken"—that is the power of God; second, "great grace was upon them all"—that is the grace of God.

The first great message in the Bible is always about the power of God. It is placed first here—it always comes first. The Gospel starts with a proclamation about God, about the being of God. It does not start with us; it does not start with our needs and problems and aches and pains. It does not matter what our condition is; it does not matter what we feel like; there is one universal message in the Bible, and it starts in Genesis 1:1: "In the beginning God." The great God, the almighty God, the God who can shake a building, the God of might, the God who, according to the Bible and therefore according to the Gospel because the whole Bible is the whole message of the Gospel, is a God of great and infinite power. He is an omnipotent God, and He sits upon the circle of the universe.

So the Gospel starts by asserting the power of God. Here in Acts we see the church meeting together, and the first thing that happened after the believers had offered up their prayers was that the building shook. Now this is not romance; this is the reporting of facts. We are not told how the building shook. It may have been an earth tremor—we do not know. But what we do know is that God produced it. I have often pointed out to people when preaching in other parts of the country that I remember this very building shaking one morning when a flying bomb landed on the Guards' Chapel. This building shook; a wall on that side trembled and was moved an inch and a half out of position. Man has the power to make bombs that can shake a building like this, and the Bible tells us that God is all-powerful.

Of course, we see God's power supremely in the great act of creation. Would you know something about the power of God? Well, here it is: "God said, Let there be light: and there was light" (Gen. 1:3). His word, His fiat, was enough. That is some indication of the power of God. The apostle Paul makes that very point: "That which may be known of God is manifest in them; for God hath showed it unto them. For the invisible things of him from the creation of the world are clearly seen, being understood by the things that are made, even his eternal power and Godhead; so that they are without excuse" (Rom. 1:19-20). The powerful God who exists in eternity and decides to create a world out of nothing does so just by a word! The feat is incomprehensible, of course. He is omnipotent. "For with God nothing shall be impossible" (Luke 1:37). And He has given proof of it in all the wonder and magnificence and perfection of creation.

But then we also see the power of God in providence and history, as described in both the Old Testament and the New. We live in an amazing world, a world that was made, as I have said, out of nothing. But then God decided that He would destroy that world because of its sin, its evil, its rebellion against Him. When He saw that "every imagination of the thoughts of his [men's] heart was only evil continually" (Gen. 6:5), that men and women were living much as they are living today, not only in immorality but in foul and unmentionable perversions, He decided that He would destroy the world.

Peter's second letter reminds us of this (see 2 Pet. 2:5; 3:5). There was "the earth standing out of the water and in the water," and God decided to destroy it by a deluge. Here we see the same power. He can bring a world into being, and He can destroy it whenever He chooses.

Then the flood was made to recede, and God restored order. He went on sustaining and guiding the world. Read for yourselves Psalm 104 where you will find the psalmist working out in detail how God not only made everything but keeps it all going. He controls it. He gives everything breath and life. If He were to withdraw the Spirit, everything would collapse. Those are some of the accounts in the Old Testament of this amazing power of God.

Then we see God's power in providence and in historical events. The children of Israel went down to Egypt because of a famine, and when they were there, they grew and multiplied. They did so well that the Egyptians began to be jealous and maltreated and victimized them. Pharaoh was a great dictator, one of the most powerful men in the world, with armies and chariots and horses, and here were these slaves who had nothing at all. But they were God's people, and God acted on their behalf.

You can read the story in the Old Testament. God leads His people out of Egypt, and there they are, suddenly confronted by the Red Sea. The armies of Pharaoh are behind them, the Red Sea in front of them, and two mountains, one on each side, Pi-hahiroth and Baal-zephon. What can they do? Nothing. But God can. He suddenly opens the Red Sea, and across they go.

The hosts of Pharaoh try to follow, but the sea closes upon them, and they are destroyed. Pharaoh and all his boasted army are vanquished and destroyed. The same God!

The story goes on, often recapitulated in the great psalms in the Old Testament collection. As we read of God's dealings with people and with nations, we see His great power. Another dictator arose, a man called Nebuchadnezzar, the dictator of the Babylonians, a mighty man, a great soldier and statesman. But, like so many such men, he became inflated with pride. Beginning to think that he was a god, he commanded people to worship him. What an ignorant fool! He did not know the power of the God who dwells in the heavens. This God suddenly struck him, and there he was in the field, eating grass, with his hair grown like that of an ox and his nails like great talons. Nebuchadnezzar was humbled, made a fool of before his own people.

Well, I am just giving you a summary of the Old Testament and its history. It simply tells us that we are under the eye of an almighty God. "The place was shaken"—the all-powerful God! We live in a world that is under His hand, made by Him, controlled by Him, governed by Him, determined by Him. You and I are face to face with such a God. That is the first message of the Gospel.

And, of course, we find the same truth in the New Testament. We have been thinking about the babe born in Bethlehem in the stable, whose little body they put into the manger. When we read the stories about Him in the Gospels, we find that He was always astonishing people. He performed mighty works, miracles, marvels: "The blind see, the lame walk, the lepers are cleansed, the deaf hear, the dead are raised" (Luke 7:22). Who was this? He could calm the storm, silence the raging of the wind, feed five thousand with five loaves and two fish—who was this? That was the question they all asked. "We have seen great things today," the people said. "What is this power?"

Oh, it is the power of God! These are the attestations of His person. These are the things that tell us that Jesus of Nazareth, the babe of Bethlehem, is not merely a man. He is God come in the flesh. He is the one by whom and through whom all things were created. "In the beginning was the Word, and the Word was with God, and the Word was God. The same was in the beginning with God. All things were made by him; and without him was not any thing made that was made" (John 1:1-3). God! The almighty Creator! And our Lord manifested this might in His works of power. They are recorded for us in the Gospels in order that we might realize who He is and what He came into the world to do.

But, of course, one of the most amazing demonstrations of power that has ever taken place or ever will take place occurred when He was taken, tried, condemned, and nailed to a cross. He died, and when a soldier thrust a spear into His side, out came a mixture of blood and water. Then His friends took down His body and laid it in a tomb. His enemies were all triumphant. They thought they were finished with Him, and that was the end, but they were so terribly wrong. On the morning of the third day the tomb was found empty. There was nothing left but the grave clothes. He had risen from the dead—God had raised Him from the dead.

In his letter to the Ephesians, the apostle Paul writes of the Resurrection. He wants the Ephesian Christians to know something of God's power toward them, and this is how he describes it:

> *And what is the exceeding greatness of his power to us-ward who believe, according to the working of his mighty power, which he wrought in Christ, when he raised him from the dead, and set him at his own right hand in the heavenly places, far above all principality, and power, and might, and dominion, and every name that is named, not only in this world, but also in that which is to come.*
>
> *Eph. 1:19-21*

Here is a power that can conquer death, a power that can conquer the grave. Here is a power that can conquer the devil and hell: "the power of the resurrection," the power of eternal life. "The last enemy," death, has been destroyed by the power of God.

Then we read in Acts 2 of what happened on the day of Pentecost at Jerusalem. These waiting believers, we are told, had been praying together for ten days, and they were praying again on that morning. Then: "When the day of Pentecost was fully come. . . . And suddenly there came a sound from heaven as of a rushing mighty wind, and it filled all the house where they were sitting. And there appeared unto them cloven tongues like as of fire, and it sat upon each of them. And they were all filled with the Holy Ghost." "A rushing mighty wind"! Here is the same power. And in our story in Acts 4, we find another example of the same power. These people were in desperate straits, not knowing what to do or where to turn. So they prayed to God, and the building was shaken.

Now all these are but adumbrations of a mightier manifestation of the power of God that is yet to come. Peter writes about this in his epistle: "The day of the Lord will come," he says, ". . . in the which the heavens shall pass away with a great noise, and the elements shall melt with fervent heat" (2 Pet.

3:10). Have you seen on your television sets explosions of atomic bombs? Have you seen the power lifting up the earth, rising into the heavens, causing the sea to mount up like a mountain? What mighty power there is in that! But, my dear friends, that power is nothing by contrast with the tremendous cataclysm that will take place at the end of time when "the day of the Lord will come."

What is this? It is God's last judgment when He will demonstrate that He is the Governor of the universe and the Judge of the ends of the earth. He has shown His power throughout history in order to prepare us. He is teaching us, calling us to be ready, and that is why I am addressing you on this subject. The authorities condemned the apostles, telling them to be silent. But they said to God: "We don't want to be silent; we want to go on. Tell us that You will enable us."

And God shook the building—His answer. "Yes. Go on! I am with you."

A day was coming when those judges, the men in that council, would have to stand before this mighty Judge. The author of the letter to the Hebrews warns:

> *See that ye refuse not him that speaketh. For if they escaped not who refused him that spake on earth, much more shall not we escape, if we turn away from him that speaketh from heaven: whose voice then shook the earth. [He is talking about the giving of the law to Moses on Mount Sinai when we read that "the whole mount quaked greatly" (Ex. 19:18), and any animal or human that touched that mountain died immediately.] But now he hath promised, saying, Yet once more I shake not the earth only, but also heaven. And this word, Yet once more, signifieth the removing of those things that are shaken, as of things that are made, that those things which cannot be shaken may remain. Wherefore we receiving a kingdom which cannot be moved, let us have grace, whereby we may serve God acceptably with reverence and godly fear: for our God is a consuming fire (Heb. 12:25-29).*

Have you heard this God speaking? First of all, this gospel message proclaims that God the Almighty is over all, that we are all under Him, and that we hold our lives and our being and our existence under His almighty hand. The power of God!

But, thank God, the message does not stop there. If it did, it would be the most terrible message ever heard. But the second ingredient in this message is a proclamation of the grace of God: "great grace was upon them all."

Oh, what a wonderful word, this word *grace*. That is why there is a Christian church; that is why these people were praying in the room that was shaken; it was because of the grace of God. The power of God, yes, but the grace of God is equal to His power.

What do we mean by grace? Grace is "favor shown to people who are utterly undeserving of it." When man sinned against God, he deserved immediate annihilation; he and his world deserved to be blotted out. But he was not. Why? Because God is long-suffering, full of mercy and compassion, summed up in the word *grace*. The world is still in existence because of this amazing quality, this grace of God.

Our human definitions are inadequate, of course; you cannot describe God's grace. But you can see it in operation, and you can see it very clearly in the Old Testament. God had made a nation for Himself—the children of Israel. He had given them His laws and had promised to bless them. But they constantly rebelled against Him. They turned to other gods and did everything they could to insult Him. They deserved retribution, annihilation. Yet repeatedly having, as one of them put it, "played the fool" (1 Sam. 26:21), having turned their backs on God and gone their own way, thinking that this was the way to find life and happiness and pleasure, they would come up against some brick wall. They would lose everything, and their enemies would defeat them. Then in utter desolation and despair, they would turn back to God and ask Him to help them. The amazing thing is that He would listen to them and come down again, as it were, to help them. That is the measure of His grace, that time and time again He was prepared to forgive them, take them back, and give them another chance.

Today I am a preacher because of the grace of God. If God were only power, I would not be here. None of us would be here; there would be no message. But God is a God of grace—"great grace was upon them all."

If you really want to know about the grace of God, then you must go to that inn in Bethlehem and out into the stable. Because all the rooms were booked, there was no room for a pregnant woman. Nobody had the decency to vacate a room for her. It is "my room." "I'm all right, Jack. It's their own business; they should have booked." So he was born in a stable and placed in the manger.

What was that? It was the grace of God! "God so loved the world, that he gave his only begotten Son, that whosoever believeth in him should not perish, but have everlasting life" (John 3:16). God loved the world, remember—the world that had rebelled against Him and ridiculed Him, spat into His face and thought it knew better than He did. And He did not merely send

His Son into the world, but, above all, He sent Him to the death of the cross, to bear the sins of men and women, to "endure scoffing rude" and shame and ignominy and everything that is hurtful. That is the grace of God.

Paul makes a magnificent statement in his letter to Titus: "For the grace of God that bringeth salvation hath appeared to all men" (Titus 2:11). The grace of God! "For ye know the grace of our Lord Jesus Christ, that, though he was rich, yet for your sakes he became poor" (2 Cor. 8:9). Oh, how poor! Though He was God, He "thought it not robbery to be equal with God: but made himself of no reputation" (Phil. 2:6-7). Why? That you and I might be delivered and redeemed and restored to God. That is grace. God has done everything. We deserve nothing but punishment and hell, but because of the grace of God, this amazing Gospel is offered to us.

God's power and God's grace—those are the two strands of the Gospel. But let me show you how the poet Isaac Watts has put them before us in a most wonderful hymn:

> *Now to the Lord a noble song,*
> *Awake, my soul; awake my tongue;*
> *Hosanna to the Eternal Name,*
> *And all His boundless love proclaim!*

Listen:

> *See where it shines in Jesu's face,*
> *The brightest image of His grace;*
> *God, in the person of His Son,*
> *Has all His mightiest works outdone.*

Then Watts argues it out. He starts, as I have been doing, with the power of creation:

> *The spacious earth and spreading flood*
> *Proclaim the wise and powerful God;*
> *And Thy rich glories from afar*
> *Sparkle in every rolling star.*

> *But in His looks a glory stands,*
> *The noblest labour of Thy hands;*
> *The radiant luster of His eyes*
> *Outshines the wonders of the skies.*

We see the power of God in the skies and the rolling stars. But look at the grace of Jesus Christ. Watts says:

> *The radiant luster of His eyes*
> *Outshines the wonders of the skies.*

> *Grace, 'tis a sweet, a charming theme;*
> *My thoughts rejoice at Jesu's name:*
> *Ye angels, dwell upon the sound;*
> *Ye heavens, reflect it to the ground!*

There it is, is it not? The power of God! The grace of God!

The Gospel proclaims the power of God and the grace of God, but the most wonderful thing of all is that it proclaims the *powerful grace* of God. The Gospel brings them together. And if it did not, I would have no message to give you. Before you and I or anybody else can be saved, we need power and grace! The two must operate together, and in Christ they do.

Powerful grace! Here is the paradox of Christianity, a paradox that men and women do not understand. The apostle Paul, writing to Timothy, says, "God hath not given us the spirit of fear; but of power, and of love, and of a sound mind [discipline]" (2 Tim. 1:7). Power and love! Of course. The world thinks they are antitheses, and so they are to people with finite minds, but not with God. Power and love. Power and grace. They become one; they operate together. In Christ you see this to perfection. The miracle of redemption is made possible because God combines His power and His grace in His dealings with us.

Why is this necessary? It is because grace alone cannot save us—power is needed. God combines the power with the grace because no man or woman can ever be saved unless he or she is first of all "quickened from the dead." Paul says to the Ephesians, "You hath he quickened, who were dead in trespasses and sins" (Eph. 2:1). As the result of the Fall, everyone born into this world is spiritually dead. That is why the world does not believe in the babe of Bethlehem. The world is so dead that it does not know that it is dead. That is its whole trouble. The dead do nothing and know nothing. Those who are spiritually dead do not know God; they do not know the truth about Him; they do not realize they are living in the universe God created; they do not know anything about the coming judgment. Before anyone can be saved, therefore, and raised out of the death of sin, a power is needed that is greater than death, a resurrecting power. This power is all there in Jesus Christ. Powerful grace! He is able to quicken by His Holy Spirit.

The world needs power for a further reason, and perhaps this is one of its greatest needs today. The world needs to be "shaken," shaken out of its complacency, carelessness, and sense of safety. Is not that the real curse of this country of ours at the present time? Does not that account for most of our problems? It certainly accounts for the godlessness and vice and increasing immorality. Affluent society! "Never had it so good!" Plenty of money, plenty of everything. People say, "Everything is all right! We don't want preaching. We don't want Christianity. We've made a perfect world for ourselves." Oh, the complacency of the modern world—the carelessness, the heedlessness, the sense of security! Oh, the tragedy of men and women living on a volcano and unaware of it! The world needs to know about the God who can shake, the God who did shake the building where the first believers were praying—just a touch of His power to let them know that He was there and that He is almighty.

Shall I ask you a simple question: How often have you thought about your soul? How often have you thought about your death? How often have you visualized yourself standing before God at the eternal bar of judgment? You need to be reminded that you will stand before a God who is all-powerful, an almighty God, who is "the Judge of all the earth" (Gen. 18:25). We all need to be shaken out of our complacency, thoughtlessness, and carelessness, and He does it. He does it by the grace He has shown in His Son through the Gospel.

We need power that can convict us of sin. No argument or demonstration can do it. "I try my best," you say; or, "That is just what *he* thinks." Only one thing can ever convict a man or woman of sin, and that is the power of the Holy Spirit. He can do it, and He does it. He did it on the day of Pentecost. Peter was preaching, expounding Scriptures, taking Old Testament passages and bringing them together. You might say, "What a poor sermon—no eloquence, no art." I know, but he was filled with the Spirit, and as he was preaching, "They were pricked in their heart, and said . . . Men and brethren, what shall we do?" (Acts 2:37). The power of conviction! If you read the stories of the great revivals of history, you will see men and women not only convicted of sin, but falling to the floor, staggering home in agony, not able to sleep, in trouble for weeks. It is the power of conviction produced by the Holy Spirit—this power that "shakes" and disturbs and demolishes all that we have relied upon.

This is the power needed to put us right. We need to be created anew. Our Lord said, "Ye must be born again" (John 3:7). You do not want just a new idea; a new teaching is not enough for you; you do not merely want an example. You must be born again. There is only one power that can do that—the power of God. Good advice, sentimental thoughts about the babe of Bethlehem—all this has never saved anybody and never will. We need a new nature, a new life, a new orientation. The power and the grace of God combined—and that alone—can do it for us.

Then we need to be delivered from the power of the world, the flesh, and the devil. Oh, what power! Have you been able to stand up against it? Can you stand up against the jeering and the mockery and the insinuations of your friends in the office or factory? Can you stand up to the ridicule and scorn, the suggestions on the television and in the newspapers, all against the Gospel? Have you stood up? There is only one power that can defeat the power of Satan and sin and evil. It is the power of the Lord Jesus Christ—God's power and God's grace combined in this one blessed person. He alone can deliver us from these enemies that are set against us.

Then think of the work of perfecting us, of getting rid of the evil and the sin that is in us, purifying us, cleansing us, and making us fit to stand in His holy presence. There is only one power that can do that, and Paul mentions it at the end of Ephesians 3. "Now," he says, "unto him that is able to do exceeding abundantly above all that we ask or think, according to the power that worketh in us, unto him be glory in the church by Christ Jesus throughout all ages, world without end" (v. 20).

Finally, there is the power that every one of us will need when we die and our bodies are placed in a grave or cremated or drowned in the sea or blown to nothing in the air—the power to reassemble, raise the body, glorify it, make it perfect, and put it in the presence of God. There is only one power that can do that—the power of God. And the power of God combined with the grace of God purposes to do this. God's grace and power have done it for millions who are in the glory at this moment, and God is doing it for us who believe. That is the message of the Gospel. The power of God! The grace of God! The powerful grace of God!

You see how this message divides humanity. At the beginning of the church, the Sanhedrin hated this message. It hated Christ and crucified Him. It hated His disciples, the apostles. It arrested them, condemned them, and threatened to put them to death.

But there is another reaction, and it is this: "Great grace was upon them all." What a contrast! And that is what I want to leave with you now as a great and most momentous question. We are all of us in one of these two positions, and there is no third.

Some people will only know the shaking power of God. "Yet once more I shake not the earth only, but also heaven" (Heb. 12:26). There are men and women—God forbid that it should be any who are considering my words now—who will know nothing but the power of God to shake, and when they stand before Him they will shake to nothing. They are like the man described in the first psalm: "Therefore the ungodly shall not stand in the judgment, nor sinners in the congregation of the righteous" (v. 5). They will be swept away. "The ungodly are not so: but are like the chaff which the wind driveth away" (v. 4). The shaking consigns to eternal perdition. What a terrible prospect. What an awful thought. But that is the fate of all who do not believe the Gospel, who turn a deaf ear to the overtures of the grace of God, the powerful grace of God in Christ Jesus. These people will see nothing but the power, the demonstration of the might, the awfulness of the final calamity, and it will be too late to change.

But there are others, thank God, who know "great grace." Is not this an amazing thing? Here was a group of Christian people threatened by the authorities, threatened even with death, but "Great grace was upon them all." The favor of God was upon them in a mighty and unusual manner. That is why God shook the building. It was God's way of saying to the people, "Do not be troubled. You have heard their threats and have reminded Me of them. They have it in their power to put you to death if they choose to, but I am with you. Do not be frightened of them. You know Me; you have described My power to Me; you have reminded Me that I am the Creator. And I am behind you. I love you. You are My people. I will never leave you. I will never forsake you. Hold on—all is well."

"Great grace was upon them all." So though they were threatened, they were filled with a wonderful spirit of rejoicing and of praise, of love for one another and love to God.

Would you like to know in which of the two positions you are? You can know by answering this question: Is great grace upon you? Do you know something of it?

"How can I know it?" asks someone.

God forbid that anybody should not be quite clear about this. Those who have great grace upon them do not worry about their past because they know that it is cleansed. They know that God in his infinite, all-powerful grace has laid all their sins upon one who could take the punishment and still rise from the dead, setting them free. Do you know that? That is the past.

What about the present? Are you resting in Him? Do you have life in you, the life of Christ? Have you gotten rid of the restlessness that is so characteristic of the world? Have you found peace? Have you found satisfaction? Look again at these people in Acts. In spite of the threats, they had never been so happy in the whole of their lives—great grace was upon them all.

> *When all things seem against me*
> *To drive me to despair,*
> *I know one gate is open,*
> *One ear will hear my prayer.*
> Oswald Allen

Listen to Paul putting it to the Romans:

Therefore being justified by faith, we have peace with God through our Lord Jesus Christ: by whom also we have access by faith into this grace wherein we stand, and rejoice in hope of the glory of God. And not only so, but we glory [rejoice, make our boast] in tribulations also: knowing that tribulation worketh patience; and patience, experience; and experience, hope: and hope maketh not ashamed.

Rom. 5:1-5

Are you able to rejoice in tribulations? Are you happy in spite of the world? Do you have contentment? Are you independent of the world and all its noise and bustle, its empty show and all that may happen in it? Do you have a place of rest and peace and quiet—a calm, undisturbed joy that the world can neither give nor take away? If you have these things, "great grace" is upon you—the grace of God in Jesus Christ. That is the present.

What of the future? This little company of people is threatened, but they are full of rejoicing and of praise. Why? Well, because they have complete assurance with respect to the future. When great grace is upon you, you are not only not afraid of life, but you are not afraid of death. Nothing can make you afraid. You are like the apostle Paul who writes from prison in one of his last letters, "For the which cause I also suffer these things: nevertheless I am not ashamed: for I know whom I have believed, and am persuaded that he is able to keep that which I have committed unto him against that day" (2 Tim. 1:12).

Do you know anything about that? As you face the future, are you afraid of it, filled with terror? As you look forward and contemplate the end of life and your own dissolution out of this mortal frame, how do you react? Can you look steadily in death's face? What if war comes, persecution, bombs?

Here are the questions that matter. And Paul's answer?

Who shall separate us from the love of Christ? shall tribulation, or distress, or persecution, or famine, or nakedness, or peril, or sword? . . . Nay, in all these things we are more than conquerors through him that loved us. For I am persuaded, that neither death, nor life, nor angels, nor principalities, nor powers, nor things present, nor things to come, nor height, nor depth, nor any other creature, shall be able to separate us from the love of God, which is in Christ Jesus our Lord.

Rom. 8:35, 37-39

Can you say that? If you can, I can assure you "great grace" is upon you, the powerful grace of God. You know that you are His and that nothing can ever separate you from His love. You are therefore "more than conquerors" against any conceivable eventuality.

Let me test you further by asking if you can say something like this:

> *All the way my Savior leads me,*
> *What have I to ask beside,*
> *Can I doubt His tender mercy*
> *Who through life has been my guide?*
> *Heavenly peace, divinest comfort,*
> *Here by faith in Him to dwell,*
> *For I know whate'er befall me*
> *Jesus doeth all things well.*
>
> Frances Jane van Alstyne

Or take the words of another great hymn:

> *I shall behold His face,*
> *I shall His power adore,*
> *And sing the wonders of His grace*
> *For evermore.*
>
> Augustus Toplady

"The place was shaken!" "Great grace was upon them all." To every believer the power here is a gracious power. It is the power that saves them, that keeps them, that protects them, and eventually will put them in the glory everlasting.

My dear friends, the old year is dying, and life is moving on. I am privileged and glad to be able to tell you that the day of grace is not yet ended:

"Now is the day of salvation" (2 Cor. 6:2). There will be an end to the day of grace. But not yet, thank God. "Now is the accepted time" (2 Cor. 6:2). Remember the ten virgins—the five wise and the five foolish. The door of mercy will be shut. But not yet—it is not too late. Have you entered through the gate of grace? Go through now if you have never done it before. Cry to Him. Thank Him for this grace, for this open door that is still there. Thank Him for the invitation and say:

> *Just as I am, without one plea,*
> *But that Thy blood was shed for me,*
> *And that Thou bidst me come to Thee,*
> *O Lamb of God, I come.*
>
> Charlotte Elliott

17

THE UNSEEN REALITY

And with great power gave the apostles witness of the resurrection of the Lord Jesus: and great grace was upon them all. Neither was there any among them that lacked: for as many as were possessors of lands or houses sold them, and brought the prices of the things that were sold, and laid them down at the apostles' feet: and distribution was made unto every man according as he had need. And Joses, who by the apostles was surnamed Barnabas, (which is, being interpreted, The son of consolation,) a Levite, and of the country of Cyprus, having land, sold it, and brought the money, and laid it at the apostles' feet. But a certain man named Ananias, with Sapphira his wife, sold a possession, and kept back part of the price, his wife also being privy to it, and brought a certain part, and laid it at the apostles' feet.

—Acts 4:33—5:2

We have now reached the end of the fourth chapter of the book of Acts, and we have seen wonderful things. We have looked at historical events, and it has all been very thrilling. But now we arrive at a remarkable incident, something that comes as a shock, especially after all we have been considering together in the first four chapters. There we saw the pouring out of the Spirit on the day of Pentecost; we saw the church come into being and the idyllic picture of the joy and happiness of the believers as they had all things in common. Of course, we saw the opposition, but the church—oh, what a wonderful picture!

Then suddenly we turn a page and come across this amazing incident at the beginning of Acts 5. Judged from any standpoint, this is an extraordinary passage, and I freely confess that it is one that I approach with a considerable measure of fear and trembling. No one, it seems to me, would choose to deal with a subject like this, but I am not to pick and choose. I am to expound the record, and here it is. God give me grace to do so in a right and fitting and worthy manner, and God give you grace to consider it in the same way.

Let me start by making some general points about this incident. We cannot deal with it exhaustively now, so I shall just introduce it. It is of vital importance, and God forbid that any of us should miss its message. My first point is that this incident is a fact, a bit of history. I start with that because there are those who say, "Of course, if you are a psychologist, you realize that things like this do not happen. People may imagine they do, but in reality they never do." However, this is a definite piece of history; it is as much history as everything that we have considered hitherto. It is as much history as the stories of the birth of our Lord recorded in the Gospels, His miracles, His death upon the cross, His burial, His resurrection, His ascension, and the coming of the Holy Spirit.

Notice that the record makes it quite plain that this incident was greatly used in the spread of the Christian Gospel. It led to a kind of revival. It was a very remarkable incident in the life of the early church. It gave a new impetus to the church and helps us to understand how this message, which was first delivered by one who appeared to be just an ordinary carpenter, this message from this unknown person in the land of Palestine, was able in a very short space of time to dominate the civilized world. The author was guided by the Spirit to put this incident in Acts because it is as vital an element in the understanding of the great story of the early church as are the other things that he records for us.

Secondly, one cannot but comment upon the honesty of this record. This forthrightness is particularly striking, and it is very important for us to realize that. I claim that the Bible is the most honest book in the world. Indeed, I would be prepared to go so far as to say that there is no book in the world, apart from the Bible, that is completely honest, that really tells us the truth. Here is an account of the early church, but you notice at once that it is not an idealized account or a doctored history. The bad is included as well as the good. I emphasize that fact because there are people who seem to think we are claiming that the Christian church is a perfect society, that there has never been anything wrong in it, and that there is nothing wrong now. What utter folly that is! No, it is all put down before us in this terrible event almost as soon as the church came into being.

You find the same honesty in the Old Testament. Of course, the modern critic is so confused that he contradicts himself. On the one hand, he tries to tell us that the Bible is a collection of fairy tales, idealized pictures, untrue to life, and then, with the same breath almost, he says that parts of the Old Testament are unfit for women and children to read—the shocking things we are told about David, for example, his terrible acts of adultery and murder and so on. But what these critics are really saying, howbeit unconsciously, is that they, too, think that the Bible is completely honest. It gives us the truth about every one of its characters, warts and all. You see them with terrible defects. And here in Acts we find the same openness with regard to the Christian church.

Do you get honesty in your newspapers? Do you believe what you read? Reporters and editors have completely lost all sense of proportion. The television is the same. What is greatness? It is very difficult to tell, judging by the things that are reported from week to week. Everything is painted up, idealized, beautified, and you do not have the truth. You do not get the truth about men and women in your newspapers nor in your secular history books. There is bias, a covering over, special pleading. But there is nothing like that in the Bible. This book will tell you more against the Christian church than you have ever imagined or would ever think of. It is a book you can trust. It is not here to wheedle you. It is here to give you a message that is of vital import to your soul and to your eternal destiny.

But let me make a further point quite clear. Let us understand what this man Ananias and his wife, Sapphira, had done. People have often misunderstood, which is why I have included those few verses from the end of the previous chapter. There was no compulsion upon anybody to sell their goods and to put the money into a common pool. People were taking this action voluntarily. Some, like Barnabas, felt called to do so and obeyed. Ananias and Sapphira need never have sold their possession at all. Indeed, even after they had sold it, as Peter pointed out to Ananias, nobody was forcing them to give the money (Acts 5:4). If there had been a commandment, and everybody had to do it, then you could put in some kind of plea or excuse for them, but there was not. We should emphasize that fact in order to understand exactly what Ananias and Sapphira had done. Here were people who voluntarily sold a possession and then deliberately deceived the church. It was dishonest; a case of hypocrisy.

There is one other general point. I think we must be clear as to what happened to Ananias and Sapphira. It is almost amusing to notice the way some of the commentators try to evade the central and obvious teaching. Some say that the moment Peter confronted Ananias with the fact that he had done this wrong thing, Ananias was so convicted and shocked that he fell down dead. Of course, that kind of thing is possible. People do sometimes drop dead when they hear bad news, but it seems to me to be totally inadequate as an explanation here, if only for the reason that Peter clearly knew beforehand that Sapphira was also going to die. He made this quite clear in the way he spoke to her, and that is an important point in the whole incident. Moreover, people dying of shock does not happen twice like this. So it is not just a question of them receiving a sudden shock that killed them. No, we must reject this explanation.

Secondly, some commentators say that Peter pronounced a judgment upon Ananias and Sapphira. It is important to realize that he did not—it was not Peter's place or his function to do that. I believe that the apostles had the power to strike people blind or dumb, and I have no doubt that they also had power, if necessary, to take people's lives away, just as they could also resurrect the dead. But there is no indication here that Peter was acting in a judicial manner. He merely convicted Ananias and Sapphira of the truth. He was the mouthpiece of God in exposing the enormity of their sin. It seems clear that this was a judicial action on the part of God Himself. Here at the very beginning of the life of the church, God did something to lay down a great principle. The event is like a great monument, if you like. There it stands at the beginning. God gave an indication to His own people as to who He is and how He acts. He was teaching the church, and teaching people through the church a vital truth concerning themselves.

People may ask, "Are you saying that Ananias and Sapphira were damned and that they were immediately consigned to hell?" There is only one honest answer I can give: I do not know, and neither does anybody else. In 1 Corinthians 11, in connection with the passage about the Communion service, the apostle Paul writes, "But let a man examine himself, and so let him eat of that bread, and drink of that cup. For he that eateth and drinketh unworthily, eateth and drinketh damnation to himself, not discerning the Lord's body. For this cause many are weak and sickly among you, and many sleep" (1 Cor. 11:28-30). "Sleep" here means dead, and Paul is teaching that they have died before their time as a part of the punishment of their sin. It is conceivable that God terminated the lives of Ananias and Sapphira in this world without their necessarily going to hell.

Neither do the deaths of Ananias and Sapphira mean that sudden death is always a punishment of sin. People have assumed all sorts of erroneous things from this incident. They say that if you teach that God caused the death of these two as punishment, then the conclusion must be that if anybody dies suddenly, it must be God's punishment. Not at all. It may be; it may not be. There is nothing in the record to say that this is a universal law.

So having cleared these preliminary matters, let us now look at the great lessons taught in this passage. First, here we are shown something about the nature of the church and of the whole Christian message. The very atmosphere of the story, it seems to me, tells us that the Christian church was something new and unique in the world. Now it is not unique when you compare it with the children of Israel—that was the church in the Old Testament. What I am saying is that the church, the people of God, constitutes something unique in the history of the whole human race.

The church is not just a society of people. There are many societies in the world—political societies, cultural societies, literary societies, scientific societies, and so on. People meet, take up a subject, discuss it, pass resolutions, and decide to act together. Now there are people who think of the Christian church as being like that, and I do not blame them. They have the impression that the church is just a human society, an ethical or even a political society, but essentially a human society. People who happen to be religious come together and consider religious subjects. They sing hymns and have a certain amount of ritual and ceremony. But the essential point is that a church is a meeting place for people who are concerned about living good moral lives, who try to help other people, and who try to spread a spirit of goodwill and friendship in this world of time.

Now if nothing else is taught us in this story in Acts 5, the idea I have just described is immediately put out of court. The church is not just a human society. It is true that the church is a gathering of men and women. You cannot read the story at all without seeing people meeting together. But this incident in Acts 5 at once establishes that the church goes much further than that. There is also another unseen element. In every "meeting" there is a power that is not visible. Strange things happen that cannot be explained in purely human terms. An agenda is drawn up, but something breaks into that agenda, and everything is upset. That is the church.

Now this incident we are considering is in series with all the great actions and events of the Bible. If you read again the account of the giving of the law to Moses found in Exodus 19, you will see the mountain quaking with fire and smoke. Here in Acts people were gathering together, but that is not the important factor. What is important is what happened when they met together, this other mysterious element, this strange manifestation of power. Something similar happened on the day of Pentecost. The disciples had been in the Upper Room for ten days, and they could have spent ten years or a hundred years there, and nothing would have happened had they been just an ordinary society. But, we are told, "Suddenly there came a sound from heaven as of a rushing mighty wind." It was not somebody making a proposition and somebody else seconding; it was not a decision to follow a course of action. No, something happened!

The deaths of Ananias and Sapphira are also in series with what Peter and John did to the man at the Beautiful Gate of the temple. Two men walking into the temple saw a man lame from his mother's womb. They did not decide to start a benevolent society, did they? They did not decide to take up a collection for him. That is what you and I can do, what human societies do, and it is right that we should. All I am pointing out to you is that this is not what happened. What happened was something that men and women can never do in and of themselves: The man was healed! The man who had never walked went into the temple walking and leaping and praising God.

Furthermore, Acts 5:1-11 is in series with that other incident from Acts 4 that we have considered together. There they were, men and women meeting together and talking to God. They were expressing their worship and adoration and were bringing their petitions to Him. You and I can do that, but that was not the only important thing in connection with the life of the early church. What was as important was that when they had prayed, "the place was shaken where they were assembled together." It is this other element that makes the church unique. When the church lacks this element, she is nothing but a human society, an institution without any uniqueness. She is like the politicians and their societies and their clubs and parties. No, the place was shaken, and that is what makes the church. In other words, the first thing we must realize about the church, and about the truth it represents and holds before the people, is that what matters is not what people do but what happens to them.

What matters above everything else in the world is the reality of the unseen spiritual realm. If you really get hold of this, it will transfigure your whole life and experience. That is the second great lesson this incident teaches us. The apostle Paul, as is often the case, has put it all for us in a memorable statement: "Our light affliction, which is but for a moment, worketh for us a far more exceeding and eternal weight of glory; while we look not at the things which are seen, but at the things which are not seen: for the things which are seen are temporal; but the things which are not seen are eternal" (2 Cor. 4:17-18).

Now if there is one message needed more than any other in this modern world of ours, it is just this. The basic trouble with the world and with this generation is that it has forgotten the unseen. This is the age of materialism, the affluent society, which has never had it so good. This is the age of prosperity, the age of machinery and gadgets, the age of comfort and of amenities. This is an age entirely earthbound with science and its discoveries, science and its insistence upon the visible, the tangible, and the measurable. That is the realm of science, but what has happened is that science has turned itself into philosophy and tells us that there is nothing apart from what can be seen, handled, and measured.

In other words, man has become the measure of everything. Only what people can understand, know, discover, and sanction can be believed. That alone is real—what belongs to this world of time. All else is poetry and imagination. If you are presented with anything that people cannot encompass with their minds, it is ridiculed and dismissed as fantasy. All right, they say, you can read a novel or read your Bible now and again—it does not matter which. They are the same sort of thing, and you will get temporary relief. But, of course, the Bible and novels are not real and true; you still have to come back and live in this same old world. Some psychologists say that children must not be taught Scripture, and you must not teach them religion, therefore, because it does violence to them. Others say that religion disturbs a person's emotional balance. The unseen world is actively and militantly denied and dismissed.

Above anything else, the modern world needs to be told that its central fallacy is its denial of the unseen and the spiritual. Will they take it, I wonder, from Shakespeare if they will not take it from the Bible?

> *There are more things in heaven and earth, Horatio,*
> *Than are dreamt of in your philosophy.*
> Hamlet

The unseen real, in a sense, is the great message of the Bible, though it has a better way of putting it. Furthermore, as a consequence, the modern world does not even understand the nature of its problem. Modern men and women are more bewildered as to the nature of their problem than they are with regard to anything else. They falsify everything because they believe, they really do believe and have done so for a long time, that if you only educate people and train them and give them knowledge and understanding, their problems will be dealt with. But we have done all that, and the difficulties are greater than ever. If people do not understand the nature of the problem, how can they possibly hope to find any solution? I repeat that this failure in diagnosis is entirely due to the fact that people have forgotten the supernatural and have banished everything outside human comprehension.

But the business of the Bible is to assert the reality of the unseen. Not only that, the Bible asserts the primacy, the all-importance, of the unseen. "The things which are seen are temporal; but the things which are not seen are eternal" (2 Cor. 4:18). What we see around us is not the real world; this is the passing phantom. That other world is the real one, the absolute. This world is the appearance; that world, says the Bible, is the great reality. There is no greater blunder than to confuse the appearance with the reality or the temporary with the permanent. So here is the basic postulate of the Bible, and it is put before us in this story in a striking manner that I trust we shall never, any of us, ever forget again.

Now the unseen is all-important, for we are in its hand. The Bible puts this before us in many ways. It is there in Genesis: "In the beginning God," and in all the subsequent Old Testament history. Shakespeare and others feel after this, but they never quite get there.

> *There's a divinity that shapes our ends,*
> *Rough-hew them how we will.*
>   Hamlet

The author of those lines is a man beginning to think profoundly and seriously. It takes a long time to bring people to that. All they are aware of is what some have called "fate." When the ancients had drawn up their philosophies and plans, they always saw a further element—fate, "kismet"—that guides our destiny and of which we are but playthings. There are other powers. The world has come very near to this truth, feeling after it. People have a vague awareness of how small we are, how little we know, and how great are these forces above us and beyond us and around us. The message of the Bible, the teaching of biblical history, is the all-importance of the unseen reality that controls our lives.

The reality of the unseen world is particularly taught in the prophetic books of the Bible. There is no other explanation. The prophets were able to forecast eight hundred years or so before the time things that later happened. How did they do it? Poetic imagination is a wonderful thing, but no poet has ever been able to imagine or foretell history in the minute detail that we find in the Old Testament prophecies. No, there must be another source that gives the knowledge, the revelation. Men must have been in touch with the unseen and the eternal, the real, the true, and the everlasting.

Above all, in the coming of our Lord into this world, we see the breaking of the eternal into time. He is the unseen and the invisible become visible; He is the Word made flesh and dwelling among us; He is God manifest in the flesh. We see it in His birth; we see it in the manifestation of His miraculous powers; He said it Himself. One day when the people were saying that He was casting out devils by the power of Beelzebub, He refuted the argument and then said, "But if I with the *finger of God* cast out devils . . ." (Luke 11:20, emphasis mine). People were amazed and said that they had seen strange things. They were aware of the supernatural and the eternal—the finger of God.

The power of the eternal is seen above all in our Lord's resurrection when all the laws of nature were broken. Of course, clever, modern people, even those calling themselves Christians and leaders in the Christian church, deny a physical resurrection. "You cannot expect modern people to believe that," they say. I do not expect them to believe it, but I am telling them that if they do not, there is only one end for them.

I do not expect anybody to believe these things. As a natural man, I myself do not believe them. "The natural man receiveth not the things of the Spirit of God" (1 Cor 2:14). Why not? Because he is a natural man. That is his whole trouble. He is blind. How can mortal man understand and receive the spiritual unseen and eternal? It cannot be done. Yet the Bible asserts that it has been done: "God hath revealed them unto us by his Spirit" (1 Cor. 2:10). This is the history that the Bible puts before us. A Gospel that the modern person can accept is, by definition, not a gospel at all; it is politics or sociology or whatever. The very basis of God's Gospel is that it baffles us, and we can only stand back with Paul and say, "Great is the mystery of godliness" (1 Tim. 3:16). We bow down before God in humble worship and praise and adoration.

These, then, are the events of the book of the Acts of the Apostles—Pentecost, miracles, buildings shaken, and then Peter's knowledge of what was going to happen to Ananias and Sapphira. Peter did not surmise that the news was going to kill these two people. No, that outcome had been revealed to him, and that is why he spoke as he did, particularly to Sapphira. He virtually announced her death to her. The intimation Peter received was part of the breaking in of the unseen and the eternal. Then, above all, there were the two deaths. They were what is called an act of God. You cannot explain them in any other terms.

So this is the great teaching of the Bible—the reality, the primacy, of the unseen, the spiritual, and the eternal. In an amazing way, this teaching is all summarized here before us. Is the message of the Gospel just an appeal to all of us to get together and pull the world back on to an even keel? Is it just an international appeal that says to the nations, "Now come along, let's solve this whole problem of color and of race. Let's be sensible and meet at the conference table." Is that Christianity? I find it very difficult to know how people who have ever read the Bible can think that. No, the message of the Bible is God, and God in three persons—the one who keeps on breaking into time. "Why hath Satan filled thine heart to lie to the Holy Ghost. . . . Thou has not lied unto men but unto God." Here it is.

"But I cannot understand the doctrine of the Trinity," says someone, "and because I cannot understand it, I don't believe it."

Stop for a moment and think about what you are trying to understand. God in three persons: Father, Son, Holy Spirit. That is the message of the Bible. Not "the ground of all being," not "the ultimate," not "the absolute," not some vague spirit of goodwill, not "a spirit of love"—but persons who think, who act, who intervene, who do things. God the Father, creating at the beginning: "In the beginning God created." God is not a force that brought things into being but a person who decided to create, who did so, and who, having created, goes on sustaining.

God the Son, active, appearing in various angelic forms in the Old Testament, and, when the fullness of the time was come, born as a babe in a stable in Bethlehem (see Gal. 4:4). The Son is a living person. "He that hath seen me," He said, "hath seen the Father" (John 14:9). "I and my Father are one" (John 10:30).

Here also in Acts is this great emphasis upon the Holy Spirit. "Why hath Satan filled thine heart to lie to the Holy Ghost. . . . Thou hast not lied unto men, but unto God."

Oh, I am not saying that I understand the Trinity, and I am not asking you to understand it. I am simply telling you that you will go to a Christless eternity unless you believe this message of the God who is and always was, the three persons in this blessed Godhead—coequal, coeternal in every respect, God acting in this world of time. It is not our world; we did not make it; we did not bring ourselves into it. We are in the hands of the living God. He is the author of everything, the sustainer of everything, and we live our lives under Him—these measured little lives that we have in this world as we pass through it. Oh, the idiotic conceit of men and women. They cannot understand themselves, nor God, nor anything without this view of spiritual reality.

Next I am going to put before you something that to the modern man or woman is indeed the height of folly. Peter asked, "Ananias, why hath Satan filled thine heart to lie to the Holy Ghost?" Now whatever you and I might like to think, the message, not only of this incident but of the whole Bible, is that there is a personal devil—Satan. The devil is part of the spiritual realm. Here again we see the utter bankruptcy of modern thinking. Moderns not only do not believe in God; they do not believe in the devil either. That is quite consistent, of course. When the Russians went up into space, they said that they did not see God anywhere. Apart from the blasphemy, what utter rubbish. What utter, pathetic folly! They did not see the devil either. So many say that because they have not seen God, there is no God, and because they have not seen the devil, there is no devil. That is the tragedy.

It is as much a part of the purpose of the Bible to teach us the reality and the personality of the devil as it is to teach us the personality and the being of God. Why is the world as it is? Why confusion? Why pain? Why lust, avarice, jealousy, envy? Why disease? The answer is back in the third chapter of Genesis, and it is about the devil. God made a perfect world—a paradise. He looked upon it all and "saw that it was good." Then the devil, this creature that is more subtle than any other, came and tempted the man and the woman, and they fell into sin. There is a strange parallel here. At the beginning of the original creation, the devil came in and caused trouble. Then came the second creation, the church, and again the devil was at work.

"If our gospel be hid," says Paul, "it is hid to them that are lost: in whom the god of this world hath blinded the minds of them which believe not, lest the light of the glorious gospel of Christ . . . should shine unto them" (2 Corinthians 4:3). If people do not believe the Gospel, there is one main reason—the devil has blinded them. Take Ephesians 2:1-2: "You hath he quickened, who were dead in trespasses and sins; wherein in time past ye walked according to the course of this world, according to the prince of the power of the air, the spirit that now worketh in the children of disobedience." That is the teaching of the apostle Paul. He puts it again in Ephesians 6:12: "We wrestle not against flesh and blood." It is not even my own human nature that constitutes the problem: "We wrestle not against flesh and blood, but against principalities, against powers, against the rulers of the darkness of this world, against spiritual wickedness in high [heavenly] places." That is the problem.

The book of Revelation deals with the same theme, with its descriptions of the devil cast into a lake of fire and the beasts that influence and control and mar the whole of life. And the same teaching is here in Acts 5: "Why hath

Satan filled thine heart to do this?" Peter, spiritual man that he now was as the result of his baptism with the Spirit, saw exactly what had happened. I say again, this is the teaching, the reality of the unseen realm. We are surrounded in this world by unseen powers and forces, evil as well as good, by principalities and powers, by rulers of the darkness of this world. These powers organize the evil in the world today, which is what makes it so devilish. The evil does not merely come from human beings. They are driven—the victims, the slaves, the dupes. The devil is in control, and he enters into the hearts of men and women, as we are told here, and masters and controls them.

That is why the world is as it is and, alas, that is why the church is as she is. Here in Acts 5, the devil comes into the hearts of Ananias and Sapphira, who are members of the church, and he does this devilish thing in them that leads to such terrible consequences. The devil is still working in the Christian church. The devil, says Paul, can turn himself into an angel of light and still does so. So you find prominent people in the church denying the very elements of the faith, denying the deity of the Son of God, some even denying the very existence of God—all in the name of Christianity. That is Satan, this unseen power. He is too clever, too fiendish, too involved, and too subtle to be merely of human origin.

We are all surrounded by these powers, and the Bible teaches that a great cosmic fight is going on—God and the devil, the kingdom of light and the kingdom of darkness, heaven and hell. You and I with all our great scientific knowledge and all our clubs and societies and institutions and counsels, all our arrangements to make a perfect world, are going from bad to worse because we are not aware of the powers influencing us in such a subtle manner. Lack of awareness is not always bad, but the good is often the greatest enemy of the best. Moral men and women have generally been the ones who have resisted the preaching of the Gospel more than anybody else—they have felt no need of it. Cheating tax-collectors and sinners are always more ready to listen than the Pharisees and scribes; that is the trouble. It is the devil.

So here is this great battle going on: The Holy Spirit and Satan are both operating upon this world, on you, on me—trying to win us. The devil was a created angel who rebelled and fell. He hates God and would drag the whole universe down to his own ultimate perdition. The devil was at work in the early church. He is still at work today. It is not your great brain that makes you reject the Gospel; it is the devil influencing your heart and making it impossible for you.

Finally, I must warn you that the last general message taught here is the fact of final judgment. This judgment is not something theoretical and remote and academic—a point of view in which we may or may not be interested. Final judgment is the truth about us, every single one of us. Men and women are responsible beings, responsible to God who made them, and they will have to stand before Him, before that God who knows everything. Ananias and his wife could agree to keep back a bit of money, saying to themselves, "The apostles won't know; nobody will know. We'll give the impression that we're great spiritual people, but we're also looking after ourselves—and how clever we are!" Clever? It was sheer madness. Why did they do it? Because they had forgotten the unseen, the spiritual; they had forgotten God. "But all things are naked and opened unto the eyes of him with whom we have to do" (Heb. 4:13).

Yes, according to the book of Revelation (20:12), the day is coming when the books will be produced and opened to your record. There is nothing that you have ever done or said or thought that is unknown to God. Men and women cannot escape God or evade him. They can do many things while they are in this world, but their times are altogether in the hands of God. They can be struck in a second, in a moment. They did not create their lives; they do not control them; nor, in an ultimate sense, can they end them. When they think all is well, sudden destruction comes. This is the great message of our Lord Himself. The end will come, and God will judge all those who have rejected the knowledge of Him, all who have remained dupes of Satan and have refused God's offer in Christ, His only begotten Son whom He sent into this world that "whosoever believeth in him should not perish, but have everlasting life" (John 3:16).

In the light of this fact, God calls upon us to repent, to acknowledge and confess our sin and shame and folly and ignorance of Him, and to believe His Gospel. That is the first great message that comes to us from the tragedy of Ananias and Sapphira. May God open our eyes to see it.

18

THE HEART AND ITS ENEMIES

But a certain man named Ananias, with Sapphira his wife, sold a possession, and kept back part of the price, his wife also being privy to it, and brought a certain part, and laid it at the apostles' feet. But Peter said, Ananias, why hath Satan filled thine heart to lie to the Holy Ghost, and to keep back part of the price of the land? Whiles it remained, was it not thine own? and after it was sold, was it not in thine own power? why hast thou conceived this thing in thine heart? thou hast not lied unto men, but unto God. And Ananias hearing these words fell down, and gave up the ghost: and great fear came on all them that heard these things. And the young men arose, wound him up, and carried him out, and buried him. And it was about the space of three hours after, when his wife, not knowing what was done, came in. And Peter answered unto her, Tell me whether ye sold the land for so much? And she said, Yea, for so much. Then Peter said unto her, How is it that ye have agreed together to tempt the Spirit of the Lord? behold, the feet of them which have buried thy husband are at the door, and shall carry thee out. Then fell she down straightway at his feet, and yielded up the ghost: and the young men came in, and found her dead, and, carrying her forth, buried her by her husband. And great fear came upon all the church, and upon as many as heard these things.
—Acts 5:1-11

We are continuing with the story of Ananias and Sapphira, the couple who decided to join with the other members of the early church in sharing their possessions. But they had a reservation. They pretended that they were giving all the money received from the sale of a piece of property, but they conspired together to keep back some of it. Because of that action God dealt with them in the terrifying manner described in this passage.

Now we have seen from this story that the first great purpose of the gospel message is to get us to realize that we are living in a spiritual world, a spiritual realm. The greatest lie of the devil is materialism, whatever form it may take. So the world forgets the unseen, the supernatural, the eternal, and ultimately that is the cause of all its tragedies. We are reminded of that truth here. The believers were meeting together and praying when suddenly God acted, and the whole situation was changed. But we are reminded equally of the constant operation of Satan who, in his hatred of God, is always doing his utmost to mar God's work, whether it be the original creation or this "new creation" called the Christian church.

So the message of the Gospel is that we are all responsible to God, as Ananias and Sapphira were, that we are all of us in God's hands, whether we know it or not. They did not realize it, but they had to face up to it, and that is true of all of us. What fools we are to fail to realize that we are in the hands of powers and forces greater than ourselves!

It is in such a world that the message of the church comes, this Gospel that the apostles were sent out to preach. The Lord had said to them just before His ascension, "And ye are witnesses of these things. . . . tarry ye in the city of Jerusalem, until ye be endued with power from on high" (Luke 24:48-49). He said, in effect, "I am going to send you to tell people about Me, who I am, why I came into the world, and what I have done"—this great good news of salvation, of deliverance, leading to a "joy unspeakable and full of glory" (1 Pet. 1:8).

So why is it that everyone in the world does not believe this message? With the world in trouble as it is, at its wits' end, with everything else failing, why do men and women dismiss the Gospel without even considering it? Now I have already given you the main part of the answer. Satan, the devil, the god of this world, "hath blinded the minds of them which believe not" (2 Cor. 4:4), lest they believe the glorious Gospel of Christ. How does Satan blind people? They do not see any need of the Gospel. It is as simple as that. If they saw a need, they would be ready to listen. They are aware of certain needs, but they are not aware of their true, real need, and that is always the work of the devil.

Now this amazing incident tells us that the trouble with humanity is that it does not know what is wrong. People are mistaken with regard to the nature of their problem, their basic need, and so they do not believe the

Gospel. This fundamental problem of need divides itself into two main sections. First, people are wrong in their view of human nature—of who they are and of what their needs are. Secondly, they are completely wrong in their treatment of the forces set against them.

Everyone is conscious that something is wrong and is aware that in this life there is a fight. But the vital issue is to know exactly what is wrong and the nature of the opposing forces. If you turn to secular historians, they will give you the history of the world's attempts to deal with itself and its problems. In the so-called history of civilization, we see men and women grappling with the problem. They have been extremely busy at this task—there would be no history books otherwise. Even in their wars they are looking for peace.

But in spite of all the energy expended, the world has gotten no better. So what is it in the human race that seems to be dogging its footsteps? Why is it that just when we think that everything is going to be all right, so many things go wrong? How often has that happened in the long history of the race—so much so that many historians believe that the world just goes round in circles? It appears to be going right up to the top, and then suddenly it seems to be on a curve, and back it goes again to the bottom. We advance, we regress, and on and on. Why is this? Well, because of the two great problems that the world must of necessity face. I want to put them to you in the light of this story of Ananias and Sapphira, because here, it seems to me, we are given great insight into the nature of these problems.

What is wrong with the modern view of the problem of the human condition? First, if you read the writings of people who try to deal with all the moral and political problems facing us today, you are at once struck by the fact that these writers all have a very superficial view. Generally they are interested only in conduct. They get the statistics of juvenile delinquency and theft and robbery and ask what can be done about the behavior of men and women. The sociologists are not interested in people in themselves, in how they react and how they live. They start with what they call "society," and then "the interrelationships," and they put it learnedly and cleverly. Their question is: How can we get these people who commit crimes and disturb society to become good members of society? So the whole time they are only looking at the surface of the problem.

A second fallacy follows from that, almost of necessity. This fallacy suggests that the problems facing society are entirely the result of a lack of knowledge and instruction, that people behave as they do because they do not know any better. People have not been given the right training. The conclusion is that for a harmonious and happy society, nothing is needed but education.

People go wrong because they have not yet quite understood that they must adjust themselves to society and to other members of society. When these people have been taught how to accommodate themselves to what society requires, the problems will be eliminated.

Now I think you will agree that that is a fair representation of the commonly held view about how to deal with the problems facing society. This view underlies the approach to education in schools, and it is the controlling theory behind the punishment of crime and the treatment of prisoners, in which the emphasis is on "rehabilitation," as it is called—which means training people. You may have to call in psychotherapists, of course, but the purpose is to get people to think straight. So there is a multiplication of agencies designed to treat the mind, to give instruction, and to show a better way.

But I suggest to you that this one story of Ananias and Sapphira is enough in and of itself to show how completely superficial all that is. Look at these people and at what happened to them. Can you explain Ananias and Sapphira merely in terms of lack of knowledge or of understanding? Or take any one of the great illustrations of the same principle that we find running right through the Bible. Can you explain the conduct of men and women merely in intellectual terms? The moment you bring these modern views to the light of the scriptural teaching, you see that they are hopelessly superficial.

To put it positively, the real failure is the inability to see that the essential problem of the human race is the problem of the heart. Here is the great emphasis of the whole of the Bible. This is where, if I may so put it, biblical psychology shows its profundity. Entirely on these grounds alone, I would put out of court every current theory. People talk so much about psychology, but it is there that they are wrong, because psychology simply means the understanding of people and their behavior in totality. Here in the Bible, and here alone, you get a true assessment of human nature and an analysis that reveals a profound psychological understanding.

Peter came to the point at once. "Peter said, Ananias, why hath Satan filled thine heart to lie to the Holy Ghost?" And he said the same thing, in effect, to Sapphira when she came in afterwards. But listen to Peter again. Working out his point with Ananias, he said, "Why hath Satan filled thine heart to lie to the Holy Ghost, and to keep back part of the price of the land? Whiles it remained, was it not thine own? and after it was sold, was it not in thine own power?" In effect, you remember, Peter was saying, "To start with, you need not have sold it, but even after you had, and after you received the money, there was no compulsion even then for you to give a halfpenny. You could have kept it all. Twice over you deliberately decided to deceive. Why did you do it?" Then he continued, "Why hast thou conceived this thing?"—where? In your mind? No—"in thine heart." And there is the whole problem exposed.

So the trouble with the modern outlook is that it has never seen that the problem is in the hearts of men and women. The problem is not intellectual, due to a lack of knowledge and of information. The difficulty is much deeper. There are elements in human nature that are deeper and stronger and more profound than the mind. These elements are the controlling factors and can mar and ruin the whole of someone's life. But here is the great message of the Bible. We are told of the devil—Satan, who is mentioned here—that what caused his original fall was that he lifted up his heart against God. Jealousy! Something deep and profound. He was not merely thinking. He desired something—to be equal with God. The heart condition is what the Bible emphasizes everywhere with regard to men and women.

Now I have stressed the honesty of the Scriptures, and we take one notable example. One of the greatest men of the Old Testament is King David, that "sweet psalmist of Israel," that beautiful young man who honored God and obtained a great victory over Goliath, who established the kingdom and raised it to such great and wonderful heights, heights it never quite attained afterwards. But the Bible is honest and tells us the truth about him. It tells us that King David was guilty of adultery and murder. Why did he do that? Was it lack of knowledge? Was it that he had not been sufficiently instructed in the art of how to accommodate to others in society? Was it that he needed to be rehabilitated?

The whole idea is so superficial it is ridiculous! David himself eventually came to see the reason, and he puts it honestly in Psalm 51 when he cries out in his agony, "Create in me a clean heart, O God; and renew a right spirit within me" (v. 10). He knew where the trouble was. A man like David, who had great insight, who had received messages from God and knew what it was to be inspired by the Holy Spirit to write those incomparable psalms, a man with a knowledge of God's law and of God's truth, could commit adultery and murder. Why? Was his trouble only in the mind? God knows it was not, and David came to know it was not. It is not the mind, but the spirit, the heart, this deeper part of human nature that causes the trouble. That is what is forgotten today.

Our Lord is equally explicit. The Pharisees and scribes were wrong about this selfsame thing, but our Lord put it quite plainly to them. His own disciples did not understand it either, so He said, "Do not ye yet understand, that whatsoever entereth in at the mouth goeth into the belly, and is cast out into the draught? But those things which proceed out of the mouth come forth from the heart; and they defile the man. For out of the heart proceed evil thoughts, murders, adulteries, fornications, thefts, false witness, blasphemies: these are the things which defile a man" (Matt. 15:17-20).

The heart is the center of the personality. The heart includes the feelings and the emotions but also something even deeper. There is a center to every one of us, a great center, out of which everything comes, which controls everything, and our trouble is there. The problem is not merely intellectual. If it were, our educational systems would solve it. No, there is something in men and women that is deeper than their minds, something that will make them contradict their knowledge and trample upon it and violate it, so that they do wrong even though they know that it is wrong. That is the trouble.

Take again the way our blessed Lord puts it: "This is the condemnation, that light is come into the world"—Why does everyone not believe it then? He gives the answer—"and men loved darkness rather than light, because their deeds were evil" (John 3:19). Here is the trouble—the love of darkness. It is not that people are unaware of light. They have had light. Throughout the running centuries, civilizations have known light apart from the revelation of God. You can read the philosophers and study their noble views of life, their exhortations to rise to a higher level. They have shown the better way; they have shown the folly and futility and madness of war. There has been plenty of light and instruction and information. And never has the world had more light than it has today, and yet the statistics for crime and violence have never been so bad.

How do you explain these things? I repeat that there is only one explanation—the trouble with humanity lies in the heart, and any view that does not realize that fact is already doomed to failure. James puts this teaching clearly when he writes in his epistle on the subject of war. People are troubled by this subject. "Why," they ask, "in this enlightened age and generation, are there still wars?" "From whence come wars and fightings among you?" asks James. Then he says, "Come they not hence, even of your lusts that war in your members? Ye lust, and have not: ye kill, and desire to have, and cannot obtain: ye fight and war, yet ye have not, because ye ask not. Ye ask, and receive not, because ye ask amiss, that ye may consume it upon your lusts" (James 4:1-3).

Peter asked Ananias and Sapphira: "Why hast thou conceived this thing in thine heart?" This is the question, and the answer remains the same. Men and women are not only intellects. However much they know, they are governed by what they like, what they want. It is not merely the poor and the ignorant and the illiterate who are guilty of adultery and who pass through the divorce courts.

University professors are not paragons of all the virtues. A man or woman may have vast learning and a great brain but be a miserable failure in the art of living. Why? Because the "drives," as they are called today—the lusts, desires, and passions—may be equally great, and these are deeper than the mind; they come out of the heart! It is not the knowledge that goes into the mind that makes a person, but that which comes out. There is something that vitiates the very source and fountain of the personality so that all efforts at purification come to nothing. You can multiply the number of psychotherapists in the prisons and everywhere else. You can bring them into the schools, if you like, and that is happening. You can spend millions on educating society to adjust itself, but it will not work. The world is providing ample proof. I repeat that those methods stem from an utterly superficial view of the problem of humanity.

But let me go on to show you something else that comes out strikingly in this story from Acts. The message here is not only that the trouble is in the heart, but also that the heart is in a terrible state, that it is perverted and twisted. The truth is that the human heart is rotten. No one else tells you that, but the Gospel does. Jeremiah says, "The heart is deceitful above all things, and desperately wicked: who can know it?" (Jer. 17:9). That is what the Bible says everywhere about the hearts of men and women as they are by nature. I sometimes think that people have not really started living until they have discovered the truth about themselves and their own hearts—what the old teachers used to call "the plague of one's own heart." The heart problem is illustrated to perfection in the story of Ananias and Sapphira.

Peter expressed his amazement: "Why hast thou conceived this thing in thine heart?" What made them do it? Have you ever felt like that about yourself? You do not know yourself unless you have. Have you not been amazed at what you do and the thoughts that pass through your mind, the thoughts you accept and fondle, the marvelous thoughts, the ugly, foul thoughts? Have you never wondered, what is this evil that is in me?

Now let me analyze the problem just a little for you. The human heart is in such a terrible state that people deceive themselves. They are such fools and have such deceitful hearts that they always think they are better than they are. We are all guilty of that. We can put up a wonderful defense. Other people are worse, while we are always better!

Such is the deceit of the heart that it makes us think we are very clever.

That is always the fatal mistake that every criminal makes, is it not? Criminals are caught because they think that they have planned the perfect crime. But they always make a mistake. Our big mistake is that we think we are cleverer than we are. Ananias and Sapphira thought they could get the best of both worlds. Both agreed that it was a wonderful scheme. Yes, Sapphira knew all about it; they were in it together. They both said, "We will get all the credit for having given this gift, but we have also kept back this portion for ourselves, and we shall live on that and enjoy it. We are pleasing the church and ourselves; we are serving God and mammon! We are getting all the advantages of sacrifice, the public applause and approval, while receiving what we want by way of self-satisfaction."

We all think we can do this and that we are extremely clever. But we fool ourselves. Oh, the folly of men and women! Our Lord looked at such people and said, "Ye cannot serve God and mammon" (Matt. 6:24). Yes, you want to go to heaven, but you want to get your fill of this world, too, do you not? But it cannot be done. You must choose one or the other. You cannot walk on the broad and narrow ways at the same time. Yet many people are trying to do that, and they are stretching their legs to cover both. They think they are clever. They have everything; they are in church and outside; they believe and disbelieve as they choose.

Even further, people not only deceive themselves, but they think they can deceive others. Ananias and Sapphira thought they were fooling the whole church. Can you not see the deceitfulness here, the pretense, the sham, the hypocrisy—oh, how abominable! But is not the same thing true of every one of us? What impression do we try to give to others? Dishonesty runs through society—the lie of the compliment, the lie of the appearance. Part of the tragedy of the world is that men and women are deliberately putting on masks. That is the meaning of hypocrisy—people pretend to be what they are not. They think they are clever, that they have carried it off. "The heart is deceitful above all things, and desperately wicked: who can know it?" (Jer. 17:9).

But the height of the tragedy and the folly of the heart is that people are also quite convinced that they can even deceive God. This is the problem; this is what we are dealing with. It is not a little psychotherapy that people need. This thing down in the depths of the heart deceives the very person who is ministering the psychotherapy. And it persuades men and women, fools that they are, that even God does not know, that they are so clever, so subtle, such wonderful manipulators that even God can be deceived.

So that is the truth, and the world does not realize it. Because of this, all the surface measures and remedies are condemned to nothing before they have even started. That is the first great error in the thinking of the human race about its condition.

Then the second error goes with it—the fatal wrong view about the powers set against us. Indeed, the world does not realize that there are powers set against us. It does not recognize the existence of Satan or understand that evil is concrete and positive and objective. One of the great fallacies of modern thinking is that evil is regarded as artificial and not real. People criticize biblical teaching because it regards evil as something concrete, because it tells us that evil is headed up in a person called Satan, the god of this world, who through his powers and emissaries exercises a malign influence upon the minds, hearts, and bodies of men and women—"the prince of the power of the air, the spirit that now worketh in the children of disobedience" (Eph. 2:2).

But modern men and women ridicule the biblical view. They say that the problem of war is purely a question of lack of knowledge. Have two world wars not taught us? No, a power is determined to keep this world in a state of ruination—that is the explanation of the trouble of the world. As I have often said, the trouble is not the Hitlers and Mussolinis and Stalins. If it were, we could deal with the problem. The trouble is the one who governs them, uses them, raises them up, puts ideas to them, gives them their devilish cunning and daring, and teaches them their masterstrokes.

The evil things that happen in the world give evidence of an objective evil power at work, a great controller of the forces of evil. There is no other explanation for the recrudescence of witchcraft and devil worship. These practices are coming back by leaps and bounds today, together with all sorts of other hidden, malign, and ugly things. Educated people are going in for them, giving themselves to them, taking drugs to get a still greater experience of them.

Is all this just due to some negative qualities in humanity? That is what we are asked to believe. We are told that what we regard as biblical teaching about concrete evil is merely something negative, merely the absence of certain good qualities or the failure to develop these qualities. So the tragic cause of the trouble is that the world does not recognize the dominion of Satan or the slavery of sin. But I repeat the biblical teaching. "Sin shall not have dominion over you: for ye are not under law, but under grace" (Rom. 6:14). Dominion! That is the tyranny, the power, of sin. Or again as Paul puts it in verse 17 of that same chapter: "But God be thanked, that ye were the servants [the slaves] of sin, but ye have obeyed from the heart that form of doctrine which was delivered you." The Christians in Rome had been the slaves of sin, but not any longer. Now they had become the servants of God and of righteousness. Again Paul says in Romans: "For I delight in the law of God after the inward man: but I see another law in my members" dragging me down and "bringing me into captivity to the law of sin and death which is in my members" (Rom. 7:22-23).

That is the teaching of the Bible from beginning to end. "I am carnal, sold under sin" (Rom. 7:14). There is a power greater than myself, a power that is organizing evil and sin in me and in everyone, in the whole of the universe. In addition to the deceitful, unregenerate human heart, there is a tremendous power: "Why hath Satan filled thine heart to lie to the Holy Ghost? . . . why hast thou conceived this thing in thine heart?" It is the devil, the one who came into the Garden of Eden and said, "Hath God said?" He is still whispering and suggesting. According to this incident in Acts and to the whole teaching of the Bible, this evil power is the only true and adequate explanation of the human state and condition. I began by asking: Why does not the whole world believe this Gospel? I am giving you the answer: "The god of this world hath blinded the minds of them which believe not" (2 Cor. 4:4), lest they believe the glorious Gospel of Christ.

The devil says: "Do not listen to the Bible. The problem is just in your mind; it is only a matter of conduct, and all you need is instruction; the world is improving, and it can be improved." The devil does all he can to keep the world from realizing that the problem is down in the depths and the vitals and the center of a person's being, and that he is the one who controls the world and the flesh—he has this awful power. For the moment humanity comes to see and to believe the truth, it will realize that its only hope is in the Gospel. The Gospel says, "God so loved the world, that he gave his only begotten Son, that whosoever believeth in him should not perish, but have everlasting life" (John 3:16).

Why did the great and eternal God send His only Son into this world? Why was the Son of God ever born as the babe of Bethlehem? It is because the heart is desperately wicked and deceitful. It is because men and women are the slaves and the dupes of the devil. It is because there was nothing else that could ever set humanity right. "Education," you say. God has given it—the Ten Commandments, the moral law. Here it is. "Do you want to know how to live?" asks God. "Here is My answer. Do you want instruction? I will give you a Moses; I will give you an Aaron; I will raise My prophets." In the Old Testament we see God instructing men and women on the way to live. The knowledge is there. Some has been taught by the Greek philosophers.

But, I say again, knowledge is not enough. Because the problem is in the heart, people cannot save themselves. God must save; God alone can save. Once you realize that it is the deceitfulness of the heart and the power of the devil that causes the trouble in your life and in the world, you will see that there is only one hope. That hope is that the Son of God should come into this world and live a perfect life of obedience to God, should meet the devil and evil in all the power of their might, and defeat and rout them. Then, having done that, He should take upon Himself the load of our sin and our guilt. We have all done evil in God's sight; we have all turned our backs upon Him, and we have all done it deliberately. Like Ananias and Sapphira, we knew what we were doing. We knew God's law. Conscience spoke and said, "It is wrong; you must not do it." But we said, "I will. I like it. I want it. I must have it." That is the story of every single one of us. We have sinned against the light, against knowledge, against what we know to be the truth. Even worse, some of us may even have been hypocrites who have pretended to believe in Christ and to serve Him, while living according to our own desires, thinking that we could fool Him.

We are all guilty, and we cannot remove that guilt. We cannot undo it or change ourselves. We may promise to live better in the future—we have often promised—but we cannot do it. Our New Year's resolutions are quickly forgotten, and we are back to where we were. We have done that a thousand times.

This is where the Gospel comes in. Men and women do not see their need of the Gospel because they have never seen themselves; they have never seen the nature of the problem; they have never seen the blackness, the vileness, the perversion of their own unregenerate hearts; they have never seen their rottenness, their final hopelessness before God. They have never seen that death is followed by judgment, and that in that judgment a sentence is pronounced of either eternal bliss or eternal misery.

But once they do see these truths, they will turn to the Gospel; they will fly to Christ; they will recognize that there is only one who can deliver them from the condemnation of God's holy law and the power of the devil and of hell. There is only one who can create a new heart and renew a right spirit within them. It is the Son of God, Jesus Christ, the one who just before His ascension gave the disciples a commission, telling them, "Ye shall be witnesses unto me both in Jerusalem, and in all Judaea, and in Samaria, and unto the uttermost part of the earth" (Acts 1:8). He formed the church to call men and women to "flee from the wrath to come" (Matt. 3:7), to call them to repentance. God calls them to face themselves, not only in their actions but in that which led them to the actions—their evil, foul, unregenerate, perverted hearts—and to turn to God's amazing love in Christ Jesus.

Ananias and Sapphira died. The believers rolled up their bodies in their cloaks and carried them out. They perished in an earthly sense; maybe they perished in a greater sense. And those who die unregenerate perish not only in life and in death but through all eternity. Have you ever realized the state of your heart? Have you seen that your real need is a new heart that can love the light and hate the darkness, and love God, and follow His dear Son in the certain knowledge that in eternity you shall have the beatific vision? "Blessed are the pure in heart: for they shall see God" (Matt. 5:8). May that be the portion of every one of us.

19

HUMAN NEED AND GOD'S PROVISION

But a certain man named Ananias, with Sapphira his wife, sold a possession, and kept back part of the price, his wife also being privy to it, and brought a certain part, and laid it at the apostles' feet. But Peter said, Ananias, why hath Satan filled thine heart to lie to the Holy Ghost, and to keep back part of the price of the land? Whiles it remained, was it not thine own? and after it was sold, was it not in thine own power? why hast thou conceived this thing in thine heart? thou hast not lied unto men, but unto God. And Ananias hearing these words fell down, and gave up the ghost: and great fear came on all them that heard these things. And the young men arose, wound him up, and carried him out, and buried him. And it was about the space of three hours after, when his wife, not knowing what was done, came in. And Peter answered unto her, Tell me whether ye sold the land for so much? And she said, Yea, for so much. Then Peter said unto her, How is it that ye have agreed together to tempt the Spirit of the Lord? behold, the feet of them which have buried thy husband are at the door, and shall carry thee out. Then fell she down straightway at his feet, and yielded up the ghost: and the young men came in, and found her dead, and, carrying her forth, buried her by her husband. And great fear came upon all the church, and upon as many as heard these things.

—Acts 5:1-11

As we continue to consider the story of Ananias and Sapphira, let me point something out as a matter of principle. I will say this for the modern man and woman. They are quite consistent with themselves; they are logical. We must recognize that belief and unbelief are systems, and just as there is a consistency about belief, so there is a consistency about unbelief. My case against those who are not Christians is not that they are wrong here and there or in certain particular respects, but that they are altogether wrong. As we look into the teaching of this particular incident as it is put explicitly by the apostle Peter, and as we see that teaching demonstrated in action, we shall see that all the parts of this picture fit together. Unbelief is a system, and it is totally wrong. Belief, on the other hand, is a system that is totally right. When you discuss the Gospel with unbelievers, have you not found that it is not merely at one point that there is disagreement, but there is a divergence all along the line?

We have said that men and women reject the Gospel because they do not realize their real need. They are always ready to agree that they could be better; they may even be ready to say that they are anxious to be better. They are ready to admit the need for reform, improvement, and advance. You will find that the world is always ready to listen to exhortation and instruction. There are many cultural and moral agencies in the world; people take a keen interest in them and are zealous in these matters. Yet they reject the Gospel with scorn.

Many people are not only prepared to listen to teaching and moralizing and philosophies in general, but they are also ready to listen to preaching about Jesus. They have no trouble about Jesus when He is presented as just a man, a great man, of course, indeed, the best man that the world has ever known. They are willing to read and to hear about Him. They are ready to admire and praise Him and to go out and try to imitate Him—Jesus, the incomparable teacher, the perfect example.

Indeed, I can go further and say that such people, in a sense, have no objection to religion. By religion, I mean trying to please God, trying to worship God, trying to live a good and godly life. But they do object to the sort of thing you have in this incident in Acts 5—a living God who acts, punishment, death and hell, the amazing truth about the Virgin Birth, the mystery of the two natures in the one person, the miraculous and the supernatural and the divine. That is what they reject.

Here we come face to face with the real heart and nerve of this problem. Why the objection to the supernatural? Why the objection to all that we find recorded in the Bible? Why the objection to these events in the early chapters of the book of Acts—the descent of the Holy Spirit, the miraculous signs? The only answer is that humanity does not realize its real need. We have already seen that the trouble is in the human heart, but we see something further in this incident. Here men and women are confronted by four main enemies. What are they?

The first is sin—this indwelling evil, this power greater than our minds that ever works in us.

The second is Satan—an unseen power at work in the world, moving, manipulating, conspiring. He is the antagonist and the adversary of all human beings.

Thirdly, and we are reminded of it very forcibly here, we face death. Death, described by Paul as the last enemy, came in immediately after Satan. The moment Adam fell after being tempted by Satan, there was death—a spiritual death, but it led to a physical death also. Man and woman as they were originally created had no need to die; had they gone on obeying God's commandments, they would never have died. But God had warned them, "In the day that thou eatest thereof thou shalt surely die" (Gen. 2:17). Death is the punishment of sin, and so death has always been regarded as an enemy. Oh, what would we not do if we knew that we were never going to die! How dreadful are the thoughts of death. Shakespeare has expressed it all:

> *The undiscovered country from whose bourn*
> *No traveler returns.*
> Hamlet

We hate death because we feel that death hates us, and there he is, ever advancing toward us. Do what we will, we cannot evade him; he is ever approaching with his terrible claim. Death—the enemy, the last enemy. You can evade him for years, but in the end you have to meet him.

> *The paths of glory lead but to the grave.*
> Thomas Gray

Throughout the long story of humanity people have faced this great enemy. You never know when he will come. He came suddenly with Ananias and Sapphira. They thought they had been subtle. They had done well for themselves and were going to be right for the rest of their lives. They would be praised as saints and yet have what they wanted to keep themselves going. Then Ananias was carried out dead, and three hours later Sapphira dropped dead. That is the world we are living in.

Finally, at the back of it all, you see the law. I am following in a great tradition when I describe the law of God as our enemy. That may surprise some of you, but from the early days of Irenaeus, through Martin Luther down to today, people have described the law of God as one of our enemies. The law was not meant to be an enemy, but because of what we are, the law becomes our enemy. If we had never sinned, the law would have been our friend; it would have shown us what to do and how to live; but because we are sinners, the law is against us. We are ever confronted by its holy demands. It condemns us, and it has no mercy.

Now according to Scripture, those are the enemies of humanity, but, of course, modern men and women know nothing about all this. They just think they need to be a little better, to do a little more good and a little less evil. Reformation—certainly. Teaching—of course! Jesus as the example—no difficulty whatsoever. And they think that they need nothing beyond that. But they do need more because of these four enemies. Now here are their real needs: First, each person needs a new nature, a nature that, instead of loving and gloating in sin, will hate it. I am not talking here about improvement, but about something radical and fundamental—a new heart.

But even if there is a new nature, the devil is ever waiting, trying, tempting. The second great need, therefore, is power to conquer the devil, master him, and defeat him.

Thirdly, we need power to deal with death. Every human being is born to die. You may say of a baby born a second ago that this child has started living; I am equally entitled to say that this child has started dying. We have only a limited span, and there stands the last enemy—death. We need power to overcome it.

Finally, we need an answer to the law of God. We need an ability to satisfy God and to stand before Him in the judgment.

Now the first principle I am establishing is that people reject this Gospel, and particularly the most glorious parts of the Gospel, because they are not aware of those four great fundamental needs. Am I addressing someone at the moment who has never understood the real problem? Have you ever thought of the state of your heart? Have you ever thought of sin, that enemy that gets you down and defeats you constantly? Have you ever thought of Satan and his malign power? Have you ever considered the fact of death? Have you ever faced the Lord God? Those are the great needs, and they are all here in this story in Acts: sin, Satan, death, and God's coming in judgment. I do not expect people who have not recognized these needs to believe the Gospel. They regard it not only as unnecessary, but as quite ridiculous.

My second principle is that, having failed to realize the four great problems even when these are pointed out, people also fail to realize their total inability to solve them. These are the logical steps, and each one fits into the other. Truth is a whole, and all of these facets of the truth go together; they are a part of the same great message. Even when you tell men and women about the four fundamental needs, and even if they get a glimmering of understanding with respect to them, they then fall into the error of thinking that they are capable of dealing with them. I say this on the basis of the story of Ananias and Sapphira. Why does an event like this ever happen? As Peter puts it: "Why hath Satan filled thine heart to lie to the Holy Ghost?" And, "Why hast thou conceived this thing in thine heart?" Or again, "How is it that ye have agreed together to tempt the Spirit of the Lord?" There is a fatal something that dogs all our efforts to pull ourselves together, to defeat our enemies, and to reestablish ourselves.

This failure is the great story of the Bible, and it is the great story of the whole of civilization. The story shouts at us every day of the week from our newspapers, television screens, and radios. The world is as it is because of our total failure to deal with our real enemies. The modern world is proving the case of the Bible more clearly than perhaps ever before in its long history. The world demonstrates this case before our eyes. Yet the average person does not see it, the government does not see it, the sociologist and educationalist do not see it. Only Christian people see the problems for what they are, and this has always been the church's message throughout the centuries.

The first thing people cannot solve is the problem of their own selves because the world still believes in its own perfectibility. The so-called thinkers not only believe in human perfectibility as a possibility, but they believe that it is actually happening. People today think that they are very superior to their forefathers who believed the Gospel out of ignorance and that what is needed is dissemination of knowledge. The great modern slogan is: "Knowledge is power." Until comparatively recently it was said that the two great causes of crime are lack of education and poverty. That was the explanation put forward by the politicians, by the philosophers, and by the sociologists. But though we are better educated and better off than we have ever been, the crime figures have reached new highs.

Here is the very essence of the problem. People still believe that perfectibility is actually taking place in spite of the facts staring them in the face. Unbelief has a consistency within itself, as I said at the beginning, but the moment you begin to analyze it, you will see how it breaks down. Modern people say that they are realists. They think that Christians shut their eyes to life, pull down the blinds, take up the fairy tale, sing the choruses, and make themselves feel wonderfully happy, as primitive people have always done, not knowing the truth and not facing the facts of sin, evil, and crime. They, the unbelievers, are the people of the world who know the real problems, while we are the people who turn our backs on problems or perhaps are so ignorant that we do not even know they exist—the goody-goody people. Unbelievers may grant that we are beginning to be introduced to evil now through the television, but, they say, we used to know nothing at all. That is the picture, and it is such utter rubbish! As if every man who preaches has always been a saint, as if the history of the church does not show you men and women who had sinned almost to the very gates of hell before being retrieved and becoming preachers of the Gospel!

Yet the fact of the matter is that it is the Christians who are the realists. People who, when face to face with the facts and statistics of this modern hour, can think that perfectibility is already taking place are not realists. They are the ones living in a fantasy. Those who can believe that humanity is advancing are the romanticists. They are the ones who are not facing the facts. They are whistling in the dark to keep their courage up, pretending they are very happy. If they faced the facts, they would realize that there is something in this world—some influence, some power—that is defeating humanity and all its best and most zealous efforts.

The great teaching of the Bible at this point tells us quite plainly that the world is full of dishonest cheats like Ananias and Sapphira. It tells us that people put up a facade. They pretend to be nice when there is murder in their hearts. How affable they are at the cocktail party but, oh, the daggers in the spirit!

Why is this? It is because men and women cannot change themselves; they have been trying to, and they are still trying. Self-improvement has been the whole effort of civilization. But the Bible has put it in a famous question: "Can the Ethiopian change his skin, or the leopard his spots?" (Jer. 13:23). It cannot be done. Or again as we read in Ecclesiastes, "That which is crooked cannot be made straight" (Eccl. 1:15). Rehabilitation centers cannot change people, and neither can psychotherapists. If anything is becoming plain, it is the collapse of the whole Freudian system with its analysis and supposed therapy. This system has failed and is increasingly being recognized as a failure. As our Lord put it to the Pharisees: "Ye Pharisees make clean the outside of the cup and the platter; but your inward part is full of ravening and wickedness" (Luke 11:39). Oh, yes, we can produce a better appearance. Now you may be surprised to hear a preacher saying something like this, but to me that was the whole trouble with Victorianism. Victorianism was very successful in producing respectability, but it was not successful in changing human nature. Yes, you can produce respectability in a measure by acts of Parliament, by forming societies and offering inducements, but that will not change people. These measures will put a better suit on them, and yet leave them exactly where they were. That is "the outside of the cup and platter," but the problem is inside where there is the ravening and wickedness.

But there is a further reason why men and women can never change themselves, and it follows from what we were seeing earlier. They never know the truth about themselves. Ananias and Sapphira did not; they thought they were clever and that they were fooling the apostles and God Himself. But they did not realize that they were actually fooling only themselves. People are centrally and essentially dishonest.

The Bible gives us some terrible illustrations of this deception and dishonesty. King David, one of the best men in the Bible, committed a terrible sin—adultery covered over with murder—and he was pretty pleased. He got what he wanted—the woman. But we are told, "The thing that David had done displeased the LORD" (2 Sam. 11:27). David was not aware of the Lord's displeasure until God sent the prophet Nathan to him. Nathan told David a very clever story that mirrored exactly what David had done. A wealthy man stole a poor man's pet lamb and killed that instead of killing a lamb of his own. David was a great and noble man with a strong sense of justice. So when Nathan put the case to him, David did not hesitate for a second. He said, "A man who has done a thing like that has done a grave injustice, and he must be punished." Then Nathan looked quietly at him and said, "Thou art the man" (2 Sam. 12:7). David saw the injustice when it was presented in the case of somebody else, but not in his own case. And we are all like David, every one of us. We are the people who denounced Hitler, but so many of us have done the same as he did in principle.

The apostle Paul in writing to the Romans points out that there is no excuse for anyone because we all have a knowledge of right and wrong, but we never apply it to ourselves. He says, "Which show the work of the law written in their hearts, their conscience also bearing witness, and their thoughts the mean while accusing or else excusing one another" (Rom. 2:15). We see faults in others but not in ourselves. We are always on the defensive. We can always rationalize what we have done and explain it away, but the other fellow—there is no excuse for him at all! And while we are like that, we will never change. We are always protecting ourselves so that we will never realize the truth and have to deal with it.

The second thing people cannot solve is the problem of the devil. We cannot conquer him. The Old Testament offers ample evidence. Look at the great men and women of the Bible. Every single one was defeated by the devil. Why, Adam and Eve in a state of perfection in the Garden of Eden were conquered by the devil. Perfect man, perfect woman—defeated. If the perfect were defeated, it is not surprising that the imperfect have been defeated.

The Lord taught the same thing. He describes the devil as "a strong man armed" (Luke 11:21), the one by whom we are confronted. "Your adversary the devil," says Peter, and he describes him as "a roaring lion," who "walketh about, seeking whom he may devour" (1 Pet. 5:8). Paul refers to him as "the prince of the power of the air" (Eph. 2:2) and "the god of this world" (2 Cor. 4:4). Jude has the same teaching. He tells us not to "speak evil of dignities" (Jude 8) and reminds us that "Michael the archangel, when contending with the devil he disputed about the body of Moses, durst not bring against him a railing accusation, but said, The Lord rebuke thee" (Jude 9). The archangel knows the might and the power of the devil; so he does not speak lightly or rebuke him himself but says, "The Lord rebuke thee."

Then John reminds us in his first epistle that "the Son of God was manifested, that he might destroy the works of the devil" (1 John 3:8). And look in the last book in the Bible, the book of Revelation, and see "the great dragon . . . that old serpent, called the Devil" (Rev. 13:9). Look at that powerful being that can give power to beasts, power to states, power to churches, and can manipulate them and use them for his own malign and infernal ends. There it is—this strange and mighty power that none but he who rides on the white horse with the sword in his mouth can finally defeat. That is the teaching of Scripture.

Human beings are helpless face to face with the devil, and they are equally helpless face to face with the last enemy, death. Do what you like— make a study of old age and extend life, but you cannot touch death; all your systems and discoveries and health schemes will never abolish it. Death is the last enemy that shall be conquered.

At the end of it all and beyond and above and more important than all I have been saying is this: Human beings cannot satisfy God. And that is, I repeat, the chief thing of all: "It is appointed unto men once to die, but after this the judgment" (Heb. 9:27). What does God demand? Well, here in this story of Ananias and Sapphira, we see so plainly that "the LORD looketh on the heart" (1 Sam. 16:7). Did our Lord Himself not say that? He said to the Pharisees, "Ye are they which justify yourselves before men; but God knoweth your hearts: for that which is highly esteemed among men is abomination in the sight of God" (Luke 16:15). Oh, here is something that modern men and women know nothing about. David saw it after that terrible episode in his life with Bathsheba. In Psalm 51 he says, "Thou desirest truth in the inward parts" (v. 6). You cannot dissemble before God; you cannot fool God. Ananias and Sapphira thought they could, but God knows all about us: "All things are naked and opened unto the eyes of him with whom we have to do" (Heb. 4:13).

Does God just ask me to be a decent and nice man who does not do certain things? Oh, what a ridiculous suggestion! Do you know what God demands of all of us? It is this: "Thou shalt love the Lord thy God with all thy heart, and with all thy soul, and with all thy mind, and with all thy strength: this is the first commandment. And the second is like, namely this, Thou shalt love thy neighbour as thyself" (Mark 12:30-31). That is the demand of God's holy law, and, whether we like it or not, that is the demand we all have to face. A reckoning day is coming; the account is being kept. But modern men and women are jazzing themselves away, entertaining themselves; they do not know what God demands. That is why their world is as it is. They do not believe in law or in order; nor do they believe in discipline. They are selfish and self-centered and cause chaos in society.

Hypocrisy never pays with God. He knows all about us, and we are confronted by Him and His holy law. Let the apostle Paul put it for us in a few words: "Now we know that what things soever the law saith, it saith to them who are under the law: that every mouth may be stopped, and all the world"—all the world—"may become guilty before God" (Rom. 3:19). "There is none righteous, no, not one" (Rom. 3:10). What about the people who are doing a lot of good? "There is none righteous, no, not one." They are with the world that is utterly condemned before God. In the eyes of God there is no difference between the best moral person and the vilest sinner in the city of London—none at all. That is the gospel.

> *The rank is but the guinea's stamp,*
> *The man's the gowd for a' that.*
> R. Burns

God is not interested in the clothing, the outward appearance. He is interested in the heart and in how well we meet His demands. God does not ask how much good you have done. He says, "Have you loved Me with all your heart and with all your soul and with all your mind and with all your strength?" In the Old Testament He puts it like this: "All our righteousnesses are as filthy rags" (Isa. 64:6). Saul of Tarsus, who thought he had clothed himself in very beautiful garments and had amassed a great mound of righteousness as a Pharisee, came to see that his goodness was nothing but dung and refuse. All this talk about goodness and all that we are doing is vile, refuse in the sight of God. Self-righteousness is foul because it is self-centered and lacks the most glorious element of holiness and beauty and self-abnegation and forgetfulness of self.

When men and women realize what God demands, they are very ready to agree with Augustus Toplady when he writes:

> *Not the labors of my hands,*
> *Can fulfill Thy law's demands,*
> *Could my zeal no respite know,*
> *Could my tears forever flow,*
> *All for sin could not atone.*

I cannot atone for my sin. "How should man be just with God?" (Job 9:2). "Who shall dwell in thy holy hill?" (Psa. 15:1). Who can dwell with the Lord, with burning fire? These are the great questions. And it is because men and women know nothing about these things that they reject this miraculous, supernatural Gospel. For this reason they are complete and total failures. They cannot change themselves, they cannot fight sin, they cannot deal with the devil, they cannot deal with death, they have nothing to say before the Lord God.

And the last reason men and women reject the Gospel is because they do not realize what it has to offer them. They do not know because they are not interested in knowing; they have not seen the need. They think the Gospel is an exhortation or a kind of glorified socialism or pacifism. But that is not the Gospel, which is proved by the Old Testament where we read that God gave people a law, saying that if they kept it, it would save them. But they could not keep it.

As for the idea that the Gospel is glorified socialism or pacifism, consider the teaching of the New Testament. You who think you can put yourself right and stand before God, have you ever read the Sermon the Mount? That is how you have to live. You say you are going to imitate Jesus of Nazareth, but have you ever considered what He was like? Have you ever looked at His life? Have you ever looked at His actions? If Jesus of Nazareth only came into this world to teach, to tell me what to do, and to give me an example, then He damns me more than anything else I have ever heard of. The Ten Commandments are bad enough, but Jesus Christ's example! I am utterly undone. If I have to live like that to save myself and to stand before God, I am already in hell. I know nothing that so condemns me as the person and life of Jesus of Nazareth.

But blessed be the name of God, that is not the Gospel. What has that sort of teaching got to offer to failures? Look at your modern moral people, living their "good lives," as they say. What do they have to give to someone in the gutter? What do they have to give to someone who has sinned away chastity, purity, and honesty? What do they have to give to people who have lost their character? Nothing, nothing at all, absolutely nothing. Thank God that is not the Gospel. This is the Gospel, this that was preached by the apostles in the beginning. Our Lord Himself began to preach it, the apostles continued preaching it, and it was verified by the powers that were given to them.

What is this Gospel? Oh, this is the glorious thing. It is a Gospel that tells us that every one of our needs has been met, every problem has been solved, and it has all been done in this blessed person, Jesus of Nazareth. Who is He? A man? No, the God-man, God the Son who came into this world, two natures in one person. He is not only a man. He is a man, but he is God in the flesh: "The Word was made flesh, and dwelt among us" (John 1:14). He took on our nature. He faced our problems. He stood with us. He asked to be baptized when He had no need to be baptized, putting Himself alongside us. He met the four enemies—the four final problems. And He never sinned, never disobeyed any single commandment. He lived a perfect life.

What of the devil? Well, you can read the records. The devil tried Him in all ways—tempted Him, tested Him. But our Lord defeated him with ease. Our Lord conquered the devil, mastered him, overpowered him, routed him.

What about reconciliation with God? We are guilty before God—the whole world is. What about my sin? I cannot do anything about it, but He has done it: "Who his own self bare our sins in his own body on the tree, that we, being dead to sins, should live unto righteousness: by whose stripes ye were healed" (1 Pet. 2:24). So the apostle Paul could say to a desperate Philippian jailer on the verge of committing suicide, "Believe on the Lord Jesus Christ, and thou shalt be saved" (Acts 16:31).

What of the problem of this evil heart, the problem of sin within? Here is one who took on human nature in order to give you a new, cleansed, and renewed human nature, a new birth, a new beginning. He will make you a partaker of the divine nature. You cannot change yourself, but He can change you. The glory of the Gospel is the power of God unto salvation. He will put His Spirit into you to enable you to conquer the devil, and He will be with you, helping you, strengthening you, supporting you: "For in that he himself hath suffered being tempted, he is able to succour them that are tempted"

(Heb. 2:18). He has said, "Lo, I am with you alway" (Matt. 28:20), and He will lead you to the end of the journey.

But, wait, the Christian still has to die—"The paths of glory lead but to the grave." We still have to face the last enemy, and we are helpless. But look at this one who is with you, the one who is standing by your side. He has already conquered death. He died. His body was taken down and laid in a tomb, and they rolled the stone in front, sealed it, and set soldiers to guard it. But He came out of the tomb: "[He] hath abolished death, and hath brought life and immortality to light through the gospel" (2 Tim. 1:10). The last enemy that shall be conquered is death, but He has done it, so we can stand by Him and say, "O death, where is thy sting? O grave, where is thy victory? The sting of death is sin; and the strength of sin is the law. But thanks be to God, which giveth us the victory through our Lord Jesus Christ" (1 Cor. 15:55-57). All those who believe in Jesus of Nazareth, the Son of God, have passed from death to life, from judgment to life. They are created anew. Christians do not die—they fall asleep; they go "to be with Christ; which is far better" (Phil. 1:23).

Here, then, is the answer. Thank God for it! The need is so profound that there is only one adequate answer—a supernatural, miraculous, divine answer. Modern people reject most of all what they need most of all. It is, I repeat, because they have never seen the need that they are not open to receiving this good news of salvation that "God was in Christ, reconciling the world unto himself" (2 Cor. 5:19). Fly to Christ; give yourself to Him; realize your helplessness and hopelessness and cry out for mercy. You will be heard; you will be delivered. The problem is deep and terrible, but, thank God, the Gospel is "the power of God unto salvation to everyone that believeth" (Rom. 1:16). Whatever your past may have been, to everyone who believes, the Gospel is the power of God for salvation.

20

THE GREAT CONFLICT

And when they had prayed, the place was shaken where they were assembled together; and they were all filled with the Holy Ghost, and they spake the word of God with boldness. . . . But Peter said, Ananias, why hath Satan filled thine heart to lie to the Holy Ghost, and to keep back part of the price of the land?
—Acts 4:31; 5:3

We come back once more to the story of Ananias and Sapphira now in the light of the statement in Acts 5:3 made by the apostle Peter to Ananias. I take Peter's words and put them by the side of that other sentence at the end of chapter 4, which describes what happened, you remember, after the infant church had prayed to God in their dire circumstances: "The place was shaken where they were assembled together; and they were all filled with the Holy Ghost."

"Filled with the Holy Ghost"; "Why hath Satan filled thine heart?" I put these two phrases together because I want to try to show you that they pinpoint the great message of the whole of the Bible. They certainly bring to a focus the message that we are surely intended to receive from this alarming and terrifying incident. I have already suggested to you, and it is important we should keep this in our minds, that this incident took place at the very beginning of the history of the Christian church. The event is recorded as a kind of signpost or monument once and forever directing our attention to certain fundamental truths. Of course, everything in the early chapters of this book of Acts lays a foundation of truth. These chapters were written that you and I might know what genuine Christianity is. In every period of reformation and revival, the church has returned to these events and has repeated them, showing that this model alone is true Christianity.

Now my basic proposition, indeed, the basic proposition of the whole Bible, is that the story of the human race is only really understood in the light of the fact that two great forces are operating upon us in this world. The Bible is the record of this mighty cosmic conflict between God and His forces, and the devil and his forces. Here we are shown the conflict from the beginning right until the consummation. Furthermore, what happens to us and to the world depends solely upon the preponderance of the one or the other of those two powers. The message of the Bible can be put, therefore, like this: Either Satan fills our hearts, or else the Holy Spirit fills our hearts. What makes the message of this book so wonderful and so glorious is that it simplifies the problem and brings us at once to the crucial point.

Yet, as I have been trying to show you, the whole tragedy of the modern world is that it does not begin to realize this conflict at all. People will persist in treating the human problem in terms of their understanding—what they think about, and what other people are thinking and saying—but the dilemma is always regarded as a human problem, and human beings alone, therefore, are to solve it. But we see that far from being solved, the troubles of the world grow worse. People do not see that in reality they are facing a spiritual problem, a mighty conflict between the power of God and the power of Satan. Now here in this one incident, in a very dramatic way that we can never again forget, the whole battle is depicted for us. We see the two forces, their character, their nature. We see what they do and the results they invariably produce. There is nothing more important for any one of us than just this question: Is my heart filled by Satan, or is it filled by and with the Holy Spirit? Nothing else matters, and that is the great message of the Scripture.

We have dealt with many aspects of the story of Ananias and Sapphira; so now let me just concentrate on these two forces. Take first this power that Peter refers to in addressing Ananias: "Ananias, why hath Satan filled thine heart to lie to the Holy Ghost?" We are told a great deal about Satan in the Bible. Indeed, we do not begin to understand the story of the human race apart from understanding something about him. The teaching of the Bible is that the devil was created a perfect being, a bright angelic being, unusually gifted with wisdom and understanding, given great authority and power. But he lifted up his heart, as the Bible puts it, against God; he became jealous. He resented the fact that he was under God, that he was a created being; he wanted to be a god. He rebelled against God. He fell, and ever since he has been a bitter enemy of God. His whole ambition is to mar everything that God does and to bring it into disrepute and to ruin.

So there he is, the enemy of God. Now you notice that Peter immediately concentrated on Satan's chief characteristic: "Why hath Satan filled thine heart to lie?" His dominant characteristic is that he always produces a lie. Now we say this on the authority of our Lord Himself. One day when He was preaching, certain Jews argued with Him as to who He was. Our Lord said, in effect, "What is the matter with you? Why are you like this? You seek to kill Me, a man who has told you the truth." The Jews had said that they were Abraham's seed and that God was their father. Our Lord's reply was this:

> *If God were your Father, ye would love me: for I proceeded forth and came from God; neither came I of myself, but he sent me. Why do ye not understand my speech? even because ye cannot hear my word. Ye are of your father the devil, and the lusts of your father ye will do. He was a murderer from the beginning, and abode not in the truth, because there is no truth in him. When he speaketh a lie, he speaketh of his own: for he is a liar, and the father of it.*
>
> *—John 8:42-44*

That is our Lord's own description of Satan, and the Bible constantly speaks of him in the same way. We read in the epistle to the Hebrews about the "deceitfulness" of sin, and the apostle Paul reminds the Christians in Corinth of how "the serpent beguiled Eve through his subtlety" (2 Cor. 11:3). "Beguiled"—he is a liar and the father of lies; he is a deceiver; he is, as Paul said again, a lying spirit who works "with all deceivableness" (2 Thess. 2:10). Deceit is seen in all that he does. He changes his tactics—anything to suit his own cause. He will contradict himself. He will say that something he said a hundred years ago is no longer true. He will change even from day to day. He can turn himself, says Paul, into "an angel of light" (2 Cor. 11:14). He can quote the Scriptures, as he did to our Lord, as if he believed them and meant them. There is nothing to which he will not stoop to gain his own nefarious ends. That is his characteristic. He is a liar from the beginning. Poor Ananias and Sapphira were the dupes of this master liar.

What, then, are the lies that the devil persuades humanity to believe? Unfortunately, there is no difficulty about answering that question. Having understood his methods, we recognize his lies from experience. But his lies are also laid before us plainly in the Bible. The first lie, of course, is about himself. In many ways, the cleverest of all the devil's lies is to persuade people that there is no devil. That is his real masterpiece. The art of fishing, I understand, lies in the fisherman's ability to keep himself out of sight so that the fish do not see him. You camouflage yourself—that is the way to fish. Well, the devil is a master at this, and at the present time he is succeeding admirably because the world thinks it is quite ridiculous to believe in a personal devil.

Furthermore, the devil persuades people that there is no such thing as evil. You may have heard of the philosopher C. E. M. Joad who, after years of atheism, announced that he was a Christian. He said that he was first moved out of his old position by the fact that in the Spanish Civil War he saw things that convinced him of the reality of evil as a power. Before that, as a philosopher, he had never believed that evil was concrete but merely that it was the absence of certain qualities. During that war, however, he saw things that convinced him otherwise. That was his first step.

After discovering the reality of evil, the second step is to discover that there is a devil at the back of evil, a personal power surrounded by great forces and mercenaries—if they may be so described. The apostle Paul puts it all in chapter 6 of his letter to the Ephesians: "We wrestle not against flesh and blood, but against principalities, against powers, against the rulers of the darkness of this world, against spiritual wickedness in high [heavenly] places" (v. 12). There they are, headed up by the devil—these unseen, evil, malign spiritual forces. But the devil persuades people with his lies that there are no such things—no devil, no evil spirits, no demons, none of the hobgoblins about which John Bunyan wrote in his great hymn. They are all nonsense, fairy tales. He insinuates that this kind of thing was believed by people in the past but not today. That is the first great lie with which Satan deceives the human race.

The next lie is about ourselves. Here again we see proof of the devil's mastery, of his subtle cleverness. He makes us think that we are complimenting ourselves when he persuades us to believe that human beings are only animals, that there is no such thing as a soul or a spirit. He makes us believe that we are complimenting ourselves when we say that we are reasoning animals, a little more developed than other animals, but still only animals, that the difference is only one of degree, and there is no difference in kind. Sir Arthur Keith said that after having dissected many bodies, he had never come across an organ called the soul. Great laughter among the elite!

The devil then goes on to deceive us into thinking that we are essentially good animals, that there is nothing really wrong with us, and that the biblical doctrine of sin is not true, almost a libel. Of course, you must not look at the world and see what human beings do. You must just believe this lie—and men and women are ready to believe it. They have no idea that they are holding on to a lie; they are not honest enough to face themselves, and so they believe it. Then they think that they are more sinned against than sinning. But if it is not humanity that is responsible for the state of the world, then what is?

"I don't know, but I'm not to blame. The fault must lie in other people—and yet it cannot be them somehow because they're human beings as I am, and if I'm essentially good, so are they."

So where does the evil come from?

"Well, we don't know. There's just something wrong with the works somewhere, but people are essentially good and are more sinned against than sinning."

Then as we have seen, the devil also persuades us into believing that the world is improving. Humanity is kinder, more considerate, and would not dream of suddenly blasting thousands or millions of people to death for nothing. The devil persuades people that there is an upward trend. They still believe it in spite of all we saw in the twentieth century. They believe that we will arrive at perfection as the result of the marvelous evolutionary process.

And then, of course, Satan lies about God. First, the devil always tries to say that there is no God. People think atheism is a new idea, but it is not. In Psalm 14 you will read in the first verse, "The fool hath said in his heart, There is no God." This lie is an old trick, but Satan still gets many people to believe it.

But if the devil fails with that lie, he tries another. If a person believes in God, Satan whispers, "Oh, yes, there is a God, but He is a fiend who enjoys keeping you down; He is unjust. Yes, there is a God, but why does He allow children to be born mutilated? Why does He allow war? There is a God, but He is a tyrant; He is against you." That was the lie Satan spoke to Adam and Eve in the original temptation, and they believed it. Humanity has been believing that suggestion ever since, ready to blame God whenever things go wrong and never thinking of Him when everything goes right. This is all a part of the devil's deception.

Then Satan goes on to persuade us that if we really want to be free and to enjoy true happiness, the one thing to do is to defy God, to turn our backs upon Him and have nothing further to do with Him. Again that was the original temptation: "Hath God said?" God is only concerned to keep us down and to keep this knowledge from us; if we defy Him and eat that fruit, our eyes will be opened; we will have understanding and will be as gods. We will be liberated and will really function as human beings worthy of the name. Do that and we will have true happiness.

Further, the devil goes on to tell us that there is nothing beyond this world, that when we die, it is the end of our story; so it does not really matter very much what we do. "Gather ye rosebuds while ye may." "Eat, drink and be merry, for tomorrow you die." There is nothing after life—no judgment, no eternal future. We have nothing to worry about, so we must not listen to those who preach about law and condemnation and judgment and call for responsibility. No, we must make the best of things, have a good time, enjoy ourselves.

There was always a great conflict in Israel between two kinds of prophets: the true prophet and the people described as the "false prophets." The message of the false prophets was always the same. Jeremiah brought it home to the people in these words: "[These prophets] have healed also the hurt of the daughter of my people slightly, saying, Peace, peace; when there is no peace" (Jer. 6:14; 8:11). The false prophets are still saying "peace." A lying spirit grips the minds and the hearts of people in prominent positions, and though the world is going to hell, they still say, "All is getting better; don't be alarmed or excited. There's no judgment, no eternity, no punishment—all is well. Peace, peace; carry on. Keep on with the drink and the dancing. Have a good time; everything will somehow come out all right." That is what they say even though the world is as it is. That is the lie of the devil. "Why hath Satan filled thine heart to lie?"

Finally, of course, the devil constantly lies about the Lord Jesus Christ. You would expect this, would you not? God has sent His Son to the conflict—the second Adam. Here is God's supreme act; the devil knows that, and he has manufactured lies about it. There is a great deal about this conflict in the Bible. I can only summarize it very briefly, but you can see it to perfection in our Lord's temptations in the wilderness. He was tempted by the devil for forty days and forty nights. The devil, in all his subtlety and cleverness, said, "If thou be the Son of God"—"if." That was the question on which he has always concentrated. Our Lord referred to it when speaking to the Pharisees (John 8), and Paul says, "No man speaking by the Spirit of God calleth Jesus accursed: and that no man can say that Jesus is the Lord, but by the Holy Ghost" (1 Cor. 12:3). It is the man who is *not* speaking by the Spirit of God that calls Jesus accursed.

Again John says:

Beloved, believe not every spirit, but try the spirits whether they are of God: because many false prophets are gone out into the world. Hereby know ye the Spirit of God: Every spirit that confesseth that Jesus Christ is come in the flesh is of God: and every spirit that confesseth not that Jesus Christ is come in the flesh is not of God: and this is that spirit of antichrist, whereof ye have heard that it should come; and even now already is it in the world.

1 John 4:1-3

The great fight started at the very beginning. The moment the church was born, as it were, the evil one came with his lies, and his supreme lie was that Jesus of Nazareth was nothing but a man and that this claim to be the Son of God, equal with God, was blasphemy. That claim was why they put our Lord to death. "Who is this fellow," they asked, "this carpenter, this son of Joseph? These claims are lies. This man is an impostor." So they hated Him and gnashed their teeth at Him and finally got Him crucified on that cross on Calvary's hill. They always fought most strenuously to perpetuate the lies. Peter puts it like this: "There were false prophets also among the people [the children of Israel], even as there shall be false teachers among you, who privily shall bring in damnable heresies, even denying the Lord that bought them, and bring upon themselves swift destruction" (2 Pet. 2:1).

The book of Revelation is nothing but a dramatic pictorial presentation of this great conflict between Christ and Satan, especially toward the end. In chapter 12 we are given a perfect summary as we read of the attempt of the great dragon, the devil, to drown the child and His mother by pouring water out of his mouth.

The lies continue to this day. Oh yes, people are prepared to praise our Lord as a great and a good man, but they insist that He was only a man, born like everybody else. Some are foolish enough to say, as has been said recently, that He was the illegitimate child of Zechariah, the father of John the Baptist. But the one who said that is a very poor servant of the devil. There is no subtlety about the lie; its author gives the whole game away and makes the lie obviously ridiculous. He should not have said what he did, and I am sure he has been reprimanded by his master, the devil, for saying it. The subtle method is to praise our Lord as a man because as long as it is thought that he is only a man, the supernatural, the miraculous, the divine, and His atoning death can all be dismissed—anything to rob Him of His glory and of His deity. That is the essential teaching of this liar, the devil, and he has been persuading people to believe it throughout the centuries.

What, then, are the results of listening to the devil? They are always the same. They are here in this one story of Ananias and Sapphira. The devil's teaching always ends in bondage. He promises liberty, but he never gives it. "The way of transgressors is hard" (Prov. 13:15). If the devil were speaking the truth, there would be no unhappiness in this world, no problems, no suffering, no misery, no threat of war. The devil always brings bondage because he always produces confusion. The moment people listen to him, they are under his power, what the Bible calls "the dominion" of sin and Satan. The moment the first man believed the devil's lie, what happened? He became the victim of the world and the flesh and the devil. And that is the whole trouble in the world today. Men and women are not free; they, too, are victims.

Why do people act as they do? Because everybody else does. They follow the way of the world, the social round, the thing to do, the thing the best people are doing. They have no idea why; they are just slaves. They absorb ready-made opinions from the popular newspapers, the radio, and television. They never think, and it always leads to an awful slavery.

But the aspect I want to bring to your attention now is the selfishness that always results from listening to the devil's lies. "Ananias, why hath Satan filled thine heart to lie to the Holy Ghost?" You pretend you are giving to others and helping others, but you are not. You are keeping back so much for yourselves; you are not only liars, but you are selfish liars. You are always thinking of yourself; you put yourself first. Is not the whole trouble in the world due, in a sense, to selfishness—everybody out for himself? "I'm all right, Jack. What does it matter what the other fellow gets or what happens to him as long as I'm all right!"

Of course, we put up a show about giving to charity and so on, but that is a facade. A man is not content with his own wife; he covets the wife of the other fellow. Businesses and professions are seething with jealousy and envy and spite and malice, and so are all the upper social classes. And here it is in the account of Ananias and Sapphira. Believing the devil's lie always leads to selfishness— the cause of the tragedy in the human race.

But look also at the short-sightedness that is always produced. You are happy when you are drunk but miserable the next morning. You are happy when you are spitting upon sanctities and desecrating God's holy law, but you suffer for it afterwards in remorse, and you feel a cad and worse—temporary satisfaction, temporary happiness. The author of the epistle to the Hebrews talks of Moses as "choosing rather to suffer affliction with the people of God, than to enjoy the pleasures of sin for a season" (Heb. 11:25). The pleasures of sin never last more than a season, and the seasons get shorter and shorter. The satisfaction is never permanent.

The devil is a cheat and a liar; his prospectus deceives. The pleasures he offers always lead to judgment. You think you have been clever, that you have covered all eventualities, but suddenly you are confronted by a Peter who says, "Thou hast not lied unto men, but unto God." Peter said to Sapphira, "How is it that ye have agreed together? Tell me whether ye sold the land for so much? And she said, Yea, for so much." A barefaced lie.

Judgment catches up with you. You cannot get away from it. Eventually you are collared. You are faced with the punishment and the doom that you deserve—the eternal doom to which it leads. That is the truth about this liar, this devil, this Satan, this hater of God, this hater of humanity ultimately, our enemy, our adversary. We have seen his character; we have seen what he teaches and the results to which believing his teaching leads.

But oh, what a joy, what a blessed relief to turn to what Christianity is. Listen, I say, for your lives—I have something wonderful to tell you. There is another who is ready to fill the heart. "They were all filled with the Holy Ghost." We read of this event in the second chapter of Acts. The filling of the Spirit was the promise of the Father and of our Lord Himself when He said, "It is expedient for you that I go away: for if I go not away, the Comforter will not come unto you; but if I depart, I will send him unto you" (John 16:7). Christ sent the Holy Spirit on the day of Pentecost. So the church came into being, and all the marvelous events we have considered together began to take place.

The Spirit of God, the Holy Spirit—who is He? Oh, what a contrast with the devil, what a difference in character! The Holy Spirit is called the Spirit of holiness and the Spirit of truth. Our Lord said, "He will guide you into all truth" (John 16:13). He is the eternal antithesis of the devil in every respect, but supremely in that He is the great Spirit of truth. What is so wonderful is that because He is the Spirit of truth, He is always the same in all ages. The truth I am privileged to convey to you now is "truth unchanged, unchanging." Jesus Christ is "the same yesterday, and to day, and for ever" (Heb. 13:8).

So what is my message? There is nothing new about it—oh, that you may hear it. I am simply repeating the message preached by the apostles. I am not telling you something that has suddenly been discovered. I am not telling you what I have just read in the latest book by some great philosopher. I am preaching eternal truth, the everlasting Gospel, the message preached throughout the centuries by saints, apostles, prophets, and martyrs.

What is this truth that the Holy Spirit teaches? I can only give it to you in summary form. He tells us the truth about ourselves, and what He tells us is that we are not animals. "Let us make man in our image . . . in the image of God created he him" (Gen. 1:26, 27). Each of us has a soul, a spirit; we are meant for God. We know it within ourselves; we are dissatisfied; we cry out for some "ampler ether, a divine air." Nothing else in the world but God can ultimately satisfy us. There is a thirst, a hunger, a restlessness. Augustine knew it: "Thou hast made us for Thyself, and our hearts are restless until they find their rest in Thee." He had made the rounds of sinful pleasures, kept his mistress, but his soul was too big for this.

> *Dust thou art, to dust returnest*
> *Was not spoken of the soul.*
> H. W. Longfellow

In men and women there is this intangible thing that sets them apart from the animals. This is what we read in the Bible, what the Spirit of truth, the Holy Spirit, tells us. He tells us further that we are responsible to God, that we are not just irresponsible animals that obey our lusts and passions and desires, to eat too much, drink too much, and indulge in sex too much. No, we are responsible beings, meant to exercise discipline, the lords of creation, God's representatives in this universe.

The Holy Spirit tells us that in their folly man and woman listened to the devil and fell and brought down chaos upon the whole of their world and posterity. He tells us that men and women are now fallen creatures and that all their sufferings are the result of that fall.

Then the Holy Spirit goes on to tell us the truth about God and relates the glory of God.

> *Immortal, invisible, God only wise,*
> *In light inaccessible, hid from our eyes,*
> *Most blessed, most glorious, the Ancient of days,*
> *Almighty, victorious; Thy great name we praise.*
> Walter Chalmers Smith

"God is light, and in him is no darkness at all" (1 John 1:5). He is God the Creator; God the all-powerful; God the just, the righteous, the holy, who is of such pure countenance that He cannot even look upon sin; God the Judge of the ends of the earth, in whose keeping is the moral government of the universe; God, who has made us and under whom we all exist and before whom we shall all have to appear and render an account.

That is the Holy Spirit's teaching about God as you find it in the Bible, but it is not the whole teaching, thank God! We would not be here if it were. I would not dare come anywhere near Him. I would be terrified. Who am I to speak of such a person, let alone try to enter His presence? But the Spirit goes on to tell me that God is a God of love and of infinite kindness and mercy and compassion. Listen to the apostle Paul putting it to the Ephesians: "But God, who is rich in mercy, for his great love wherewith he loved us, even when we were dead in sins, hath quickened us together with Christ"—why?—". . . that in the ages to come he might show the exceeding riches of his grace in his kindness toward us through Christ Jesus" (Eph. 2:4-5, 7).

The Old Testament psalmists and prophets had glimpsed God's love by revelation, and they had experienced it. The psalmist sinned against God and did not know what to do with himself. But he had to go back to God, for there was nobody else, and he cried out, "There is forgiveness with thee, that thou mayest be feared" (Psa. 130:4). Then he shows us the kindness of the Lord: "As far as the east is from the west, so far hath he removed our transgressions from us" (Psa. 103:12). That is the teaching of the Holy Spirit concerning God.

Far from being against us, God loves us in spite of our being what we are. When Adam and Eve rebelled against God in the perfection of paradise, He did not blast them to eternity and everlasting misery. God informed them of a plan of redemption and restoration that He had already formed. God, the God who is insulted and reviled and against whom men and women in their folly rebel, this very God conceived a way of redeeming them, of delivering them from themselves and the consequences of their listening to the devil's lies.

In the Old Testament you find announcements of God's salvation. God took a man called Abraham, turned him into a nation, and used him as the medium of his revelation. Then look at the way He handled those children of Israel—what a miserable lot they were! No worse than us, you know, but they were sinning against God and then going back to Him cringing. He forgave them and blessed them, and then they forsook Him, and back they went again and sinned against Him. This time, no, He could not forgive them—but He did! Oh, the long-suffering and the patience of God with this recalcitrant people. But that is the God whom the Holy Spirit reveals.

But above and beyond everything else, the Holy Spirit has been sent into the church to glorify the Lord Jesus Christ. Our Lord said so Himself: "He

shall glorify me" (John 16:14). Glorifying Christ is the supreme work of the
Holy Spirit. He tells us the truth about Jesus of Nazareth. Who is He? That
is the crucial question. "What think ye of Christ?" (Matt. 22:42). The Holy
Spirit answers that question throughout that amazing record we call the New
Testament. Here it is, in one verse: "God so loved the world, that he gave his
only begotten Son, that whosoever believeth in him should not perish, but
have everlasting life" (John 3:16). The babe of Bethlehem, the eternal Son of
God, the Word made flesh. "Veiled in flesh, the Godhead see," says Charles
Wesley—and it was the Holy Spirit alone who revealed that. Paul says in
1 Corinthians 2:8 that when Christ came, "None of the princes of this world
knew: for had they known it, they would not have crucified the Lord of
glory." The great men of the world rejected Him. They saw only Jesus—a carpenter. But the Spirit reveals Him as God in the flesh.

The Spirit also reveals our Lord's amazing life of perfection, His kindness. The Pharisees and scribes did not like Him; they were not sure that he
was a very nice person. He even ate and drank with tax collectors and sinners and allowed a prostitute to wash his feet with her tears and dry them
with her hair. "Ah," they said, "the fellow is an impostor." But filled with
kindness and compassion, He said, "He that hath seen me hath seen the
Father" (John 14:9). He was teaching them: God is like this. Do not listen to
what the others have told you about Him. He is not remote and against you.
He is for you, and the Son of God has come. "For the Son of man is come to
seek and to save that which was lost" (Luke 19:10). "I am come that they
might have life, and that they might have it more abundantly" (John 10:10).

As our Lord was approaching Jerusalem where He would soon be
arrested, He said, "The Son of man came not to be ministered unto, but to
minister, and to give his life a ransom for many" (Matt. 20:28). He had come
to die, and the whole teaching of the Holy Spirit about Him is that He went
to the cross deliberately. Why? Because He saw that this was the only way
whereby anybody could be delivered, forgiven, and redeemed. On the cross
He bore the punishment of my sins. He took my guilt upon Him—that is why
He came. He came to "taste death for every man" (Heb. 2:9). That is what
the Holy Spirit teaches us about Him. They laid Him in a tomb, but He rose
again. The Resurrection of the body is a fact, and it was the proof that His
work was complete. He ascended in the sight of these very apostles who had
witnessed His life and death, and He is seated at the right hand of God in the
glory everlasting. He sent down the Holy Spirit on the day of Pentecost to
make these things known, to give power to people to authenticate the truth
concerning Himself.

The message is summarized by the apostle Paul in his letter to the Romans in these words:

> *When we were yet without strength, in due time Christ died for the ungodly. For scarcely for a righteous man will one die: yet peradventure for a good man some would even dare to die. But God commendeth his love toward us, in that, while we were yet sinners, Christ died for us. . . . For if, when we were enemies, we were reconciled to God by the death of his Son, much more, being reconciled, we shall be saved by his life.*
>
> —*Romans 5:6-8, 10*

What happens to us when we believe this? Oh, you will get to know at once that your sins are forgiven, that you are reconciled to God. You will lose your fear of the judgment, and you will have peace with God. Not only that, but you will receive a new nature, a new life, a new start. You will get deliverance. This is not a philosophy. This is not an ethical teaching. The Gospel does not exhort you to pull yourself up and try to live a good life, thereby putting yourself right with God and solving your problems. It knows you cannot do that. No, the gospel message tells of a supernatural, godlike deliverance. Paul puts it like this: "I am not ashamed of the gospel of Christ"—why not?—"for it is the power of God unto salvation" (Rom. 1:16). Not the power of a sociologist, not the power of a government enactment, but it is the power of God that delivers us from the devil, translates us from the kingdom of darkness into the kingdom of God's dear Son, sets us free, and produces a new character, the character depicted here in Acts by Barnabas and others. These people honestly and genuinely sold their goods and gave the proceeds. They no longer lived a selfish, self-centered little life but were concerned for others.

I could keep on reminding you of the facts that the devil has very conveniently made people forget. The most beneficent institution that this world has ever known has been the Christian church. Before politicians ever came along with their reforms, the church had relief for the poor, had introduced education for the poor, had started hospitals. The church, Christian people—not an institution but genuine Christian people—have been the pioneers in all this work throughout the centuries. These are facts. In this country and in other countries Christians have sacrificed themselves for others. Here they are in Acts, living a new kind of life, all of one accord, and showing the fruit of the Spirit.

If you want to know the difference between the two lives—the life of listening to the devil and the life of listening to the Holy Spirit—then read the words written by the apostle Paul in Galatians 5: "The works of the flesh"—this is the life lived by those whose hearts are filled by Satan—"are manifest, which are these; adultery, fornication, uncleanness, lasciviousness, idolatry, witchcraft, hatred, variance, emulations, wrath, strife, seditions, heresies, envyings, murders, drunkenness, revellings, and such like" (vv. 19-21). Paul's description was true then, and it is true today. Those are the results of listening to the lies of the devil.

Do you want to know the result of listening to the teaching of the Holy Spirit? "The fruit of the Spirit is love, joy, peace, longsuffering, gentleness, goodness, faith, meekness, temperance" (vv. 22-23). What a contrast! The marvelous thing is that if you believe this message, you are not left to yourself to struggle against impossible odds, because the Spirit of God comes into you. "They were all filled with the Holy Ghost." A divine strength comes in and lifts people up and out of themselves and enables them to do things formerly impossible.

What does the filling of the Holy Spirit lead to? Well, in this modern world that is so materialistic and mercenary in its outlook and so interested in money and winning football pools, here is a life that gives you satisfaction without money. The early Christians were ready to sell all their possessions and put the money into a common fund. You can be happy without money; you are not dependent upon it. One of the first things that happens to men and women whose hearts are filled with the Spirit is that they become independent of the world and their circumstances and surroundings. Let all these things rise against us—they cannot touch us; we are finally safe. The Holy Spirit gives us "lasting joy and solid treasure": "joy unspeakable and full of glory" (1 Pet. 1:8). He gives us peace.

The Holy Spirit takes from us the fear of death and the grave. The end of unbelievers is certain; the enemy is already doomed; he is living on a lease, as it were. He received that mortal wound when Christ died on the cross, and his time is limited. That is why he is raging. But Christ will come, and with the breath of His mouth He will destroy that arch liar, the enemy of God and of humanity, and send him to everlasting destruction. Do not forget that when the devil plies you with his lies.

Look at the boldness of the apostles as they defied the authorities. They were no longer afraid of death. The early martyrs and confessors went gladly to the lions in the arena, praising God and thanking Him that at last He had accounted them worthy to suffer for the name of their blessed and dear Lord.

"They died well," as John Wesley put it. Why? Because they had a hope of glory; they could see that this is only a transient world. This is not the world of reality; this is the world of appearances. But there is a world that remains.

> *There is a land of pure delight*
> *Where saints immortal reign.*
> Isaac Watts

There is a glory yet to be revealed, a day coming when the glory of the sons of God shall be made manifest. A crowning day is coming, a day of ultimate victory and of triumph, when Jesus shall reign from pole to pole. In the light of that day these men and women lived the lives they did and had a joy that persisted even in the midst of tribulations.

I have put the two sides before you. I have shown you the character of Satan, and I have told you his message. I have told you the results of believing in that message. I have told you something about the Holy Spirit and His character. I have revealed His message to you, and I have told you of the results of believing the Holy Spirit's message. And now I ask you: What fills your heart? Is it filled with the lies of Satan or with the Holy Ghost? This is what matters, and I am asking you this because I am concerned about you and your eternal destiny. I see the lie—I once believed it myself, but, thank God, the Spirit opened my eyes. So I put the two before you, and I urge you to believe on the Lord Jesus Christ revealed by the Spirit and yield to the Spirit of God.

21

SIGNS AND WONDERS

And great fear came upon all the church, and upon as many as heard these things. And by the hands of the apostles were many signs and wonders wrought among the people; (and they were all with one accord in Solomon's porch. And of the rest durst no man join himself to them: but the people magnified them. And believers were the more added to the Lord, multitudes both of men and women.)

—Acts 5:11-14

The tragic story of Ananias and Sapphira has taught us many things about what the Christian church really is, how she ever came into being, how she began to grow, and how the Christian message continued to spread. Now in these verses we are told of the effect of the deaths of Ananias and Sapphira: "And great fear came upon all the church, and upon as many as heard these things." Then the record goes on to say that "by the hands of the apostles were many signs and wonders wrought among the people." These signs and wonders were used by God for the same purpose. Then we are told, "They were all with one accord in Solomon's porch. And of the rest durst no man join himself to them: but the people magnified [glorified, gave honor to] them. And believers were the more added to the Lord, multitudes both of men and women."

In other words, the record tells us that if you want to know how it was that this handful of people became such a power—how from such a small beginning, they spread far and wide—part of the answer is to be found in these events—the shaking of the building, the deaths of Ananias and

Sapphira, these signs and wonders—these miracles that were worked by the apostles. Undoubtedly the miracles are a vital part of the explanation. That is why these things are recorded in this book of Acts, which is, after all, primarily a book of history to give to Theophilus. Now Theophilus was an able, cultured man, a Gentile who wanted to know what Christianity was about. To inform him, Luke wrote first the Gospel of Luke and now this book. These two books are the explanation of what Theophilus was trying to understand.

We are, therefore, face to face with these phenomena, these facts. I know that many people find all this difficult and perplexing, and that is why I am calling attention to it. There are many who do not believe that these events happened at all. Psychology teaches us, they think, that such happenings can be explained quite simply. Primitive people are always ready to invoke the miraculous and the magical; they will believe anything, and those early Christians were very simple people. I have already told you how psychologists explain away the shaking of the building. These people deny all the miracles of our Lord—the Resurrection, the descent of the Holy Spirit on the day of Pentecost, the judicial deaths of Ananias and Sapphira, and all the reports concerning miracles. Of course, the critics' explanations sound clever but do not solve the problem of the spread of the Christian church.

Why do psychologists and others deny these events? It is because they start by putting down the postulate that miracles cannot happen; therefore, they say, miracles have not happened. Of course, the second statement is true if the first statement is right. But how do you know that a miracle cannot happen? Can you prove that? You cannot. So all I would say to those who insist that they do not believe the events of Acts is that people have often disbelieved things that have subsequently been proved to be true. You know the sort of people. They are told that the Russians have succeeded in sending up Sputnik and that it is orbiting in outer space. "I don't believe it, and I won't believe it," they say. But now they have to. Indeed, Sputnik has even landed on the moon.

However, I have a much more important answer for these doubters. How do you explain the Christian church if you deny these facts in Acts? How did it come to pass that a handful of ignorant men were able to propagate this message that spread throughout the civilized world? Are you suggesting that the people who taught the Gospel were dishonest or were so primitive that their words are irrelevant and unworthy of consideration? The whole history of the Christian church gives the lie to any such argument, for the church has been the greatest civilizing power and Christians the greatest benefactors that the world has ever known.

But some people have a more serious difficulty. They say, "All right, I'll accept that, but what I want to know is this: If that is how the church began, why don't things like that take place today?" This question is worthy of careful consideration. The answer, it seems to me, is that the very fact that there is variation is proof in and of itself of the supernatural. It is a proof of God and of the Lord as the head of the church and the controller of the activities of the church. Here I find wonderful proof that the church is not a human society and institution. To start with, human beings cannot do mighty, marvelous, miraculous things. The apostles, as we have already seen, were careful to say so. Peter and John, when the people of Jerusalem were almost ready to worship them, said, "Why look ye so earnestly on us, as though by our own power or holiness we had made this man to walk?" (Acts 3:12). They had not done this miracle. "And his name through faith in his name hath made this man strong" (v. 16). The disciples were but instruments and channels.

Then the fact that there was such a variation proves that the power came from God. If the church could have put on miracles whenever she liked, the whole position would have been very different, but though she has often tried, she cannot. No, this variation is a proof that the power is in the control of another—and that is the great message of the early part of the book of Acts. Here at the beginning of the church, God gave ignorant and unlearned people this power so that they were able to say with the apostle Paul, "We have this treasure in earthen vessels, that the excellency of the power may be of God, and not of us" (2 Cor. 4:7). Our Lord authenticated their message. The author of the epistle to the Hebrews says the same thing: "God also bearing them witness, both with signs and wonders, and with divers miracles" (2:4).

So, then, here was the initiation, the start, the authentication of the message, something to attract people's attention. You would expect that at the beginning. You would also expect that at the beginning the great principles governing the life of the church should be clearly laid down—and I suggest that they are laid down here. If you turn to the Old Testament, you will find the same diversity. The prophets Elijah and Elisha were enabled to work miracles, but we are not told that the other prophets had the same gift. Why? Well, these two were the first, the beginning, the initiation, and they were authenticated by supernatural power. Then when people were ready to listen, prophets went on delivering the message.

I will tell you something still more interesting. The same variation in these manifestations of the supernatural is seen in the subsequent history of the

Christian church. There have been exceptional periods that we call revivals in which there has been a striking manifestation of the immediate power of God, not always miracles and signs, but always an awareness of the power of the Spirit. Sometimes men and women would be literally cast to the floor; an irresistible conviction would enter into a meeting, and people, as it were, would be almost possessed. This was a direct manifestation of the power of God, the unseen power of the Holy Spirit, the very thing we have here, but manifested again in order to save the church from death, to put her on her feet, and to call men and women to listen to her message. So my answer to the question as to why we do not have those things now is that I do not really know. But I notice that this how God has acted throughout the course of history. Far from being troubled by it, my faith is strengthened. We cannot command these things; they are in God's hands.

But there is a third difficulty that people often find with miracles, and it is the one that I feel is most urgently and practically important for us. There are those who think that the fact that miracles do not happen to us now is unfair to us. They say, "If we had been alive at that time and had seen those things, we would have believed." You may have thought this yourself. *If only*, you think, *I had been alive when the Son of God was in this world! If only I could have looked into His face and seen those eyes; if only I could have heard those gracious words as they came from His lips, I would have no trouble in believing.* Now to me this is the most serious fallacy of all because it is an argument based on the assumption that such events produce automatic results, but they do not.

Read our Lord's statement in Luke 16 about Dives and Lazarus. Jesus speaks of an argument that took place between Abraham in heaven and Dives in hell. When Abraham has made it plain to Dives that there is no traffic between heaven and hell, between paradise and Hades, Dives says, "If I cannot come there, and if Lazarus cannot come and relieve me, then I beseech you, send Lazarus to my brothers. I have five brothers left in that old world, and they are still living as I did. They don't know any better. So send Lazarus to tell them the truth."

"But, son," says Abraham, "they have the Old Testament. Let your brothers listen to the teaching of Moses and the prophets."

"Oh, no, no," says Dives. "Father Abraham, if only someone went to them from the dead, if a phenomenon took place, if only this poor beggar, whom they know to have been dead and buried, could appear among them, risen from the dead, they would believe."

"No, they would not," says Abraham. "If they do not believe Moses and the prophets, neither will they be persuaded though one did rise from the dead."

Now that is the complete answer. People always think like Dives: *If only I had seen these things, then I would have believed.* But that is a fundamental error.

Or let me give you another example. Take Thomas, one of the disciples. We call him Doubting Thomas. Our Lord had appeared to the disciples one day when Thomas was not with them, and when Thomas came back, they said, "We have seen the Lord." But he said, "Except I shall see in his hands the print of the nails, and put my finger into the print of the nails, and thrust my hand into his side, I will not believe." Later when Thomas was with them, our Lord appeared again. And we are told, "Then saith he to Thomas, Reach hither thy finger, and behold my hands; and reach hither thy hand, and thrust it into my side: and be not faithless, but believing. And Thomas answered and said unto him, My Lord and my God. Jesus saith unto him, Thomas, because thou hast seen me, thou hast believed: blessed are they that have not seen, and yet have believed" (John 20:24-29).

Thomas believed, but Acts 5 tells us that many who heard and saw these things still did not. The next paragraph starts like this: "Then the high priest rose up, and all they that were with him . . . and were filled with indignation" (5:17). There is nothing at all unfair in our not seeing these things. What is important is that we have heard them: "Great fear came upon all the church, and upon as many as heard these things." That statement is repeated here several times. In verse 5 of this chapter we read, "Ananias hearing these words fell down, and gave up the ghost: and great fear came on all them that heard these things." Again in verse 11, "Great fear came upon all the church, and upon as many as heard these things." Then in verse 13 we read, "Of the rest durst no man join himself to them." And we, too, are in the position of those who have heard these things.

There is an important principle here for all of us. The great question for us is not whether we have seen these things, but whether we have understood their significance. These events are meant to speak to us, to convey a message. It is not necessary, therefore, to have seen them. We have heard them as the people here in Acts had heard them. There were different groups of people here, and their reactions were different. So the vital question is: As you hear this record in the early chapters of Acts, what is your reaction? What effect does it have upon you?

All I want to do now is to show you the true, the desired reaction, to these things, and it is put before us here very clearly. I shall, of course, at the same time be describing to you what it is that makes a man or woman a Christian. Here is this old message that has been preached for nearly two thousand years, and throughout the centuries it has had the same effect; it has been dividing humanity. There are those who believe and those who do not, those who are added to the Lord and those who are not. What is it that happens to those who truly become Christians? What should be the effect upon us of hearing these things? We have heard them as these people heard them, so how do we react?

Here, then, is the true reaction. First, these events should always arouse fear. Fear! "Great fear came upon all the church, and upon as many as heard these things." Of course, I know this is something to which people object most violently at the present time. This criticism of the Gospel and of my own preaching is, I think, one I have heard more frequently than any other. "You're trying to frighten us," people say. "This sort of preaching should be abolished. It's all wrong. You're trying to scare people into the kingdom of God. That may have worked in the past but not any longer. You're in the modern age now, remember, and we are scientific people. You cannot frighten us, and in any case, it's unfair and wrong to try to frighten people into believing your Gospel."

Now let us look at this criticism. My text says, "Great fear came upon all the church, and upon as many as heard these things." And then I read this: "Believers were the more added to the Lord, multitudes both of men and women." Not only women and children, you notice, but men and women in "multitudes." So in answer to the accusation that it is unfair to bring in the element of fear, we need only apply a little straight thinking, nothing else. The primary object of reporting and preaching these things is not to produce fear. Fear is always the result of something else, and what I am concerned about is the "something else."

But first let me say quite plainly and honestly that I agree that to try to coerce anybody into believing the Gospel is indefensible. It is absolutely unfair to try to frighten people into anything. To try to bludgeon somebody, to knock them down, as it were, is wrong—I agree 100 percent. Let me go further. I am prepared to agree that often in the past many preachers were guilty of that approach. I think there are two explanations. One is that sometimes their very concern for the souls of men and women made them go to extremes. Their motive was good, but in practice it led to something that I could not possibly defend. But there was a second reason: Sometimes I think they were carried away by their own eloquence. They started working out a picture and were carried away by it. It became so dramatic that in the end they were more interested in their illustration than in the truth. I am ready to admit all that.

But the important point is that the object of the record here is to put facts before us. Luke was led to write this to his friend Theophilus, and he was an honest historian. His facts have been checked, you know. The critics have been after him for about 150 years, and they have done their utmost to prove him wrong, but things Luke wrote, which were dismissed fifty and sixty years ago, have been proved to be right. In the early years of the twentieth century, Sir William Ramsay was able to demonstrate that Luke was a most accurate historian. Luke had but one interest. He was not trying to frighten Theophilus but to report the facts. And when events happen like those on the day of Pentecost, it is the duty of an accurate historian to report them. It is equally the business of an accurate historian to note what happened to Ananias and Sapphira. Luke was a reporter. He was simply giving facts and putting them before his friend, not primarily to frighten him, but certainly to make him think. Yes, here is the motive; here is the reason. The object of these facts and events is to make us think; it is to cause us to meditate and to ponder. The ultimate objective is to save us—not merely to get adherents, but to deliver us.

Now the moment you look at it like that, the case against reporting facts like these collapses altogether. It is a good thing to give people warnings. Is the parent who warns a child about putting a finger in the fire doing something wrong and unfair? Is he bludgeoning the child's mind? Are the authorities on certain beaches in this country being unfair to us when they put up a sign, Warning: Quicksand? Do you object to that? Fancy putting up a sign saying, "Danger!" Let us never forget that complacency and bravado are generally based on ignorance. A man says, "I don't care, I'm going on." But he does not know what he is talking about; he is a fool who is not aware of the danger, and you have to restrain him.

Is it wrong to tell people not to visit a house where there is an acutely infectious disease? Tell me, is it wrong to persuade a person who has some growth or an acute inflammation to have an urgent operation? You say to the patient, "I think this is rather serious, and you ought to have an operation."

"No, I don't want an operation," says the patient. "I'm sure I'll be all right tomorrow."

Now is it wrong for the doctor to say, "I really do press upon you to consider this very seriously. If you leave it until tomorrow morning, it may well be too late"? But still the patient does not see that there is any need. He does not want the operation. Then the doctor becomes more serious and says, "If you let this thing go on, it may burst and spread; you may get septicemia. It is most dangerous." He brings pressure to bear. Is he being unfair? Would you object to that? Would you say this is bludgeoning the mind? Of course not!

Mere fear in and of itself is of no value. Fear is no more than the ringing of the bell to call attention. Think of a man who is desperately ill and feels he is going to die. He says, "If I'm spared, I'm going to be a saint." Then he gets well, and he forgets all about his resolve. Back he goes to his old ways. That is what mere fear does. It is unintelligent, irrational, and of no value. Fear alone generally paralyzes. You may have experienced that effect—for the time being you are paralyzed, and then you panic and say, "I'm going to do this, that, and the other." But the fear wears off, does it not, and you forget all about it so that ultimately it has no effect at all upon you. But fear, when you really understand it, can be a great signpost. Fear points away from itself and indicates something you ought to be doing, somewhere you ought to be going. The business of these records in Acts is to make us face certain facts that we have forgotten. Fear is merely the introduction to the message, the help given us. So the message of this incident is that it is wise to know something of the danger in following certain courses of action.

But notice, we are told here, "Great fear came upon all the church, and upon as many as heard these things." The church herself was filled with fear, and I would emphasize that this element of fear is an essential part of the true Christian experience. Why do you believe in the Lord Jesus Christ as your Savior? Some Christian people may say, "I came to Christ because I wanted salvation; I've never known what it is to be afraid."

Well, I have only one question to ask you: Why do you call our Lord the Savior? What does He save you from? Why did you ever go to Him? Why did you ever believe in Him? You see, the very word *savior* means that we need to be saved from something. And what is it we need to be saved from? The Gospel record gives the answer—"the wrath to come." John the Baptist said to the Pharisees, "Who hath warned you to flee from the wrath to come?" (Luke 3:7). "Save yourselves from this untoward generation," said Peter, preaching on the day of Pentecost (Acts 2:40). It is no use saying that you believe in a Savior unless you realize that you are lost, under the condemnation of the law, and hell-bound.

So I cannot recognize an experience as a true Christian experience unless there is an element of fear in it—not the fear that has torment (1 John 4:18) but the fear that makes men and women flee from the wrath to come, the fear that sends them running to the Savior. Great fear! Do not misunderstand this. I am not here to frighten you, but I am here to put certain historical facts before you and to ask you to consider what they mean, what their implication is, what they say to you, and what you should be doing about them. Am I trying to bludgeon you? Am I not reasoning with you? I am not trying to frighten you or to stun you. I am saying: "Listen, these things happened—what do they mean? What do they say to me? What do they say to you?"

Now we move to the second true response to these events. A Christian knows fear, but he does not stop at this. He also responds with belief. "And believers were the more added to the Lord, multitudes both of men and women." As we have seen, the miracles that happened at the beginning of the early church were given in order to help us. As we read the records, we listen to the message to which the miracles point. Those who stop at the miracles are as wrong as those who stop at the fear. The miracles are instruments to bring us to confront and to believe the truth.

What is that truth? Why did Luke record these things in his second letter to his friend Theophilus? Ah, here is the object. He wanted to tell this man that the church is not a human institution, something you can explain in terms of men and women who have a new idea and who have founded a new society and are rather clever at propagating it. No, Luke wanted to let Theophilus know something about the power of God—this God who is over all, this unseen, mighty, glorious Spirit. When you read the four Gospels, you find the same thing coming out constantly in connection with the miracles performed by our Lord and Savior. When He worked a miracle, the effect almost invariably was at first to fill people with fear. They said: "We have seen strange things today." But you find that another time He worked a miracle, and the people gave glory to God. The miracle pointed to the power of God.

An old Puritan of some three hundred years ago described what he always did when he was near someone dying. He said, "I never find myself in the presence of death but that I always bow my head in the presence of His majesty." God! Have you not done that yourself? Someone you know has died, and so you go into the room, and there is nothing there but a dead body. You all speak in whispers. Why? The body is dead; it cannot hear. This reaction is not mere custom or a mere fear of the unseen. Oh, no. Let me sound paradoxical. You are unconsciously conscious of being in the presence of your Maker and your God. You realize that your times are in His hands. Like the old Puritan, you are bowing your head in the presence of His majesty.

That is why these things are recorded. The first believers were just men and women like ourselves, but they were in a world where things began to happen, where the Spirit descended and men were transformed, where a building was shaken and where people dropped dead. The observers were made to think: *What am I? What is this world? There is Someone here beyond me, above me.* That is the purpose of these great happenings. They are meant to remind us of the being of God, of His greatness and His glory. Oh, this foolish, superficial modern world of ours that only recognizes what it can see and does not know about the things it cannot see—the God who is ruling over all and sustains all. These things are meant to bring us to remember that we are all under God and that we are very small and finite and feeble. Supernatural events are meant to produce what the New Testament calls "reverence and godly fear" (Heb. 12:28)—not a craven fear, not a wild terror or an irrational alarm, not a kind of paralysis. No, reverence and godly fear lead to faith in God. They lead us to realize that we are in a universe controlled by the ever blessed God who is there over all and that we are, as it were, but pygmies strutting about in our self-importance, as nothing before Him.

As well as pointing to God, these wonders are recorded in order to make you think about yourself. They enable you to see that you are very much like Ananias and Sapphira, that you have the same twisted nature. All your boasting and cleverness is seen to be hollow and a wicked sham when you really face the true facts of life. These things make you sit down for a moment, switch off your television, and stop all the noise. You say: "What sort of a being am I? What am I doing in this world? What am I meant to be? Am I but an animal?" Have you ever really examined your own heart and life? Have you ever faced the evil that is in you? This evil is in everyone, and that is why the world is as it is.

This incident makes you think: *This is the sort of universe I am in, and I must face it. Ananias and Sapphira died suddenly. I may live to a very old age and die quietly on my bed, full of age and honors, but I have to die, and I have to meet God as they had to. I cannot always be running away. I'll be caught in the end.* "Be sure your sin will find you out" (Num. 32:23). This kind of event should make you think like that. You do not just say, "I don't believe it," or, "Why doesn't it happen now?" No, you say, "But I'm in a world where things like this happen. This is life. This may be very dramatic, but death happens to us all, and when I die, I have to give an account of myself and my actions and face God in the judgment."

And then—and thank God for this—these great events are meant to lead

us on to face the message of the Gospel, the message preached by these apostles. Look at these unlearned and ignorant men—here they were, working
miracles: "By the hands of the apostles were many signs and wonders
wrought among the people." We are told that the people "brought forth the
sick into the streets, and laid them on beds and couches, that at the least the
shadow of Peter passing by might overshadow some of them."

"Superstition!" you say.

There may have been an element of that, but Peter was used by God to
heal people. These healings are a part of the record, and they undoubtedly
happened. The question is: What enabled Peter to do things like this? This
fisherman, this man who cowardly denied his Lord in order to save his own
skin—what enabled him to speak as he did and to work these miracles and
wonders and signs?

There is only one answer: Peter would tell you, the other apostles would
tell you, that the miracles are just to capture your attention. You hear the stories, the accounts, and you listen to the message that Peter performed these
miracles through the power and name of Jesus of Nazareth, the one who
came into the world and was born at Bethlehem, worked as a carpenter, and
then at the age of thirty began to preach. Jesus called the apostles, and they
heard Him and saw His miracles. At first they did not understand; they were
utterly confused, and when they saw Him dying on the cross and laid in a
tomb, they gave up hope. But then He suddenly appeared to them and taught
them. He said, "Tarry ye in the city of Jerusalem, until ye be endued with
power from on high" (Luke 24:49). Then they saw Him ascend into heaven,
and the power came, and there they were, doing these amazing things.

The disciples would tell you that they are what they are because they have
been entirely changed. Jesus had taught them that they were sinners, that they
were all lost and damned, but that He had come into the world to save them.
He had told them He was dying that their sins might be forgiven, that He had
borne their punishment in His own body on the tree, that He had risen again
to justify them, and that He had gone to heaven to prepare a place for them.
They would add: "If you believe these things, He will do the same for you.
You will not necessarily work miracles, but you will know that your sins are
forgiven. You will know that He loved you and died for you and your sins.
You will know that you have new life in you and that you have the Spirit of
God in you. You will know that you are a new person, and you will feel that
you are in a new world. And it will all have come from Him!"

These people in Jerusalem were not paralyzed by terror and alarm. No,
what I read is this: "Believers were the more added to the Lord." These won-

derful events made them ask questions, and the apostles would give the answers. Their sermons are recorded. They would say: "It is not us; it is this Jesus. He is glorious. He is the Son of God." "Believe on the Lord Jesus Christ, and thou shalt be saved" (Acts 16:31). Belief! Oh yes, the first effect was to bring in an element of fear. You are convicted of your sin, but you are not left there. Listen, follow the message, and it will lead you to this glorious news that will give you the deliverance you stand in need of, and you will be led from fear to belief.

But, lastly, a great change took place in these people. Did you notice how Luke puts it here? "Believers were the more added to the Lord." He does not say that many believers joined the church; no, believers were "added to the Lord." This is absolutely vital. It means that a true change of heart had taken place in these people. But notice the statement in verse 13. Having been told that "they were all with one accord in Solomon's porch," we read, "And of the rest durst no man join himself to them: but the people magnified . . ." Who were these "rest" that dared not join the true company of believers? There is no point in saying that they were all unbelievers, because we are told that many of them did believe. No, this means that there were quite a number of people who were merely carried away by the phenomena and by a kind of curiosity. You have always had people like that throughout the history of the church—the true believers and the hangers-on.

People are always attracted by a crowd. If something strange and unusual is happening, curiosity will draw them. They may give the impression that they are true believers, but they are not—even though they may think they are and may persuade the believers that they are. These people are the superficially attracted, the merely curious. When these people saw Ananias and Sapphira dropping down dead, they said, "We don't want any of this." Until then everything had been going well; a fund had been formed, and everybody was going to share everybody else's goods. "Ah," they had said, "this is the place for us." So they attached themselves to the society of the Christian people. They were on to a good thing here. As we would put it today, they climbed on the bandwagon. But when Ananias and Sapphira dropped dead, out they went, terrified. They said, "We'll be dropping down dead next!" The power of God is an awful power. It always sifts the true from the false, pseudo believers from true believers.

I must emphasize—I am sorry to have to do it—that these people who had decided to join the church were not among those who were "added to the Lord." No, when people are "added to the Lord," it means that somebody else has added them—the Lord, the Holy Spirit Himself. We have already heard this, have we not, in the second chapter? Peter was preaching on the day of Pentecost, and we read, "Now when they heard this, they were pricked in their heart, and said unto Peter and to the rest of the apostles, Men and brethren, what shall we do?" (Acts 2:37). Then verse 47 says, "And the Lord added to the church daily such as should be saved." There is only one who can add to the church—the Lord Himself as He adds men and women to Himself. No one can make another person a Christian; nor can you and I decide that we are going to add ourselves to the Lord. Only the power of the Holy Spirit can add us to Him.

How does the Holy Spirit make someone a Christian? He enlightens the mind; He opens the understanding; He enables us to see the truth; He convicts us of our sin. Our Lord said, "When he is come, he will reprove [convict] the world of sin, and of righteousness, and of judgment" (John 16:8). The Spirit does it. He did it on the day of Pentecost; He did it here in Acts 5. Some people were annoyed, some were terrified, and some just kept away because they thought they might suddenly die. But as for these others, the Spirit opened their understanding, as He later opened the heart of Lydia so "that she attended unto the things which were spoken of Paul" (Acts 16:14). It is the Holy Spirit alone who can do this.

That is why I never try to frighten people into the kingdom of God. I do not even call people forward at the end of a service. I know that when the Spirit of God has dealt with them, has changed them, and has given them new minds and hearts, they will come and tell me or tell somebody else. I do not want an immediate decision because I know that even I can produce decisions. A man's eloquence or the use of lights or music can produce decisions. But I do not do that. I simply put the truth before people, and it is the Spirit of the living God alone who can apply that truth, and He does.

So men and women were added to the Lord. They were not terrified by the deaths of Ananias and Sapphira or by the shaking of the building. They knew it was the power of God, but they knew now that the Gospel "is the power of God unto salvation to every one that believeth" (Rom. 1:16). They had been afraid of the Jewish authorities, but now they were no longer afraid of men. They were afraid of God, but it was a kind of loving fear. They felt reverence and awe. Instead of being paralyzed, they were drawn to God. They knew that there was a heart of love behind all that happened, that righteousness and peace had embraced each other, and that God almighty had sent His only Son into the world "that whosoever believeth in him should not perish, but have everlasting life" (John 3:16). The Spirit of God had used the phenomena to enlighten their minds and lead their thinking until they had seen their own uncleanness and pettiness and smallness. They had seen the truth concerning Jesus of Nazareth, the Son of God, and had felt the mighty working of His power within them, renewing them in the whole of their being, and they had flown to Him. "Believers were the more added to the Lord, multitudes both of men and women."

You, too, have heard these things. Has that been your reaction? Have you known the fear? Have you believed the message? Have you felt the power of God in truth working in you, changing you, and making you a glad and a ready believer in this blessed message? Amen.

NOTES

1. This was dealt with by Dr. Lloyd-Jones in *Authentic Christianity, Volume 1* (Wheaton, Ill.: Crossway Books, 2000).
2. Westminster Chapel in London.
3. For example, saying, "Every day and in every way I am getting better and better."
4. These sermons were preached in 1965.